REHABILITATION OF WORKERS' COMPENSATION AND OTHER INSURANCE CLAIMANTS

REHABILITATION OF WORKERS' COMPENSATION AND OTHER INSURANCE CLAIMANTS

Case Management, Forensic, and Business Aspects

By

JOHN D. RASCH, Ph.D.

Associate Professor
University of South Florida
Tampa, Florida

CHARLES C THOMAS • PUBLISHER
Springfield • Illinois • U.S.A.

Published and Distributed Throughout the World by

CHARLES C THOMAS • PUBLISHER
2600 South First Street
Springfield, Illinois 62717

ISBN 0-398-05087-2

Library of Congress Catalog Card Number: 84-16265

With THOMAS BOOKS *careful attention is given to all details of manufacturing and design. It is the Publisher's desire to present books that are satisfactory as to their physical qualities and artistic possibilities and appropriate for their particular use.* THOMAS BOOKS *will be true to those laws of quality that assure a good name and good will.*

Printed in the United States of America
Q-R-3

Library of Congress Cataloging in Publication Data

Rasch, John D.
Rehabilitation of workers' compensation and other insurance claimants.

Bibliography: p.
Includes index.
1. Vocational rehabilitation. 2. Rehabilitation. 3. Workers' compensation. I. Title.
HD7255.R37 1985 362.4'0484 84-16265
ISBN 0-398-05087-2

PREFACE

THIS book is written primarily for use as a text in graduate and undergraduate rehabilitation education programs. This being the case, it makes relatively few assumptions as to the reader's knowledge of the field of rehabilitation in general, or the private sector specifically. Despite its orientation toward preservice education, the scope of the book is broad, and even experienced private sector rehabilitationists, claims representatives, and attorneys should find much of the book's content both informative and useful.

One of the most difficult issues to resolve in writing any human services text is how much emphasis to place on "academic" versus "applied" aspects. This book attempts to weight both approximately equally, presenting information of a historical, legislative, medical, business management and research nature; while at the same time explaining how private sector case management services are actually delivered. Both types of knowledge complement one another, and any text oriented toward preservice education must include both.

This book is divided into three parts. *Part I* is entitled, *Foundations of Private Sector Rehabilitation.* It begins with an introductory chapter which overviews the history and development of private sector rehabilitation, differentiating the private and public sectors in terms of rehabilitation philosophy and service emphases. *Chapter II* is an introduction to the insurance industry, which is the economic foundation of private sector rehabilitation. It explains basic insurance terminology, the "business" of insurance itself, and describes the lines of insurance where rehabilitation services are provided. *Chapter III* describes the workers' compensation system, addressing its rationale, history, recent developments, and benefit provisions.

Part II is entitled, *Rehabilitation Case Management.* This is an applied section containing three chapters. *Chapter IV* discusses early case management services, and describes medical management, which attempts to facilitate a maximum physical recovery, and vocational management, which is focused on the maintenance of employment with the former employer. *Chapter V* addresses vocational rehabilitation issues, specifically the development of a realistic vocational rehabilitation plan. *Chapter VI* covers the basics of job placement which is a critical and highly emphasized private sector service.

The final section, *Part III,* is entitled, *Special Private Sector Issues.* Three important but unrelated chapters are included here. In *Chapter VII* the problems of chronic pain and lower back injury are discussed. *Chapter VIII* overviews vocational expert testimony, especially as it relates to workers' compensation claims. The final chapter covers private sector business management, billing, and accountability issues.

CONTENTS

REHABILITATION OF WORKERS' COMPENSATION AND OTHER INSURANCE CLAIMANTS

Part I

FOUNDATIONS OF PRIVATE SECTOR REHABILITATION

CHAPTER I

AN OVERVIEW OF PRIVATE SECTOR REHABILITATION

IN the broadest sense, the field of "private sector rehabilitation" may be considered to encompass private-for-profit rehabilitation companies, self-employed rehabilitationists, in-house corporate rehabilitation programs, private-for-profit medical/rehabilitation centers (e.g., pain clinics), and private non-profit rehabilitation facilities (e.g., sheltered workshops). While all of the above may fall within a literal definition of private sector rehabilitation, such diverse programs and activities actually have relatively little in common. As used here, the field of private sector rehabilitation is considered to encompass *only* private-for-profit rehabilitation companies, self-employed rehabilitationists, and in-house corporate programs; all of which are involved primarily in the provision of rehabilitation case management services to industrially injured workers and other insurance claimants. The focus of private sector case management services may be on medical care coordination, vocational rehabilitation, or both.

As defined here, private sector rehabilitation means *the provision of rehabilitation case management services leading to maximum medical recovery and/or vocational rehabilitation in third party funded cases.* These third party cases are normally workers' compensation (i.e., industrial injury) or other personal injury insurance cases. In reality, there is very little private sector rehabilitation that is not in one way or another related to the insurance industry. This is because the existence of a private sector is predicated upon a third party assuming the cost of rehabilitation services. The third party is usually an insurance company, or in workers' compensation possibly a self-insuring employer, state fund, or government agency. It is rare for a client, or for the parents of a client, to directly contract for private sector rehabilitation services. When there is no third party to pay for services, handicapped individuals are normally served by the state-federal rehabilitation program.

The public and private sectors of rehabilitation are basically differentiated by the fact that case management services and services purchased for clients (e.g., medical treatment, vocational training) are supported by tax dollars in the public sector, and by insurance premiums or assessments on insurers in the private sector. Public sector rehabilitation is a federally mandated government run social service. Private sector rehabilitation is a business activity, and its roots and history are within the field of insurance. Some public sector rehabilitationists have difficulty understanding and accepting this different heritage of private sector rehabilitation. Many of the differences that exist between public and private rehabilitation simply stem from the fact that the public (government) and private (business) sectors of the economy approach accountability and manage their funds differently. The great challenge of private sector rehabilitation is to actualize a human service objective (i.e., the maximum medical and vocational recovery of injured individuals) working within the context of a free enterprise system.

Despite their funding differences, the public and private sectors of rehabilitation are closely related. Although service emphases may differ, both have vocational rehabilitation as an objective. Moreover, the private sector does not have a monopoly on insurance company referrals. Carriers can and do refer their workers' compensation and other personal injury claimants to both the public and private sectors for rehabilitation case management services. In order for a private sector to exist, and in order for it to have developed so rapidly in recent years, it must have in some way out performed the public sector in the rehabilitation of workers' compensation and other insurance claimants. The private sector has accomplished this by designing itself to specifically serve insurance funded cases by emphasizing: (a) small caseloads usually consisting of 30 clients or less, (b) good communication with referral sources and prompt contact of referrals, (c) frequent and personalized marketing activities, and (d) job placement on the basis of transferable skills before consideration of retraining. The public sector has been at a disadvantage in providing rehabilitation case management services in insurance cases for a number of reasons including: (a) the need to establish client eligibility for public sector services which is irrelevant in workers' compensation and other insurance cases, (b) by changing federal mandates such as the current requirement to first serve the severely handicapped — a group which is less frequently seen in workers' compensation cases, (c) by large counselor caseloads, (d) by poor administration and field personnel understanding of the rehabilitation provisions of their state's workers' compensation law, and (e) because of a traditional public sector emphasis on retraining.

DEVELOPMENT OF PRIVATE SECTOR REHABILITATION

The growth and development of private sector rehabilitation resulted from two concurrent processes. The first of these was the nationwide reform of workers' compensation laws, which began in the early 1970's and which was necessitated by the fact that state laws were highly variable and often failed to provide needed benefits, including rehabilitation benefits, to industrially injured workers (see Workman's Compensation: Last Chance for State Control, 1969; Workmen's Compensation Reform, 1974; Workers' Compensation Update, 1975; Can Tinkering Federal Style Make Workers' Compensation Work Better, 1978). The second reason for the growth of private sector rehabilitation was a recognition within the insurance industry that rehabilitation services positively impacted personal injury lines by: (a) containing medical costs, (b) shortening the period of disability, (c) reducing carrier exposure for lost income replacement, and (d) reducing the frequency of litigation (see Anderson, 1974; Cohen, 1981; Moskowitz, 1975; Richbourg, 1977, 1979; Welch, 1973). Together, these two processes made possible the phenomenal growth of private sector rehabilitation which characterized the late 1970's and early 1980's.

Although the roots of public sector rehabilitation can be traced to World War I (i.e., Soldiers Rehabilitation Act of 1918), the roots of private sector rehabilitation go no further back than World War II. During World War II, there was a national necessity for increased industrial production at a time when trained labor was being removed for the military. This created new employment opportunities in the national economy for women, retired persons, minority groups members, and handicapped individuals. One of the earliest events directly related to the development of insurance rehabilitation occurred in 1943 when Liberty Mutual Insurance Company opened a Comprehensive Rehabilitation Center to treat the injured employees of its policy holders (Lewin, Ramseur and Sink, 1979; Matkin, 1980). Their private rehabilitation program received considerable attention within the insurance industry, and was an early demonstration of the potential benefits of insurance supported rehabilitation services.

Insurance rehabilitation continued developing after World War II through the utilization of rehabilitation nurses. Some insurance companies hired their own nurses and others contracted with independent operators for rehabilitation nursing on an "as needed" basis. The role of the rehabilitation nurse was to coordinate medical services. This coordination essentially involved finding out what medical services claimants needed, and then arranging for their delivery in a timely manner. An important element of medical management was to see that services were not duplicated by one or more physicians or clinics. The rehabilitation nurse also provided follow-up services after medical treatment to evaluate the adequacy of results and to reduce the incidence of medical complications. It became increasingly clear, however, that medical management services did not always result in reemployment. Many claimants recovered physically, but never returned to work. The role of the rehabilitation nurse accordingly expanded to include vocational management services (i.e., working with the former employer to return the claimant to the same, modified, or new job with the company) and even vocational rehabilitation services (i.e., coordinating or delivering all services necessary to successfully place the claimant with a new employer).[1]

By the early 1960's a number of insurance companies had established in-house programs to contain or control their costs in workers' compensation cases. These programs primarily involved accident prevention, and medical management by rehabilitation nurses. In 1966, a group of insurance executives from several companies met and established the Insurance Rehabilitation Study Group (IRSG). According to Richbourg (1979), one of the early issues addressed by the IRSG was whether it made good business sense for each company to have an extensive rehabilitation staff, or if it would be better for an independent and experienced rehabilitation company to serve all insurers. One argument supporting an independent company was that it would not have a vested interest in the settlement of any claim, and would therefore be in a better position to earn the confidence and trust of the claimant and the claimant's attorney. The

IRSG gradually grew to include most of the insurance industry. The early notion of one private rehabilitation company to serve the entire insurance industry simply proved to be unrealistic.

An event of major importance in the development of insurance rehabilitation occured in 1970 when Congress passed legislation authorizing the establishment of a National Commission on State Workmen's Compensation Laws. The National Commission was formed because state workers' compensation laws were highly variable, and some failed to provide adequate medical and financial protection for injured workers. The National Commission's report was presented in 1972, and made 19 "essential" recommendations. In order to avoid the threat of federalization of the workers' compensation system, state legislatures began to review their existing laws and to move toward implementation of the 19 essential recommendations (see Chapter III).

California made an early response to the National Commission's report. Late in 1974, California enacted a law which mandated vocational rehabilitation in its workers' compensation system (Sanchez, Workman, Morris, Miller and Edelstein, 1981). The California law required that an employer/insurance carrier offer rehabilitation services to any injured worker unable to return to his or her employment. An existing rehabilitation unit expanded into a Rehabilitation Bureau with the authority to review and approve plans, and set rules and regulations to govern the provision of rehabilitation services. Private rehabilitation companies soon began to develop to help employers and carriers meet their rehabilitation obligations under the new state law. The private sector developed so rapidly in California that of 350 rehabilitation companies estimated to exist in 1979 (McMahon, 1979), over 200 were presumably based in California (Lewin, Ramseur and Sink, 1979).

While the private sector developed most rapidly in California, other states also began to modify their workers' compensation laws to mandate or encourage rehabilitation. As this occurred (and this trend is still continuing) private sector rehabilitation companies developed in other states as well. While no reliable statistics exist on the number of full and part-time private sector rehabilitationists, by 1984 the number was probably close to 10,000 nationwide, and still growing. If present trends continue, the private sector will employ as many if not more rehabilitationists than the public sector. The manpower needs of the private sector for the rest of the century will essentially be determined by how many workers' compensation claimants are referred for rehabilitation services, and this will be based upon the rehabilitation provisions of state laws. One recent estimate is that the private sector is serving between 150,000 and 200,000 clients annually (Gutowski, Harder and Koshel, 1980).

The first major private-for-profit rehabilitation company on the scene was International Rehabilitation Associates (IRA) which began in 1970. IRA grew out of and then later assimilated the Medical and Educational Needs DevelopmentProgram (MEND Program) which had been established in 1966 by George Welch at the Insurance Company of North America (INA). No discussion of the development of insurance rehabilitation can fail to acknowledge the early contribution of George Welch, the first president of IRA. George Welch began working as a claims adjuster after World War II, and he was later a supervisor, manager, and home office executive at INA. He noted that personal injury lines of insurance often had adverse loss ratios, and that insurance companies were frequently in litigation with their claimants. He subsequently developed the MEND Program to help counter this trend at INA, and later encouraged the company to form IRA where he assumed the role of president and later chairman of the board. George Welch as an effective and articulate advocate for insurance rehabilitation, and probably did more than any other individual to convince the insurance industry that disability was its enemy, and not the insurance claimant.

Although there was unquestionably a widespread need for rehabilitation services in personal injury lines of insurance, when it began in 1970, IRA had only 33 cases (Richbourg, 1979). Initially the company was primarily oriented toward medical management services but quickly recognized the need for vocational services and expanded to emphasize these as well (Lewin, Ramseur and Sink, 1979). By 1981, IRA was serving approximately 28,000 cases annually from more than 500 different referral sources ("Who's Who in Rehabilitation," 1981). Moreover, the company employed approximately 1500 rehabilitation specialists, and had offices in the United States, Canada, and Australia.

Another early and very successful private-for-profit rehabilitation company that began in the early 1970's was Crawford Rehabilitation Services. This company was formed as a subsidiary of Crawford and Company (an international insurance adjusting firm), but was independent in that it maintained separate offices and staff. Like IRA, Crawford Rehabilitation Services has served thousands of insurance cases, and in 1981 had offices in 35 different states (Office Location Directory, 1981).

Although IRA and Crawford Rehabilitation Services were formed within the insurance industry itself, the vast majority of private rehabilitation companies are not insurance subsidiaries. There are a number of regionally prominent and independent companies, such as Vocational Placement Services, which employ hundreds of rehabilitationists. There are also many smaller companies which are operated as individual proprietorships or partnerships, rather than as corporations. More recently, however, other insurance companies and even home health services have started to open rehabilitation companies. Larger employers are increasingly following examples set by 3M, Sears Roebuck, Dupont, and others; and are developing in-house rehabilitation programs for their own employees. Such programs can result in substantial savings even for employers who choose not to self-insure their workers' compensation risk (see "Rehabilitation in Industry," 1982). While it is still possible to successfully open new non-affiliated rehabilitation companies, the trend in the 1980's will be toward larger companies with offices in at least several states and in-house corporate rehabilitation programs (Ashton, 1979).

PRIVATE SECTOR PROFESSIONAL ISSUES

The phenomenal growth of private sector rehabilitation during the late 1970's overtook the national rehabilitation movement, as represented by the National Rehabilitation Association (NRA), by surprise. NRA had traditionally focussed its attention almost exclusively on the state-federal rehabilitation program, and the changing NRA leaderships did not recognize the rehabilitation implications of workers' compensation reform, and were unable to effectively respond to the different needs and interests of private sector practitioners. While not enough time has passed to write a history of private sector professionalism, which is still very much in a developmental stage, an overview of early events and recent developments can be offered. What is clear is that the early history of private sector professionalism has been characterized, unfortunately, by a sometimes adversarial and competitive relationship with the public sector. Cooperation and collaboration, which is in the best interest of clients, is a goal which both sectors must continually strive to achieve (Griswold and Scott, 1979; Smith and Sawisch, 1983).

The first private sector professional association was formed as recently as 1975 when a group of California based practitioners organized the California Association of Rehabilitation Professionals (CARP). According to Roberts (1981), one of the main reasons for forming this association was to defeat state legislation which would have made the public rehabilitation agency the sole recipient of referrals under the new state workers' compensation law, in effect ending a private rehabilitation sector in California. Largely through the efforts of the newly formed CARP, the adverse legislation was defeated. While the California experience is unique it nevertheless demonstrates that the public and private sectors are potentially competitors or at least providers of the same basic service. The established public sector controlled the existing state rehabilitation association and was not adversely affected by the proposed legislation. The private sector had to organize independently to protect its own interests.

According to Roberts (1981), the first national challenge to private sector rehabilitation occurred in the mid 1970's when NRA adopted a policy statement calling for every industrially injured worker to be referred to the state-federal rehabilitation program. While a group of private sector practitioners successfully worked during 1976 to have NRA include the private sector, a realization that the private sector would need its own national organization was rapidly developing. Paul Scher, chief of rehabilitation at Sears Roebuck, put a notice in the *ARCA News* asking for anyone interested in industrial rehabilitation to contact him. Groups of private sector rehabilitationists began meeting at the annual NRA and American Personnel and Guidance Association (APGA) conventions, and in 1977 formed the National Association of Rehabilitation Professionals in the Private Sector (NARPPS). Paul Scher was elected as the organization's first president. He served two terms, and was later succeeded by Bill Roberts, Richard LaFon, and Jim Wilson.

The formation of NARPPS was especially interesting in that this organization not only began, but started to grow very rapidly during a period when NRA and its largest professional division, the National Rehabilitation Counseling Association (NRCA), were losing thousands of members. In order to reverse these declines there were calls during 1979 for NARPPS to organize within NRA (e.g., Organist, 1979), and for NRCA to withdraw from NRA to form divisions of its own that could respond to new practice areas such as private sector rehabilitation (Rasch, 1979). While NARPPS explored and continues to explore cooperative relationships with NRA and other organizations, NARPPS will remain an independent organization representing the interests of private sector professionals. This is necessary because if there were any future conflict of interest between public and private sector rehabilitation, NRA might favor the public sector. While many private sector rehabilitationists are active members of NRA and NRCA, the private sector needs an independent voice that is all its own.

As of late 1981, NARPPS represented approximately 5,000 private sector practitioners ("President's Notes," 1981). These included institutional (for all practitioners employed by a company), individual, and student memberships. More importantly, the association was reported to be growing at a rate of about 30% per year. While meetings were still being held at the NRA and APGA conventions, the rapid growth of the organization made it possible for a first annual convention to be held in Dallas, Texas during November, 1981.

In its short history, NARPPS has attempted to address a number of professional issues of critical importance to the private sector including practitioner standards, credentialling, ethics, and research and training. Late in 1981, for example, the membership approved an important *Standards and Ethics* document (see Appendix II). Major aspects of the document were:

1. Minimum requirements for a *professional rehabilitation practitioner* were established as one of the following: (a) graduate degree in health support services and one year of rehabilitation experience, (b) baccalaureate degree in health support services and two years of rehabilitation experience, (c) diploma in nursing plus current R.N. license and three years of rehabilitation experience, (d) any other baccalaureate degree plus three years of rehabilitation experience, or (e) associate degree or high school diploma plus continuing education and five years of rehabilitation experience for an associate rehabilitation practitioner.
2. Court testimony in fields of expertise was recognized as an acceptable practitioner role. The determination of practitioner fields of expertise was deferred to each court.
3. Confidentiality and client advocacy issues were delineated with reference to third party involvement.
4. Thirteen specific points covering ethical rehabilitation business practices were adopted. These addressed issues such as: (a) representation of services and advertising, (b) necessity for professional liability insurance, (c) provisions against claims practices, (d) reviews of another practitioner's service delivery, (e) employee recruitment, and (f) fee arrangements for testimony.
5. A Peer Review Committee was established to investigate and rule on alleged infractions. This committee includes a rehabilitation counselor, rehabilitation nurse, vocational evaluator, placement specialist, insurance claimsperson or buyer, general private practitioner, and company administrator (Rasch, 1982).

NARPPS also formed a Training and Research Committee in 1982 to review research proposals, and advocate private sector curriculum issues in higher education. Because of the insurance context and issues that arise from it, private sector preservice and inservice training needs are not identical with those of the public sector (see Lynch and Martin, 1982; Matkin, 1980; McMahon, 1979; Sales, 1979).

Certification is unquestionably the professional area where NARPPS and private sector practitioners have had the most impact. There has been such a strong demand for a private sector certification process that the Certified Insurance Rehabilitation Specialist Commission was established. This Commission will oversee a "CIRS" certification process, and is administratively housed with the Commission on Rehabilitation Counselor Certification under the Board for Rehabilitation Certification.

This new certification process is in no way a replacement of the Certified Rehabilitation Counselor (CRC) designation, but is rather an additional credential for all private sector practitioners, especially those with educational backgrounds in disciplines other than rehabilitation counseling (e.g., nursing, education, psychology). This new certification will help claims representatives, workers' compensation agencies, employers, and attorneys judge who, other than CRC's, are "qualified" practitioners (see Matkin, 1983).

Another development in private sector professionalism has been the formation of state associations. Private sector rehabilitationists had, by the end of 1982, formed rehabilitation associations in Arizona, Colorado, Florida, Michigan, Minnesota, New York, Oregon, Pennsylvania, and Washington ("The Association Bulletin Board," 1982). The development of new private sector state associations, where state rehabilitation associations already existed, again suggests the different interests of the two rehabilitation sectors. Such associations are important because private sector rehabilitationists must closely monitor proposed legislative changes in workers' compensation. The industrially injured worker does not have an inalienable right to rehabilitation, and with the "stroke of a pen" rehabilitation benefits can be written into or out of a state workers' compensation law.

VOCATIONAL REHABILITATION PROCESS IN THE PUBLIC AND PRIVATE SECTORS

In comparing the public and private sectors of *vocational rehabilitation* there are several issues which should be kept in mind. First, the public sector is governed by the provisions of the Rehabilitation Act of 1973 and its amendments. Although run on a state by state basis, the program must fulfill its legislated mandate and comply with rules and regulations adopted by the Rehabilitation Services Administration (RSA). The private sector, on the other hand, is governed by each state's workers' compensation law and workers' compensation rehabilitation bureau (if any), and by the claims practices of employers and insurance carriers. Second, the public sector, due to its history, nature of clients served, and philosophy; has traditionally interpreted its mission as being that of actualizing the vocational potentials of its clientele (Diamond and Petkas, 1979) to whatever extent funding would allow. In private sector rehabilitation, the goal is to *restore* the client to the *former* level of vocational functioning or to as close an approximation of that level as is *reasonably* possible. Third, in the public sector only the agency itself oversees the provision of rehabilitation services. In the private sector there are a number of interested parties including the rehabilitation bureau, employer, claims representative, and possibly even attorneys for the plaintiff and defense.

Despite these and other important differences, the public and private sectors share a generic vocational rehabilitation process which in its most basic form may be considered to involve: (a) case finding and referral processing, (b) evaluation and assessment, (c) vocational rehabilitation plan development, (d) service delivery and coordination, (e) job placement, and (f) follow-up. In order to better understand convergence and divergence within the two sectors, it is helpful to consider each of these areas separately.

Case Finding and Referral Processing

Referrals come to the public rehabilitation agency from a variety of sources including physicans, schools, family and friends, social service agencies, and even self-referrals. Private sector referrals, on the other hand, usually come from a workers' compensation agency, insurance company, or employer. Case finding activities in the public sector must be wide ranging and extensive or handicapped individuals eligible for and truly needing rehabilitation services will be missed. Private sector case finding is often called marketing, and is directed toward third parties known to have regular or occassional statutory liability or cost savings incentives for providing rehabilitation services.

While the public sector can, and in some states does engage in direct and substantial case finding activities with insurance carriers and employers, its mission is broader than that of private sector rehabilitation, and public sector case finding activities must therefore target a wide variety of potential referral sources. Case finding in the public sector is usually accomplished by developing liason or cooperative relationships with agencies that frequently encounter handicapped individuals (e.g., hospitals, schools) so that potential clients are not missed and can be contacted at an appropriate time. Private sector rehabilitationists may market their services at local, state, regional, and/or national levels, but they solicit only referrals with third party funding. They subsequently work closely with the referral source, maintain good communication concerning case activities and developments, and identify needed services. They provide only services "authorized" by the carrier or rehabilitation bureau.

Evaluation and Assessment

Before the public sector can serve a client the eligibility of the client must be assessed and documented. Public sector eligibility criteria require: (a) the presence of a disability, (b) a resulting handicap to employment, and (c) a reasonable potential or expectation that services will result in vocational rehabilitation. While the public sector sometimes uses an extended evaluation status where the client's response to services will help assess rehabilitation potential, in most cases an eligibility decision is made before any non-diagnostic services are provided. In the private sector, the rehabilitationist normally works with any client referred by a carrier or workers' compensation agency. Eligibility and/or entitlement for rehabilitation benefits are decisions usually made by the carrier's claims representative or by the workers' compensation agency. In general, referrals for rehabilitation services are made whenever a long disability period or high medical costs are anticipated (i.e., for medical management services) or when there is reason to believe the claimant may be unable to return to the former job (i.e., for vocational rehabilitation services).

In the public sector, the assessment of vocationally significant client characteristics has become a highly developed science. In addition to medical and psychological examinations, extensive vocational evaluations may be obtained. Public sector assessment and evaluation has traditionally been quite effective in determining what limitations and assets a client has, and in identifying training potentials. A weakness of the public sector assessment process is that it is often overly focused upon the client, neglecting the local labor market and jobs currently available for which the client might qualify.

The private sector assessment process, on the other hand, has a strong labor market focus. More limited rehabilitation benefits under workers' compensation laws and insurance cost containment issues have resulted in a vocational assessment process which emphasizes transferable skills. A transferable skill is any client quality, unaffected by the disability, that may have work or reemployment relevance. The private sector rehabilitationist identifies, and whenever possible enhances these skills, and relates them to jobs existing in the local labor market.

Vocational Rehabilitation Plan Development

In public sector rehabilitation the evaluation and assessment process culminates in the formation of an Individual Written Rehabilitation Program (IWRP). The program or plan is developed with the active participation of the client, and the client must sign the plan to indicate review and consent before services are implemented. In developing the plan the rehabilitationist and client relate evaluative data (e.g., medical reports, testing and vocational evaluation reports) to the client's vocational interests and real world training and employment opportunities. The IWRP specifies a job objective, rehabilitation services which will be provided to actualize the objective, the cost of different services, who will provide the services, and a time frame for service delivery. The IWRP is reviewed by the rehabilitationist's supervisor to ensure that the job objective is realistic and authorized services appropriate and reasonable.

Private sector plan development varies on a state by state basis. In workers' compensation cases the vocational rehabilitation plan is written with the client, and is normally sent to both the carrier and rehabilitation bureau of the workers' compensation agency for approval. Reporting requirements and the actual form on which the plan is written vary in reference to different state requirements, carrier-specific requirements, and the procedures of different rehabilitation companies. As in the public sector, the vocational rehabilitation plan specifies the job objective, services to be provided, cost of services, service provider, and the time frame for different services.

Plan development issues are complicated in the private sector by the fact that rehabilitation services are overseen and approved by other parties. Moreover, rehabilitationists may be involved in the provision of medical and vocational management services during the early stages of the claimant's recovery, long before it is possible to develop a vocational rehabilitation plan. Moreover, in some cases only one specific service will be authorized, such as job placement in a certain occupation, and when this is appropriate and reasonable, an actual rehabilitation plan may not be written.

Service Delivery and Coordination

Once the rehabilitation plan is developed and approved, the next step is to deliver and coordinate authorized services. The service delivery and coordination process is essentially the same in both the public and private sectors. The basic difference between the two is again that third parties are involved in private sector rehabilitation. The carrier and/or workers' compensation agency normally oversees the entire process. In addition to the carrier and workers' compensation agency, attorneys may also become involved in the rehabilitation process when there is some dispute or complaint.

With more than two parties (i.e., client and counselor) interested in private sector rehabilitation, good and effective communication between all parties is essential. Because the rehabilitationist is under contract with the carrier or workers' compensation agency to provide rehabilitation services, periodic progress reports and time charges must be made. Bills for purchased services (e.g., medical evaluation, treatment, job training) are paid by either the claims representative or workers' compensation agency.

Job Placement

The most distinctive aspect of private sector rehabilitation is the preeminence given to job development and placement activities. Welch (1979) stated that private sector placement priorities were sequentially placement into: (a) the same job with the same employer, (b) a different job with the same employer, and finally (c) a new job with a new employer. Placement is approached by identifying the claimant's transferable skills and matching them with job opportunities. Retraining for new employment and self-employment are normally considered only when transferable skills are insufficient for job placement.

As indicated earlier, the public sector has historically sought to maximize client vocational potentials. The public sector also serves more severely disabled clients and clients with no or minimal work histories, such as the developmentally disabled. These factors have naturally led to a stronger emphasis on prevocational training (for work enculturation) and vocational training (to develop marketable work skills) than direct job placement. It is probably fair to say that in the public sector, more energy is generally expended on getting the client "job ready" than "job placed." There is increasing recognition, however, of the importance of job placement as a distinct rehabilitation service, and more emphasis is now being given in the public sector to this aspect of the rehabilitation process.

Follow-Up

In the public sector, cases are normally closed after the client has been successfully employed for 60 days. Certain post-employment services designed to maintain employment can be provided up to one year after closure. Periodic reviews of both open and closed cases contribute to quality follow-along and follow-up services.

Again, in the private sector, provisions for following-up a placement are more variable. If a placement is lost and employment is not readily reestablished, and this situation is related to the covered injury/disability, and rehabilitation benefits have not been exhausted; then rehabilitation benefits should again be provided. If they are not, the claimant may wish to hire an attorney and/or appeal the decision. In some cases, however, the carrier and claimant will agree to what is called a "lump sum settlement" of the carrier's obligations to the client. For a certain dollar value, which is often paid as a lump sum, the carrier discharges its present and future obligations to the claimant, and closes its file.

Summary

The public and private sectors have a common objective, vocational rehabilitation, but they serve different populations and have different rehabilitation philosophies. The state-federal rehabilitation program serves all individuals meeting its eligibility requirements with the first priority for services going to the severely disabled. The private sector primarily serves workers' compensation and other insurance claimants. The public sector has historically sought to maximize the vocational potentials of its clients through training, and is as much involved in vocational habilitation (serving individuals who have never worked) as vocational rehabilitation. The private sector, on the other hand, seeks to return its clients to suitable employment as quickly and cost effectively as possible, first utilizing transferable skills in the job placement process.

Although the public and private sectors approach vocational rehabilitation differently, this does not preclude extensive cooperation between the two sectors. In some states this cooperation has been excellent, but in others the relationship between the sectors has been more competitive. Cooperation benefits the client by providing access to strengths existing within each sector, such as evaluation and training in the public sector, and placement in the private sector. Both sectors will continue to exist side by side, and it is important for handicapped individuals that they learn to work and cooperate together.

Finally, it is essential to remember that public sector rehabilitation is a federally mandated program, and private sector rehabilitation an insurance benefit. Insurance is one of the greatest inventions of mankind, protecting individuals from personal disasters that could lead to impoverishment and subsequent dependence on the social welfare system. In a very real sense, insurance is a type of social welfare program that is paid for before it is needed, with full realization that it may never be needed. When a major catastrophy does occur, the insurance benefit becomes operational, and the individual's needs, which were anticipated in advance, are addressed. In order to understand private sector rehabilitation it is necessary to have some understanding and appreciation of insurance principles and the insurance industry itself.

Reference Note

[1]A distinction is sometimes made between vocational management and vocational rehabilitation services, although the latter term may be used for both. Vocational management is an extension of medical management and essentially involves: (a) keeping the employer informed of the injured worker's condition and probable release date for return to work, (b) evaluating the post-injury suitability of the former job and identifying any modifications in the job which might be necessary, (c) identifying other jobs in the business that the injured worker might do, and (d) encouraging the employer to transfer the worker to a new position if the old job is unsuitable. Vocational management is often considered to end and vocational rehabilitation to begin when reemployment will require job placement with a new employer.

References

Anderson, H.B.: Second Chances. *The Wall Street Journal,* May 20, 1974, p. 1.

Ashton, P.C.: Rehabilitation in a major corporate setting. *Journal of Rehabilitation,* 1979, *45*:26-29.

Can tinkering federal style make workers' compensation work better? *Journal of Insurance,* 1978, *54(3)*: 6-11.

Cohen, A.P.: Rehabilitation and the insurance industry. *Best's Review,* January 1981, pp. 76-77.

Diamond, C.R. and Petkas, C.R.: A state agency's view of private-for-profit rehabilitation. *Journal of Rehabilitation,* 1979, *45(3)*:30-31.

Griswold, P.P. and Scott, J.W.: The state rehabilitation agency and private rehabilitation: A partnership long overdue. *Journal of Rehabilitation,* 1979, *45*:32-33, 70.

Gutowski, M., Harder, P. and Koshel, J.: *Forecasting Manpower Needs in the Rehabilitation Industry.* Washington, D.C.: The Urban Institute, December, 1980.

Lewin, S.S., Ramseur, J.H. and Sink, J.M.: The role of private rehabilitation: Founder, catalyst, competitor. *Journal of Rehabilitation,* 1979, *45(3)*:16-19.

Lynch, R.K. and Martin, T.: Rehabilitation counseling in the private sector: A training needs survey. *Journal of Rehabilitation,* 1980, *46*:51-53, 73.

Matkin, R.E.: Credentialing the rehabilitation profession. *Journal of Rehabilitation,* 1983, *49*:25-28, 67.

Matkin, R.E.: Public/private rehabilitation during recession. *Journal of Rehabilitation,* 1980, *46*:58-61.

Matkin, R.E.: The rehabilitation counselor in private practice: Perspectives for education and preparation. *Journal of Rehabilitation,* 1980, *46,* 60-62.

McMahon, B.T.: Private sector rehabilitation: Benefits, dangers, and implications for education. *Journal of Rehabilitation,* 1979, *45(3)*:56-58.

Moskowitz, L.: Rehabilitation seen as moral duty. *Business Insurance.* August 1975.

Organist, J.: Private sector rehabilitation practitioners—organize within NRA. *Journal of Rehabilitation,* 1979, *45(3)*:52-55.

President's notes. *NARPPS Newsletter,* midyear 1981 (undated), pp. 4-5.

Rasch, J.D.: Private sector establishes standards and ethics. *ARCA News,* June 1982, p. 4.

Rasch, J.D.: The case for an independent association of rehabilitation counselors. *Journal of Applied Rehabilitation Counseling,* 1979, *10(4)*:171-176.

Rehabilitation in industry: State of the art. *Conference Proceedings,* D.E. Shrey (Project Director), Department of Rehabilitation Counseling, Boston University, 1982.

Richbourg, H.: Impact in rehabilitation. *Rehabilitation Forum.* October 1979a, pp. 3-4.

Richbourg, H.: Impact of rehabilitation. *Risk Management.* June 1979b, pp. 20-25.

Richbourg, H.A.: Rehabilitation: Game without losers. *Journal of Commerce and Commercial,* June 3, 1977.

Roberts, B.: Professional associations: A view from the private sector. *Journal of Applied Rehabilitation Counseling,* 1981, *12(2)*:72-74.

Ross, E.M.: Legislative trends in workers' compensation rehabilitation. *Journal of Rehabilitation,* 1979, *45(3)*:20-23, 70.

Sales, A.: Rehabilitation counseling in the private sector: Implications for graduate education. *Journal of Rehabilitation,* 1979, *47*:59-61, 72.

Sanchez, I., Workman, E.L., Morris, G.M., Miller, J. and Edelstein, M.: *The California Workers' Compensation Rehabilitation System.* New York: Macmillan, 1981.

Smith, H.R. and Sawisch, L.P.: Injured worker rehabilitation in Michigan: Two decades of maturation. *Rehabilitation Counseling Bulletin,* 1983, *27*:5-11.

The association bulletin board, *Rehabilitation Reports.* January 1982, pp. 9-10.

Welch, G.T.: The relationship of rehabilitation with industry. *Journal of Rehabilitation,* 1979, *45(3)*:24-25.

Welch, G.T.: The right to work. *National Underwriter* (Property and Casualty edition). April 13, 1973.

Who's Who in Rehabilitation. *Rehabilitation Reports,* December 1981, pp. 5-8.

Workers' compensation: Update 1975. *Journal of Insurance.* 1974-75, *50(4)*:23-27.

Workmen's compensation: Last chance for state control, *Journal of Insurance.* 1969, *45(3)*:25-28.

Workers' compensation reform, *Journal of Insurance.* 1974, *50(1)*:27-30.

CHAPTER II

THE INSURANCE INDUSTRY

INSURANCE and rehabilitation are both extensive and complex fields, and professionals within each must develop a basic understanding of the other. This is necessary because mutually shared knowledge provides a foundation for communication and eventually for consensus. If a claims representative, for example, does not understand rehabilitation, the representative may be very reluctant to pay for testing, vocational evaluation, or on-the-job evaluation, insisting instead on the immediate placement of a claimant for whom no truely suitable position has been identified. Likewise, the rehabilitationist who does not understand the liability limits of the carrier may recommend a vocational training program that cannot be justified from a prudent claims practice perspective. Both scenarios reflect insufficient understanding of the other field, and in both cases the claimant suffers.

When insurance industry personnel study rehabilitation, a logical starting point for their study is the rehabilitation process. Mastering this process involves understanding typical rehabilitation services including their rationale, sequence, and interrelationships. Rehabilitation is far more than a synonym for job placement, and multiple services are often required before a claimant can be successfully restored to a productive role in society. Rehabilitationists work to place claimants in jobs which they can maintain, which will not result in reinjury, and where they can earn enough to support themselves and their families. Providing multiple services which actualize these objectives, in a timely and cost effective manner, is what private sector rehabilitation is all about.

While the study of rehabilitation can efficaciously begin with the rehabilitation process, there is no logical point to begin the study of insurance. Insurance is a complex and multifaceted field in which an uninformed reader can become quickly lost. In discussing the problem of studying insurance, Mehr and Cammack (1966) stated:

> The trouble with insurance — and we mean the trouble with the subject of insurance — is that the student needs to know everything at once. In geometry, one can begin with a few axioms and postulates and proceed to build the whole apparatus. In history, one can begin at the beginning, or any intermediate point, and proceed so far as he likes. But in insurance, what really is needed is comprehensive knowledge of most facets of the subject from the very beginning. Since that, unfortunately, is

> impossible, the next problem is at what point to plunge into the subject. Should study be made first of the theoretical background of insurance; should it be treated as a branch of mathematics, for instance? Should it be examined from the viewpoint of history? Or should the first concern be a study of the companies engaged in the business or of the policies of insurance they offer? Or should the study begin with the problems in risk management that insurance can solve? (p. 3)

While there may be no logical starting point for the study of insurance, this discussion begins by introducing two critical insurance concepts — *loss* and *risk*.

BASIC CONCEPTS

Loss

Why do individuals or businesses buy insurance? Although the answer to this question is certainly very involved, let us say that they purchase insurance to protect themselves against losses. Bickelhaupt and Magee (1970) described loss as a "decrease or disappearance of value, usually in an unexpected or at least relatively unpredictable manner" (p. 7). Losses occur because of *exposure* to *perils* which exist in the world. Examples of perils include robbery, fire, flood, automobile accidents, vandalism, etc. In insurance terminology a *hazard* is distinguished from a peril in that a hazard is said to be something which increases the probability of financial losses. For example, old rags piled up in a corner would constitute a fire hazard. Through insurance, individuals and businesses (the *insured*) shift losses resulting from perils to another party (the *insurer*).

In a fundamental sense, the purpose of insurance is to shift losses from one party unable to bear them to another more capable of bearing them. Mankind's realization that losses did not need to remain where nature or circumstance randomly placed them was no small enlightenment. The shifting of losses made it feasible for individuals to place or invest their assets in areas subject to substantial perils. Without this transfer of economic losses made possible by insurance, most individuals would be very reluctant to expose their assets to perils, and trade and business could not flourish.

If the purpose of insurance is to transfer the economic consequences of losses from where they naturally fall to some other party, then the next logical question is how is this transfer accomplished? The basic insurance solution is to have those *units* (individuals) exposed to a peril agree to collectively share the losses of units that actually encounter the peril. If, for example, the peril is fire and the group exposed to the peril home owners, the home owners would agree to collectively share the economic loss resulting from fire in any group member's house. The contract by which this agreement is legalized is called an *insurance policy*. The writer, manager, and executer of the contract is the *insurance company* or its representatives.

Risk

It has now been established that the basic purpose of insurance is to transfer losses from one party to another. If this is to be accomplished, the insured units should collectively provide the insurer with a total payment that will: (a) cover all economic losses which the insurer actually encounters, (b) cover the operating or overhead costs of the insurer, and (c) provide a reasonable profit for the insurer. The payment of the insured is called a *premium*, and collectively the premiums of the insured should allow for the fulfillment of the three conditions noted above. The insured benefit from this arrangement is that they change potentially catastrophic losses into small sums which can be budgeted and payed to the insurer on a regular basis. The insurer expects to benefit through the realization of a profit.

In order to determine what premiums to charge the insured, the insurer must make some assessment as to the probable loss and potential extremes of loss which may be encountered under each *line* or type of insurance offered. This problem is known in insurance as risk, which was defined by Williams and Heins (1981) as "the variation in outcomes that could occur over a specified period in a given situation" (p. 4). The insurer attempts to estimate its risk as precisely as possible using past measures of central tendency and dispersion with losses attributed to different lines of insurance, taking into consideration qualities or different classes of insured (Greene and Serbein, 1978). If the insurer is not reasonably certain of the risk involved in *underwriting* a loss, the insurer will normally refuse to provide a policy. The insurer's goal is to minimize losses and accurately predict them. Successful *risk management* allows the insurer to offer comparable or superior policies at competitive prices.

To briefly illustrate the importance of accurately assessing risk, let us return to the example involving fire insurance. Assume that on average, one of every 10,000 Class A houses has a fire each year, and during the past several years these fires have averaged $10,000 in damages. If an insurer has written 100,000 fire insurance policies on Class A houses, it would expect to assume losses resulting from 10 fires averaging $10,000 each. However, it is unlikely that there will be exactly 10 fires in its 100,000 units in any given year. The insurance company's risk is the uncertainty of how many fires there will actually be, and also how much damage they will do. If the insurer should estimate its risk at 10 fires with each averaging $10,000 in losses, and there are 15 fires averaging $20,000 in losses, then the insurer underestimated the risk by 200% ($100,000 estimated losses versus $300,000 actual losses). Since premiums are based on these estimates, this type of error can produce serious financial problems for the insurer. Fortunately, as the number of insured units increases, the prediction of losses becomes more accurate. This is a basic statistical phenomenon which is known in insurance (and in other fields) as the *law of large numbers*.

Although insurance companies exist to assume the risks of others, it is important to remember that they will not, at least voluntarily, assume all risks. As noted earlier, they will not assume risks that they cannot accurately assess. They will also refuse risks where the probability of loss is too high or the potential economic consequences too great. It is socially desirable, however, for many poor insurance risks to nevertheless have insurance protection (e.g., auto insurance for high risk drivers, workers' compensation coverage for dangerous types of work or for businesses with poor safety records). Government regulations therefore require, in certain cases, the formation of *assigned risks* pools where insurers randomly draw and insure otherwise non-insurable units.

The types of risks which are normally insured against fall into four broad categories: (a) personal risks — threats to income or material well-being such as death, disability, old age, or unemployment, (b) property risks — involving physical damage to or loss of income from property, (c) liability risks — stemming from injury to another or their property, and (d) risks that result when others fail to meet contractual obligations. All of these risks are known as *pure risks*, and they reflect situations where loss may or may not occur. A second broad class of risks are *speculative risks*, such as business ventures, where there is an expectation of gain but a potential for loss. Insurance companies normally do not insure speculative risks (Green, 1971).

TYPES OF INSURANCE

Although lines of insurance may be subdivided a number of ways, traditionally there have been three broad classifications of private insurance. These are: (a) life insurance, (b) health and accident insurance, and (c) property and liability insurance (Crane, 1980). While the private insurance industry developed on a mono-line basis where each company characteristically wrote only one type of coverage (e.g., life insurance), most large insurance companies now provide multiple-line or all-line coverages (Huebner, Black and Cline, 1976).

Life Insurance

Life insurance has two principal purposes: (a) to protect dependents against the early death of the "breadwinner," and (b) to provide economic security in old age. The two basic types of life insurance are *term insurance* and *whole life insurance*. Term insurance provides protection against early death, and whole life protection against the economic uncertainties of old age. Many individuals buy *endowment insurance* or other combination policies which provide both term and whole life coverages. In practice, there are many ways in which the features of term and whole life may be combined, based upon the needs of the insured (Greene and Serbein, 1978).

While life insurance represents a very large portion of the insurance industry, its focus is on death and superannuation benefits. There is accordingly no need or rationale for rehabilitation services. Life insurance is not, therefore, a line of insurance that generates private sector rehabilitation referrals.

Health and Accident Insurance

Health and accident insurance protects against losses which result from sickness or injury. Losses fall into one of two categories: (a) loss of income, and (b) medical expenses. The health and accident insurance market has traditionally been divided between the individual and group policies written by private insurance companies, and the policies of Blue Cross and Blue Shield associations (Mehr and Newman, 1972). More recently, Health Maintenance Organizations (where subscribers pay an annual fee for a wide range of health services) have developed as an alternative to other forms of health and accident insurance.

Within the health and accident insurance area, vocational rehabilitation services are most frequently provided under *long term disability* (LTD) *policies*. The purpose of LTD policies is to provide income replacement when the insured cannot return to work. If, through vocational rehabilitation services, the insured can again work, then the insurance company is released from its obligation to replace the insured's income.

Insurance companies write LTD policies for individuals, groups (i.e., the employees of a business), and associations (e.g., fraternal orders, professional organizations). Many LTD policies include or are sold in association with short term income replacement coverage and accidental death and dismemberment coverage. The difference between short term and LTD coverage is that short term coverage lasts for only a few years, while LTD coverage may last until age 65 or for life in cases of total disability.

The income replacement benefits provided under LTD policies are variable, but benefits are computed as a certain percentage of the preinjury or base period wage, exclusive of overtime. A typical benefit under group LTD policies is 66.66% or two thirds of gross weekly wages. Because this benefit is tax free income, most individuals find a two thirds replacement of gross income adequate. The benefit, however, is normally somewhat less than preinjury net income, thereby providing a financial incentive for returning to work.

Group LTD policies are usually written with a clause that allows for the offset of LTD benefits by Social Security Disability Insurance, workers' compensation, and/or retirement and pension benefits. This means that if an injured worker, for example, was entitled to $800/month in group LTD benefits, but received $500/month in other insurance benefits, the group LTD payment would be $300/month. This reduction for similar benefits occurs because the employer normally contributes to group LTD coverage, and the offset substantially reduces the overall cost of the insurance. Individual and association LTD policies, however, are not always offset by other benefits, and in some cases the insured may collect more than they received in salary or wages.

In relation to vocational rehabilitation services, the most critical aspect of LTD policies is how "total disability" is defined. The LTD policy may consider the insured to be totally disabled and therefore entitled to benefits if the insured: (a) cannot return to his or her preinjury occupation, or (b) cannot perform any suitable occupation for which he or she is reasonably qualified. This aspect of LTD coverage has become known in rehabilitation circles as the "HIS OCC/ANY OCC" clause. Typical LTD coverage will provide benefits for "HIS OCC" disability for about two years, and for "ANY OCC" disability until age 65 or for life.

Vocational rehabilitation services can be provided in LTD coverage whether the insured is under the HIS OCC or ANY OCC clause. There is, however, no placement flexibility under the HIS OCC clause, and longer existing disability in cases falling under the ANY OCC clause. Both situations complicate the task of the rehabilitationist. Some LTD policies have *trial work clauses* which allow for the partial continuation of LTD benefits during a trial work period. These clauses allow the insured to keep all work earnings and a portion of LTD benefits equaling a total amount greater than what would have been received under LTD alone, creating a financial incentive to return to work. Some policies also have *cooperation clauses* whereby LTD benefits can be reduced or lost by the claimant's obstruction or refusal to cooperate with rehabilitation services.

In working with LTD cases the rehabilitationist should remember that the LTD carrier is liable for only income replacement and not medical expenses. The carrier may agree to support reasonable medical services that are directly related to the objective of vocational rehabilitation, but if there is another carrier liable for medical services, the rehabilitationist may need to arrange needed medical services through that carrier.

Property and Liability Insurance

The category of property and liability insurance is far broader than either life insurance or health and accident insurance. Four major areas within this category are: (a) fire insurance, (b) marine insurance, (c) fidelity and surety bonds, and (d) casualty insurance. The area of casualty insurance is where rehabilitation referrals are generated, and the casualty insurance area is in itself diverse, including a number of seemingly unrelated coverages such as: (a) automobile insurance, (b) workers' compensation, (c) liability insurance, (d) title insurance, (e) plate glass insurance, (f) boiler explosion insurance, and (g) insurance against theft and robbery.

Workers' compensation is the line of casualty insurance that accounts for the vast majority of private sector referrals. In a survey of the 33,916 IRA cases closed during the ten year period preceeding 1979, Field (1979) reported that 22,493 (66.3%) were workers' compensation, 4,923 (14.5%) automobile no-fault, 4,149 (12.2%) automobile liability, 1,562 (4.6%) disability income, 522 general liability (1.5%), and 234 (.7%) referrals from other sources. While there is an increasing tendency to use rehabilitation services in insurance lines other than workers' compensation (see Rasch, 1983), the caseloads of most private sector rehabilitationists are largely workers' compensation referrals.

Liability lines of insurance are the second largest source of private sector referrals. Liability insurance covers the insured for both property damage and the effects of personal injury wrongfully inflicted on another, and rehabilitation services are involved in the personal injury aspect of this coverage. The four basic liability lines are: (a) automobile liability — covering all auto-related injuries to another party, (b) product liability — protecting against injuries from defective machinery or goods, (c) malpractice liability — covering injury from professional negligence or misconduct, and (d) general liability — representing all other liability exposures. States with automobile no-fault laws (at this writing 24 states and the District of Columbia) have restricted the automobile liability exposures of carriers by requiring injured parties to collect damages up to certain threshold limits from their own carrier before suing an "at fault" party.

It is important to recognize that liability insurance is the economic underpinning of our *tort* or civil law system. Without this type of insurance there is no satisfactory way to collect for *damages* wrongfully inflicted by another party (unless that party is wealthy). Motorists, for example, are required by law to carry liability insurance in the event they are responsible for an automobile accident which injures another's property or person. The injured party is able to collect damages because the responsiblity for the loss is transferred from the driver (who may have few resources) to an insurance company.

In liability insurance the insured is called the first party, the insurance company the second party, and the injured person the third party. In order for the third party to collect damages from the second party, the third party must establish that the first party was *negligent* in a way that the second party, through an insurance contract, assumed liability for. Negligence essentially means that the injury occured through a wrongful act of commission or ommission by the first party. The situation is often complicated in that the third party, through *contributory negligence,* may have some responsibility for their own injury.

When carriers write liability lines of insurance they specify the maximum amount of financial liability that they will accept in consideration of the insured's premium. This is normally stated as *X* dollars for any one individual who is injured, and a larger *Y* dollars for the total occurrance. Carrier payments under personal injury liability insurance involve the medical expenses of the injured third party (both present and anticipated in the future) and also the replacement of lost income. There may also be a payment for *pain and suffering* stemming from the injury. These payments may be negotiated in an out-of-court settlement by attorneys representing the parties, or if there is disagreement the issues may be settled in a court of law. In all cases, the carrier's liability is limited to the amounts specified by the insurance contract. The first party is responsible for any excessive court award, such as *punitive damages*, which may be over and above the carrier's exposure.

Clients referred under personal injury liability lines have usually engaged the services of an attorney, unless the carrier makes the referral shortly after the injury. Whenever a client has an attorney, regardless of the type of insurance line involved, the rehabilitationist should contact the attorney and request permission to work with the client. This permission is normally granted over the telephone without difficulty, but the request should nevertheless be made as soon as the rehabilitationist learns that the client has an attorney. If this information is revealed in the initial interview, the attorney should be contacted before the interview proceeds further. This is necessary because the rehabilitationist is technically an extension of the carrier, and there are some attorneys who will object to the rehabilitationist's involvement, or who will want to be present for the initial interview. The client's attorney has the right to be present whenever the client is interviewed, but this is usually unnecessary and is seldom conducive to rehabilitation. The evaluations and progress reports written by the rehabilitationist go to the carrier, and if the client's attorney wants these reports they must be obtained from the carrier.

Liability cases are often in litigation, and this presents special rehabilitation problems. The foremost problem is that the more severe and incapacitating the injury, the higher settlement or award the client should rightfully receive. Moreover, because the client's attorney is usually paid on a *contingency fee* basis (i.e., a certain percentage of the settlement or award goes to the attorney), the attorney has no real financial incentive to encourage rehabilitation. Successful vocational rehabilitation may actually undercut the award which the client would receive if unable to work again, and has the overall effect of making the client appear less severely injured. All of this unfortunately creates an incentive for some clients to try to appear as disabled as possible, at least until their litigation is resolved. Litigation culminates in a cash settlement or award which may range from nothing to a substantial sum of money. However, once the carrier has settled, usually by a lump sum payment, the carrier has no further obligation to support rehabilitation services. Many clients unfortunately make poor use of their settlement or award (which is usually only moderate), and years later may have few remaining financial resources and little chance to work again.

In the "average" personal injury liability referral, the carrier is seeking two outcomes. The first is for the claimant to reach maximum medical improvement at the earliest possible date and at a reasonable cost. The second is for the claimant to maintain his or her employment, and if that employment is lost, to find new employment. For maximum effectiveness, cases should be referred early for medical and vocational management. Early referral may also reduce the likelihood of litigation and facilitate a reasonable out-of-court settlement (Rasch, 1983).

When working with liability cases an important rehabilitation issue is the quality of the relationship developed with the claimant and the claimant's attorney. When this relationship is positive and both are full participants in the rehabilitation process, the probability of early medical recovery and vocational rehabilitation increases. The carrier must also be involved in this "good faith" relationship. If the carrier is or is perceived as interested in only cost containment issues, rehabilitation will be undercut and the probability of protracted litigation becomes greater (Rasch, 1983).

Although personal injuries stem from many types of accidents, in our society the automobile is the major agent of trauma and premature death ("Auto Accidents," 1980-81). When two parties are involved in an automobile accident one is usually at fault (or more at fault than the other) and therefore responsible for the injuries suffered by the other. Depending on the state law, insurance which covers auto-related injuries is known as automobile liability insurance or automobile no-fault insurance. Automobile liability is like other liability lines, but automobile no-fault is substantially different.

As indicated earlier, approximately half of the states currently have automobile no-fault laws, but their provisions and benefits are highly variable. Under automobile no-fault, each injured party collects benefits up to certain set limits from their own insurance company, regardless of who was at fault (Mehr and Hedges, 1974). No-fault limits for income loss and medical benefits, for example, might be $10,000 and $20,000, respectively (some states provide unlimited no-fault medical benefits). Losses above these amounts are the responsibility of the negligent driver and his or her insurance company (automobile liability). In cases of severe injury, suits for pain and suffering are allowed. The overall objective of no-fault insurance is to keep automobile accidents that involve only minor losses out of litigation by having the injured party deal first with their own insurance company.

Automobile no-fault insurance laws characteristically provide rehabilitation benefits to injured parties either as part of their medical benefit provisions, or as separate rehabilitation provisions. The first party coverage in automobile no-fault which generates rehabilitation referrals is called Personal Injury Protection (PIP). While PIP benefits normally include income replacement as well as medical benefits, the carriers exposure is usually higher for medical benefits than income replacement. For this reason, no-fault cases are more often referred for medical management than vocational rehabilitation services (Rasch, 1983).

FUNCTIONS OF INSURANCE COMPANIES

Like all large businesses, insurance companies have divisions within themselves to address specific or circumscribed tasks. This is true whether the insurance company is owned by its stockholders (stock insurance company) or by its policy holders (mutual insurance company). The basic functions (see Crane, 1980; Greene, 1977; Vaughan and Elliot, 1978) of an insurance company are:

1. Ratemaking
2. Sales and Marketing
3. Selection of Risks
4. Claims Processing
5. Investment

Ratemaking

As indicated earlier, the price of any unit of insurance is based upon company predictions of probable loss. These predictions may be made by the *actuarial* staff of the company or obtained from outside *rating bureaus*. Most rates are *class rates*, meaning that the insured are sorted into different groups based upon characteristics which predict loss. For example, a construction company will have a higher per unit workers' compensation rate than a telephone answering service because of greater expectations of injury in the former line of work. Class rates may be adjusted by *experience ratings* if the insured has a loss record better or worse than expected for their class.

To determine the rate charged per unit of insurance coverage (exposure unit) within a given class, the insurer divides the average expected loss for each exposure unit (which is determined by dividing total expected losses by the number of exposure units), by one minus their probable expense or overhead ratio in offering the line of insurance. For example, if an insurer expected annual malpractice losses of \$100 per insured rehabilitationist, and had operating cost requiring 20% of every premium dollar, the annual rate for each exposure unit would be \$125:

$$\frac{\text{Average Malpractice Loss}}{1 - \text{Expense Ratio}} = \frac{\$100}{1 - .20} = 125$$

Sales and Marketing

Once insurers have determined the coverages they will write and their rates, the next function is to find buyers for the insurance. This is the sales and marketing function of the insurer, and this function is often referred to in the insurance industry as *pro-*

duction. This is because there is no insurance product until a buyer is found and a contract signed. The signing of the contract "produces" the tangible insurance product (Green, 1977).

Insurance companies utilize sales and marketing divisions and outside agents to produce their product. It is critical that the company generate an adequate number of exposure units in each line of insurance, for this is the only way losses can be accurately predicted. Insurance policies are normally sold either by *direct agents* who work for the insurance company or by *independent agents* who represent many companies.

Selection of Risks

Although insurance companies are in the business of selling insurance, they will not insure all applicants. The selection of risks is known in insurance as *underwriting*, which is the process of deciding which risks will be accepted and rejected. The purpose of underwriting departments is to secure not only a safe distribution of risks, but also a profitable distribution (Mowbray, Blanchard and Williams, 1969; Greene and Serbein, 1978). Underwriting policy must assure that truly poor risks are rejected, that reasonable risks are accepted (too strict underwriting rules choke off business), and that risks are adequately distributed so that one catastrophy cannot cause losses in many exposure units.

In determining whether a risk should be accepted or rejected, underwriters normally determine the "class" into which the risk should fall, and then decide whether the rates set for that class seem appropriate in reference to pertinent information available on the applicant. According to Vaughan and Elliot (1978), there are five sources from which underwriters can obtain information to make this decision: (a) statements made in the insurance application, (b) information from agents or brokers, (c) investigations, (d) information bureaus, and (e) physical examinations or inspections. The underwriting function is obviously very critical for insurers, and each company has underwriting policies which its representatives and agents must follow. At times, the underwriting and production functions clash when business generated by direct or independent agents is subsequently declined by company underwriters.

Claims Processing

Regardless of how successful underwriting decisions are, losses invariably occur. When a loss occurs the insured presents a *claim* to the insurer. The claim normally specifies the nature and extent of damages, and assigns a monetary value to the loss. When a claim is filed under an insurance contract the process of *loss adjustment* or *claims processing* begins.

When an insurance claim is made, the first step of the insurer is to determine whether a loss covered by the policy in fact occurred. Insurance companies are routinely presented with invalid claims (e.g., a business property fire set by the owner, an injury reported to have occured while at work that actually occurred during nonwork hours). Obviously, the identification and denial of claims not covered by the insurance contract is an important loss reduction function. In addition to losses not covered by the insurance contract, false claims may be presented (i.e. where no loss occurred) or the amount claimed may be far in excess of true damages.

Insurance companies cannot pay claims presented under a contract without first investigating and determining that: (a) a real loss occurred, (b) the loss is covered by the insurance contract, and (c) the amount claimed for the loss is accurate. When insurers pay excessive claims, or claims which are not legally binding, they increase their costs, reduce profits, and if poor adjusting occurs regularly the company will eventually cease to be competitive. This is because the insurer will eventually need to charge its customers higher premiums to cover losses under the line of insurance where poor adjusting occurs. It is therefore in the interest of both the insurer and its customers that the loss adjustment function be fair and accurate.

In personal injury lines of insurance, the injured claimant will be assigned to a *claims representative* who will investigate the claim and subsequently supervise the payment of benefits for which the injured claimant is entitled. The claims representative may be an employee of the insurance company or the employee of an independent adjusting firm. Outside adjusting services are most frequently used when the carrier has insufficient business in a given local to justify an office with claims representatives of its own. Regardless of who processes the claim, the goal of the adjuster is to meet the legal obligations of the insurer at a minimum cost. Insurance companies are not social welfare agencies, and they will enter into adversarial relationships with claimants when they believe injuries are exaggerated or claims excessive. At times, the insurer and insured are not able to reach an agreement on what benefits should be paid under an insurance contract and the arguments of both are presented to an overseeing agency or in a court of law.

Although the insurer and insured can find themselves in an adversarial relationship regarding benefits entitled under a contract, this situation is the exception rather than the norm. When rehabilitation case management services seem needed, the claims representative (or workers' compensation agency) will refer the case to a rehabilitation service provider. This provider is normally a private rehabilitation company or the public VR agency. The rehabilitationist assigned to the case interviews the client, evaluates medical and vocational data, coordinates medical services, and develops a vocational rehabilitation plan.

In personal injury lines of insurance, the rehabilitationist must work closely not only with the injured claimant, but also with the claims representative and/or workers' compensation agency. From an insurance perspective, rehabilitation is part of the claims adjusting process. How well the client responds to vocational rehabilitation services will largely determine the financial or economic losses resulting from the injury. The carrier's liability for claimant losses is limited by the insurance contract or state workers' compensation law, and economic losses above the carrier's liability will be born by the injured party. Because the insurance indemnity seldom fully replaces lost earnings, the injured party also has a strong financial incentive for vocational rehabilitation.

Investment

Insurance companies have two major sources of income — premiums and investment earnings. Premiums are paid before losses occur, and as it would be foolish to let these funds remain idle, they are invested to cover future liabilities and to generate a profit for the insurer. The insurance industry controls substantial financial assets, and it is an important source of funds in American money and capital markets (Mowbray, Blanchard and Williams, 1969; Greene, 1977).

Insurance company investments are largely determined by the nature of the liabilities assumed by the insurer. Property and liability insurers require more liquidity than life insurers (life insurers have only a long-term obligation to their clients) and so the former's funds are more heavily invested in stocks and government bonds, and the latter in mortgages and corporate bonds (Greene, 1977; Preffer and Klock, 1974). In some cases, anticipated investment earnings are taken into consideration in calculating premiums. This practice is more common in life insurance than in property and liability insurance as the earnings of long-term investments are more predictable.

THE GOVERNMENT AND INSURANCE

Federal and state governments have two major roles in insurance. One is to directly provide various insurance coverages for their citizens, the other is to regulate the private insurance industry. Both of these roles are very important. Government sponsored insurance is necessary because there are some insurance needs, that for various financial or risk selection reasons, are beyond the capabilities of the private insurance industry. Government regulation is necessary because insurance is an industry in which the public has strong vested interests.

Government Sponsored Insurance

When most people think of government sponsored insurance they think of "social insurance" programs such as the Old Age, Survivors, Disability and Health Insurance (OASDHI) program, which is of course better known as Social Security and Medicare. In reality, federal and state governments operate a variety of insurance programs. While some are compulsory, participation in many government sponsored programs is voluntary. In some cases, government insurance programs are in direct competition with privately offered coverages. For example, many states have their own workers' compensation insurance fund that competes with private companies licensed to write workers' compensation coverage within the state. In some states (six at this writing), the state workers' compensation fund operates as a monopoly (Vaughan and Elliott, 1978).

While it is not possible to present an exhaustive list of government sponsored insurance, some additional examples of government insurance programs are: (a) railroad retirement, disability, and unemployment programs; (b) state unemployment insurance; (c) federal crop insurance; (d) Federal Housing Administration (FHA) and Veterans Administration (VA) mortgage loan insurance; (e) national flood insurance; (f) VA life insurance; (g) federal crime insurance; (h) state title insurance funds; (e) federal insurance of deposits in banks and savings institutions; and (j) state funds to insure against the insolvency of insurance companies. While most government insurance programs are voluntary, federal and state governments have the power to make insurance programs compulsory for their citizens. This makes it possible for the government to use the insurance mechanism as an instrument for social welfare, as is the case in workers' compensation insurance.

Social Security

The most far reaching example of how government has used insurance as a mechanism for social welfare is the Old Age, Survivors, Disability and Health Insurance (OASDHI) program. This program, which began with the Social Security Act of 1935, has been modified over the years so that it covers most workers and their dependents providing: (a) retirement benefits, (b) survivor benefits, (c) disability benefits, and (d) health insurance in old age (Medicare). The part of this program which is of most interest to rehabilitationists is Social Security Disability Insurance (SSDI) and a companion non-insurance welfare program, Supplemental Security Income (SSI), both of which are operated by the Social Security Administration.

The basic purpose of disability benefits under SSDI and SSI is to provide economic maintenance for those citizens who are too severely handicapped to work. SSDI covers workers who paid into the Social Security System and their dependents, and SSI the developmentally disabled and noninsured poor. In 1981, SSDI was paying annual benefits of $18 billion to 4.6 million people, and SSI, $4 billion to 2.3 million people (Fialka, 1981). In order to receive benefits under either program the applicant must: (a) have a physical or mental impairment which prevents them from doing any substantial work existing in the national economy, and (b) the disability must have existed or be expected to exist for at least 12 months, or be expected to result in death. In order to determine if an applicant is eligible for benefits, state employed disability examiners collect and review medical and other pertinent data. In addition to new applicants, disability examiners annually review the eligibility of approximately 200,000 recipients (Fialka, 1981). If the disability determination unit rules an applicant or recipient ineligible for SSDI or SSI benefits, the individual can appeal the decision to a Social Security administrative law judge. A hearing is then held and all pertinent data regarding the applicant's eligibility for benefits is reviewed. Frequently, administrative law judges will ask for an "outside" opinion on the applicants' employability and a vocational expert registered with the Social Security Administration's Vocational Consultant Program will review the data and offer an opinion on the applicant's work ability. Many rehabilitationists are registered with the Vocational Consultants Program and provide vocational opinions in cases that arise in their local communities.

All applicants for and beneficiaries of SSDI and SSI are screened to determine if they might benefit from vocational rehabilitation services. The purpose of this is to assure that applicants with employment potential are not provided benefits, and that beneficiaries who "improve" are helped to return to work. Although the Social Security Administration has always had a contractual service relationship with the state VR agencies, new regulations and reimbursement guidelines are making it more feasible for private rehabilitation companies to work with Social Security Administration cases (see Rasch, 1982).

Regulation of the Insurance Industry

As indicated earlier, insurance is an industry in which the public has vested interests. It is socially undesirable to have insurers become insolvent, or to have them realize unreasonably high profits at the public's expense. For these and other reasons states regulate insurance practices within their boundaries (Post, 1976). Each state has its own insurance laws or *code*, and an administrative apparatus (usually a commission or board of insurance) which enforces the code and monitors insurance companies operating within the state.

The head of a state's regulatory agency is often called the *Commissioner of Insurance*. The duties of the Commissioner's office include: (a) setting administrative rules which operationalize state laws, (b) licensing insurers within the state, (c) assuring that assets on deposit with the insurance commission are adequate to cover the reserves (liabilities) of the insurer, (d) periodic examination of the insurer's business practices and solvency, (e) reviews and approval of existing and new rates to assure that they are adequate, not excessive, and not unfairly discriminatory, and (f) overseeing the liquidation of assets of insolvent insurers. State insurance commissioners have been organized since 1871 (Grant, 1979) in the National Association of Insurance Commissioners (NAIC). Through this voluntary association, the commissioners study each others insurance practices, coordinate regulatory activities, review the adequacy of existing state insurance laws, and recommend needed legislation to state legislatures (Vaughan and Elliot, 1978).

Although there are federal laws that specifically address the insurance industry (e.g., McCarran-Ferguson Act of 1945), the regulation of insurance practices is a responsibility of each state. This situation has resulted in the development of 50 different insurance codes and a lack of uniformity in the regulation of the insurance industry. There are those who strongly advocate the "federalization" of insurance regulation. According to Greene (1977), proponents of federal regulation argue that state regulation of national and international companies is relatively ineffective, and nonuniform regulation adds to insurance costs. According to Vaughn and Elliot (1978), there may eventually be a dual system of regulation where insurance companies may operate under a federal or state charter, with those operating under a federal charter being exempt from state insurance laws.

Within rehabilitation, the impact of state rather than federal regulation of insurance practices is most keenly felt in the area of workers' compensation. Presently, there are 50 state workers' compensation laws which provide variable medical, income replacement, and vocational rehabilitation benefits. The result is that regularly since 1973, legislation has been introduced in Congress that would, in effect, federalize workers' compensation (Lewin, Ramseur and Sink, 1979). In response to this and other developments, many states have recently reviewed their workers' compensation laws, with one of their objectives being to increase rehabilitation benefits for injured workers. NAIC has strongly endorsed rehabilitation as a needed component in state workers' compensation laws. If the federalization of workers' compensation should ever occur, rehabilitationists must advocate for strong vocational rehabilitation provisions in a federal law. Presently, rehabilitationists must become intimately familiar with their own state laws, and must work toward the adoption of state laws which adequately provide for the vocational rehabilitation needs of injured workers.

References

Auto accidents: The dollar takes its toll. *Journal of American Insurance*, Winter 1980-81, p. 15.

Bickelhaupt, D.L. and Magee, J.H.: *General Insurance*. Homewood: Richard D. Irwin, 1970.

Crane, F.G.: *Insurance Principles and Practices*. New York: John Wiley and Sons, 1980.

Fialka, J.J.: Wielding the ax. *The Wall Street Journal*, November 19, 1981, pp. 1, 22.

Field, S.J.: Data base analysis. *Rehabilitation Forum*, December 1979, p. 2.

Grant, H.R.: *Insurance Reform: Consumer Action in the Progressive Era*. Ames: Iowa State University Press, 1979.

Greene, M.R.: *Risk and Insurance*. Cincinnati: South-Western Publishing Company, 1977.

Greene, M.R.: *Risk Aversion, Insurance, and the Future*. Bloomington: Indiana University, 1971.

Greene, M.R. and Serbein, O.N.: *Risk Management: Text and Cases*. Reston, Virginia: Prentice-Hall, 1978.

Huebner, S.S., Black, K. and Cline, R.S.: *Property and Liability Insurance*. Englewood Cliffs: Prentice-Hall, 1976.

Lewin, S.S., Ramseur, J.H. and Sink, J.M.: The role of private rehabilitation: Founder, catalyst, competitor. *Journal of Rehabilitation*, 1979, *45(3)*:16-19.

Mehr, R.I. and Cammack, E.: *Principles of Insurance*. Homewood: Richard D. Irwin, 1966.

Mehr, R.I. and Hedges, B.A.: *Risk Management: Concepts and Applications*. Homewood: Richard D. Irwin, 1974.

Mehr, R.I. and Neuman, S.: *Inflation, Technology, and Growth: Possible Long-Range Implications for Insurance*. Bloomington: Indiana University, 1972.

Mowbray, A.H., Blanchard, R.H. and Williams, C.A.: *Insurance: Its Theory and Practice in the United States*. New York: McGraw-Hill, 1969.

Post, J.E.: *Risk and Response*. Toronto: Lexington Books, 1976.

Preffer, I. and Klock, D.R.: *Perspectives on Insurance*. Englewood Cliffs: Prentice-Hall, 1974.

Rasch, J.D.: Insurance rehabilitation of nonindustrially injured clients. *Rehabilitation Counseling Bulletin*, 1983, *27*:12-17.

Rasch, J.D.: New act may open SSA cases to private rehabilitation providers. *ARCA News*, March 1982, p. 4.

Vaughan, E.J. and Elliot, C.M.: *Fundamentals of Risk and Insurance*. New York: John Wiley and Sons, 1978.

Williams, C.A. and Heins, R.M.: *Risk Management and Insurance*. New York: McGraw-Hill, 1981.

CHAPTER III

WORKERS' COMPENSATION

REHABILITATION services may be delivered under any personal injury line of insurance, but the vast majority of referrals are generated by the workers' compensation system. Workers' compensation is the foundation upon which private sector rehabilitation developed, and it will remain the major source of referrals to private sector rehabilitationists for the foreseeable future. Unlike the state-federal rehabilitation program where federal guidelines result in a uniform program, workers' compensation is the concern of each state. This has naturally resulted in considerable variability as each state has a unique workers' compensation law. While each rehabilitationist must become familiar with the legislation in the state(s) where they operate, there is enough similarity in existing state laws to allow for a generalized discussion of how rehabilitation services relate to the workers' compensation system.

HISTORY OF WORKERS' COMPENSATION

People have always worked to survive, producing through their efforts shelter, food, clothing, other necessities, and of course the amenities of life. In any society, it is necessary for most people to produce the goods and services which characterize that society. Unfortunately, it is inevitable that some people will be seriously injured or even killed while working. Although it is true that many deaths and injuries may be prevented by greater attention to safety, it is a simple fact that accidents will invariably occur in work activities. Workers' compensation is the mechanism which Western society developed to assist workers and their dependents who are the victims of industrial accidents.

While work activities are not the only activities that can lead to death or disability, the idea that "special" provisions should be made for those injured while working can be traced to antiquity. For example, the Old Testament called for a master to set a servant free if the master willfully injured the servant. In ancient Rome and Greece, it was generally accepted that masters were responsible for their servants' health and physical condition. Throughout the middle ages, and probably long before, soldiers injured in the service of a king or prince looked to their master for sustenance until they were well enough to fight again (Oberman, 1965). While servants expected their masters to care for their health, injury in the service of another gave one only a strong moral claim for charity or relief, but rarely legal rights. The extent of aid was usually determined only by the master's resources and sense of personal obligation to the servant.

Early American laws governing injured workers were based upon *common laws* (legal precedents from court decisions) which had developed earlier in England. Although English common laws protected injured workers from arbitrary discharge by their employers (because with discharge they subsequently became economic burdens on their community), common laws made it very difficult for injured workers to successfully petition their employer for medical care or financial compensation from work-related injuries. With the increasing urbanization and industrialization of the American and European continents during the later 19th and early 20th centuries, thousands of injured workers found their suits for damages frustrated by common law defenses which came to be known as *employer liability laws*. These defenses greatly restricted the liability of employers for injuries suffered by employees performing their duties, in effect giving them fewer rights than if they were injured strangers. The result was that a serious work injury often lead to chronic poverty for workers and their dependents (Cheit, 1961).

Tort Law and Common Law Defenses

In order to understand the development of workers' compensation, it is necessary to overview *tort law*. Under tort law when someone is injured by the negligent act of another (the act may be by commission or ommission), the injured party (plaintiff) is entitled to collect damages from the negligent party (defendant). Damages may involve payments to the plaintiff for medical expenses, lost income, and for inconvenience or pain and suffering. In some cases, courts may even award punitive damages to an injured party in order to punish a negligent party. However, before any damages are awarded, the plaintiff must prove that some other party or parties were negligent and therefore have responsibility (liability) for the injury. In cases where several defendants are shown to have contributed to an injury, the court assesses some percent of negligence to each as a basis for determining what percentage of the damages each must pay. However, some states (Vaughan and Elliot, 1978) have doctrines of *contributory negligence* where if the injured party was also negligent, the injured party is then not entitled to damages. Most states, however, have *comparative negligence* doctrines which allow a partially negligent plaintiff to recover some portion of their loss from other negligent parties.

When a plaintiff sues a defendant for damages from a personal injury, the plaintiff must prove (or establish to the satisfaction of the court) that: (a) the plaintiff was actually injured and that there were (or will be) adverse economic consequences from the injury, and (b) the defendant negligently contributed to the occurrence of the injury, and is therefore fully or at least partially liable for damages. It follows that if the plaintiff must prove the above, the defendant's task is to prevent this from occurring. When it is clear that the plaintiff was actually injured (in some cases this may be contested), the defense normally presents evidence to indicate that the actual injury or economic consequences of the injury are less severe than claimed by the plaintiff. However, the first priority of the defense is to defeat or weaken the accusation of negligence, thereby eliminating all or at least a portion of the defendant's liability for the injury.

A claim of negligence in a personal injury can be defended a number of ways. These include establishing for the court that the negligence claim is frivolous or unfounded, or by identifying another party liable for the injury. The contributory or comparative negligence doctrines are almost always used as a defense against negligence. Another common defense is the *assumption of risks* doctrine, which states that if an injured party knew that risks were present and voluntarily choose to place him or herself in a situation or activity where they might be injured, then they are not entitled to damages from another negligent party. For example, if someone at a bar decided to ride a mechanical bull, and was subsequently thrown off the machine and injured, a suit for damages could be defended on the basis that by choosing to ride an obviously dangerous machine the injured party had assumed the risks inherent in the ride.

In the 19th and early 20th centuries employers naturally used the common law defenses of contributory negligence and assumption of risk to defeat law suits brought by injured workers. Another common law defense available to employers was the *fellow servant doctrine* which held that an employer was not liable for an employee injury if the injury resulted from the negligent act of another employee. With these three common law defenses (contributory negligence, assumption of risks, and fellow servant) it was very difficult for injured workers to successfully sue their employers. Even when injured workers could show that the employer was negligent, the suit for damages would be defeated if the employer could show that the injured worker or a co-worker were in anyway negligent (Cheit, 1961). In the event the employer failed to establish such negligence, the assumption of risks doctrine often provided a sufficient defense in itself.

In addition to legal problems caused by the common law defenses available to employers, injured workers faced many "technical" problems in bringing successful suits against their employers. First, filing such suits almost always resulted in the dismissal of the injured worker and subsequently poor work references. This being the case, a law suit could be seriously considered only in cases of profound injury. If the injury produced only temporary or partial disability, it was often better for the injured worker to bear the economic losses rather than risk dismissal by an angered employer. Second, in order to successfully sue an employer it was characteristically necessary to have co-workers testify against the employer. Fellow workers naturally feared reprisals from the employer, making it difficult to find competent witnesses (Berkowitz, 1960). Third, law suits are long, time consuming activities, which offer no immediate relief or guarantee of eventual success. Finally, even if an injured worker won a law suit there was no assurance the court award would justify the effort. Court awards were and still are highly variable, ranging from outrageously generous to totally inadequate sums for injuries sustained. Moreover, the injured worker's attorney was usually paid on a contingency fee basis, meaning that a set percentage of the award (often as high as 50%) went for legal services.

It became increasingly clear in the late 19th and early 20th centuries that the common laws which had developed to define employer liability unfairly discriminated against injured workers, and actually supported employer indifference to safety in the work environment. Gradually, states began to pass employer liability laws to modify (in favor of injured workers) some principles of employer liability, especially the fellow servant doctrine. In some states contributory negligence doctrines were dropped and comparative negligence doctrines adopted (Turnbull, Williams and Cheit, 1968). Also, under common law only the injured worker had a right to sue for damages, and if the worker was killed in an industrial accident the dependents had no legal recourse. This gradually changed to allow suits by the dependents of deceased workers. However, despite modifications in the system of employers' liability, it became increasingly apparent that a system based on negligence could not adequately deal with the personal and social consequences of industrial injuries.

Rationale For Workers' Compensation

Prior to the industrial revolution, business enterprises generally operated on a relatively small scale. Employers usually resided in the same community where they did business, often knew their employees personally, and perhaps even worked beside them. The industrial revolution, however, changed the nature of business activity from small to large scale production of goods and services. In this change from craftmanship to factory production, injuries became far more prevalent and serious. Although no reliable data exists, it is estimated that beginning around 1900 there were more than 2 million serious industrial injuries and 25,000-35,000 deaths each year (Turnbull, Williams and Cheit, 1968; Vaughan and Elliot, 1978). While the industrial revolution created great wealth for Western society, it became increasingly clear that many of the workers who produced that wealth paid a terrible toll.

The principle underlying workers' compensation is that *industrialization benefits everyone in society, and since injury and death are inevitable in industrial activity, everyone in society should help bear the economic consequences.* In other words, industrial accidents are seen as a cost of production. The statistical frequencies for accidents in different types of industrial activity are predictable, and their economic consequences can be passed along to consumers as a price factor in the production of goods and services. Viewing industrial accidents as an inevitable by-product of industrialization, and as a cost of production, removes the need to establish that some party was negligent and therefore liable for the injury. In workers' compensation, the employer is liable for all work related injuries whether they result from the employer's negligence or not (Post, 1976).

In addition to making industrial accidents a cost of production, workers' compensation changed the nature of the recovery to which injured workers were entitled. Under employer liability laws, injured workers winning their law suits received a single recovery in the form of a lump sum payment. As indicated earlier, amounts paid were highly variable and often poorly related to the actual economic losses of the worker, and more importantly payment was delayed by the litigation process. The workers' compensation system established a procedure where the employer's liability was extended over a period of time equal to the length of the disability. During this period the employer paid employee medical, surgical, and hospital expenses, and also made periodic payments to partially compensate for lost wages. A lump sum settlement was often arranged after the injured worker reached maximum medical improvement to discharge the employer from any further liability in the injury, and to compensate the injured worker for residual impairments (e.g., lost body members, disfigurement), future medical expenses, and/or lost earning potential. In cases where death resulted from an injury, the workers' compensation system provided benefits to dependents in the form of a burial allowance and periodic payments to compensate for the lost wages or salary of the deceased worker (Vaughan and Elliot, 1978).

It is important to emphasize that the workers' compensation system is a compromise between the economic interests of injured workers and employers. In this compromise injured workers are suppose to exchange the right to sue their employers (even when the employer is clearly negligent) for a guaranteed partial compensation of their economic losses regardless of fault. Injured workers normally receive full compensation for medical expenses and a partial replacement of lost wages. The partial replacement of lost wages is designed not so much to hold down the cost of the workers' compensation program, but rather to create an incentive for injured workers to seek reemployment. The employer benefits from the workers' compensation system in that potentially devastating law suits are avoided. The cost of industrial injury becomes a predictable factor in production, payable in regular installments to an insurance company or state managed workers' compensation fund.

Early Laws

The first workers' compensation legislation was passed in Germany in 1884. The original German law only covered workers engaged in manufacturing and mining, but was extended over the next few years to cover government employees (1886), agricultural and forestry workers (1886), and seamen (1887). The German law required employers engaged in similar types of industry, usually within a given district, to form and make payments to accident associations. The accident associations were non-profit bodies which functioned under the auspices of the Federal Insurance Office, and were responsible for ensuring that injured workers received all benefits to which they were entitled. Benefits for injured workers included medical expenses and partial income replacement for temporary and permanent disability. For temporary disability, workers were reimbursed for 50% of wage loss during the first four weeks and 66⅔% for the next nine weeks. Permanent disability benefits were payable at 66⅔% of the last year's wage for the "continuance of disablement." Partial disability benefits were provided at some fraction of the above based upon degree of impairment. Rehabilitation benefits (physical and vocational) were added in 1925. Survivors benefits provided funeral expenses and moderate pensions for dependents (Gordon, 1963).

The passage and implementation of the German law helped focus attention on the problem of industrial accidents, and gradually other European nations began to adopt workers' compensation legislation. The Austro-Hungarian Empire adopted legislation similar to that of Germany in 1887. In 1897, Great Britain passed the British Workmen's Compensation Act which stated that employers were liable for industrial injuries to their employees. The British legislation departed from that of Germany in that employers were not forced to make arrangements to cover their liability (in practice most purchased insurance) and benefit levels were not as substantial. The British legislation, nevertheless, influenced similar legislation throughout the British Empire and in the United States (Gordon, 1963).

In the United States, the first workers' compensation legislation was passed by Maryland in 1902. Maryland's law provided a schedule of benefits for injured workers in more dangerous occupations such as mining, quarrying, municipal construction work, and railway work. The law was operational for scarcely a year before the Baltimore Court of Common Pleas declared it to be unconstitutional because it denied the right to trial by jury and gave the state excessive powers (Mehr and Cammack, 1966, Oberman, 1965). The states of Massachusetts (1908), Montana (1909) and New York (1910) also passed laws which were subsequently declared unconstitutional. The first effective legislation was the Federal Workmen's Compensation Act of 1908, which provided benefits to employees of the federal government and District of Columbia (Huebner, Black and Cline, 1976). The first effective state law was passed by Wisconsin in 1911 (Bickelhaupt and Magee, 1970).

In the early days of workers' compensation, the most intensely debated issue was not whether workers and their dependents needed protection against the economic consequences of industrial accidents, but whether it was constitutional to deprive employers of their property without due process of law. Many employers had earlier resisted trends to liberalize employer liability laws, and later strongly argued that government could not rightfully hold them liable for industrial injures when they were not at fault. The result was a series of court challenges to the early workers' compensation laws based upon the due process and equal protection clauses of the Fourteenth Amendment to the Federal Constitution, and upon similar guarantees in state constitutions. The Fourteenth Amendment states:

> No state shall make or enforce any law which shall abridge the privileges or immunities of citizens of the United States; nor shall any state deprive any person of life, liberty or property without due process of law; nor deny to any person within its jurisdiction the equal protection of the laws.

Early workers' compensation laws were frequently declared unconstitutional on the basis of: (a) they took an employer's property without due process of law (i.e., trial by jury), and (b) they transferred powers to state executive offices which were properly judicial powers (Huebner, Black and Cline, 1976).

In order to circumvent constitutional challenges, many states adopted elective rather than compulsory workers' compensation laws. This was because compulsory laws were more vulnerable to constitutional challenges. Elective laws gave employers the option of not participating in the state workers' compensation system. However, states concurrently passed legislation which denied the three common law defenses (i.e., contributory negligence, fellow servant, and assumption of risks doctrine) to employers who chose not to participate. With these defenses denied, it was foolish for employers to decline to participate in the state workers' compensation system. Workers also had the option of declining to come under workers' compensation, but in that event the employer retained the three common law defenses. Although at one time approximately half the states had elective laws, today almost every state law is compulsory. The constitutionality issue was finally settled in 1917 when the U.S. Supreme Court ruled in the case of *The New York Central Railroad vs. White* that a state could pass a compulsory law under its police powers.

Despite constitutionality problems, workers' compensation laws were adopted, and by 1921 45 states and territories had passed workers' compensation legislation. In 1927, Congress passed the U.S. Longshoremen's and Harbor Workers' Act which provided workers' compensation benefits to longshoremen, stevedores, and workers outfitting or repairing ships for sea (Huebner, Black and Cline, 1976). However, it was not until passage of the Mississippi Workmen's Compensation Act in 1948 that every state had an operational system (Mehr and Cammack, 1966).

Recent Developments

According to the Chamber of Commerce of the United States (1978), there are six basic objectives which underlie workers' compensation:

1. To provide sure, prompt, reasonable income and medical benefits to work accident victims or their dependents, regardless of fault.
2. To provide a single remedy and reduce court delays, costs, and work loads which arise as a result of personal injury litigation.
3. To relieve public and private charities of financial drains which result from uncompensated industrial accidents.
4. To eliminate payment of fees to lawyers and witnesses as well as time consuming trials and appeals.
5. To encourage maximum employer interest in safety and rehabilitation — through appropriate experience rating mechanisms.
6. To promote a frank study of the causes of accidents (rather than concealment of fault) — reducing preventable accidents and human suffering.

Each of these objectives is important, and it is unfortunate that they have been unequally met by many state workers' compensation laws. While some states have provided excellent benefits to the victims of industrial accidents, others have provided inadequate medical, income replacement, and rehabilitation benefits. How injured workers and their dependents fair under workers' compensation is determined by the adequacy of each state law. In the late 1960's there was a growing recognition that many state laws did not adequately meet the basic objectives of workers' compensation, and this lead to calls for reform.

The effort to reform the state managed workers' compensation system began when Congress enacted the Occupational Safety and Health Act (OSHA) of 1970 (Public Law 91-596). While the main purpose of OSHA was to establish and enforce mandatory federal standards for industrial safety and health, Section 27 of OSHA called for the creation of a National Commission on State Workmen's Compensation Laws. The National Commission was authorized to study and analyze state workers' compensation laws to determine if they provided an adequate, prompt, and equitable system of compensation for injury or death in the course of employment. The National Commission was composed of 15 members appointed by the President. Their report on the state managed workers' compensation system was presented on July 31, 1972.

The 1972 report of the National Commission was highly critical of the workers' compensation system. While 80 specific recommendations for reform were made, 19 were designated by the National Commission as "essential" for an adequate and equitable workers' compensation program. These essential recommendations may be summarized as follows:

1. Coverage should be compulsory with no waivers permitted.
2. Employers should not be exempted from workers' compensation coverage because they employ only a few workers.
3. Farm workers should be provided workers' compensation coverage.
4. Household workers should be covered under workers' compensation at least to the extent they are covered under Social Security.
5. Coverage should be mandatory for all government employees.
6. There should be no exemption from coverage for any occupational group (e.g., professional athletes, employees of charities).
7. An injured employee or survivors should have the choice of filing a claim either in the state where injury or death occured, in the state where employment was principally performed, or in the state where the employee was hired.
8. All states should provide full coverage for occupational diseases.
9. Subject to the state's maximum weekly benefit, *temporary total disability* benefits should be at least 66⅔ % of the worker's average gross weekly wage.
10. The maximum weekly temporary total disability benefit should be at least 66⅔ % of the state's *average weekly wage* by July 1, 1973; 100% by July 1, 1975; and 200% by July 1, 1981.
11. While the definition of *permanent total disability* was judged adequate in most states, some states were found to pay these benefits to individuals with substantial earning capacity. Benefit proposals contained in the report should be applicable only to individuals who meet the definition of permanent total disability used in most states.
12. Subject to the state's maximum weekly benefit, permanent total disability benefits should be at least 66⅔ % of the worker's average gross weekly wage.
13. The maximum weekly permanent total disability benefit should be at least 66⅔ % of the state's average weekly wage by July 1, 1973; 100% by July 1, 1975; and 200% by July 1, 1981.
14. Benefits for total disability should be paid for the duration of the disability without any limitations on time or amount.
15. Subject to each state's maximum weekly benefit, death benefits should be at least 66⅔ % of the worker's average gross weekly wage.
16. The maximum weekly death benefit should be at least 66⅔ % of the state's average weekly wage by July 1, 1973, 100% by July 1, 1975, and 200% by July 1, 1981.

17. A surviving spouse should receive death benefits for life or until remarriage, and in the event of remarriage two years' worth of benefits should be paid in a lump sum. Benefits for dependent children should continue until age 18 (longer if actually dependent) or age 25 if a full-time student in an accredited educational institution.
18. There should be full coverage for medical and physical rehabilitation services without limitations on time or amount for work-related impairments.
19. The right to medical and physical rehabilitation services should not terminate simply by the passage of time.

These and the other recommendations in the National Commission's report helped direct state legislatures toward needed workers' compensation reforms. In May of 1974, the President appointed an Interdepartmental Workers' Compensation Task Force (as recommended by the National Commission) to undertake further research and provide the states with technical assistance in meeting the 19 "essential" recommendations. The Task Force was also to monitor and report on state progress toward the needed reforms.

While the National Commission's report had affirmed the value of the workers' compensation concept, the many faults it found in the existing state managed system resulted in calls for federalization. Senator Jacob Javits (who had earlier worked toward establishing the National Commission) introduced in 1973 with Senator Harrison Williams legislation known as the National Workers' Compensation Standard Act (92nd Congress, S2008). This bill called for the establishment of federal standards for state workers' compensation laws, and provided for the Federal Longshoremen and Harbor Workers' Compensation Act to apply in place of any state law that did not meet the required standards by January 1, 1975. Legislation requiring minimum state standards has been repeatedly introduced in Congress since 1973 (Lewin, Ramseur and Sink, 1979), but there has never been enough support for its passage. Such legislation has, however, put state legislatures, employers, and the insurance industry on notice that the alternative to reform is federalization.

Since 1972 the states have been very active in reviewing and rewriting their workers' compensation laws. In 1973 alone, over 200 state law amendments were adopted in 49 states and Puerto Rico (Mehr and Hedges, 1974). This attention to reform is still continuing as evidenced by the fact that more than 1500 bills related to workers' compensation were introduced in 49 state legislatures during 1981. Of these, approximately 108 became law in 35 states. Five of the 1981 bills addressed rehabilitation related issues (*Workers' Compensation Rehabilitation Laws and Programs*, 1981).

While much of the attention in workers' compensation reform has been directed toward issues such as the adequacy of income replacement benefits, mandatory insurance protection for all workers, and full coverage for medical expenses and occupational diseases; the importance of vocational rehabilitation has by no means been overlooked. In addressing vocational rehabilitation, the National Commission recommended that every workers' compensation agency: (a) establish a medical/rehabilitation division with authority and the necessary resources to supervise medical care and rehabilitation services, (b) that employers or insurance carriers be required to cooperate with the medical/rehabilitation division in every instance where an injured worker needs rehabilitation services (c) that the medical/rehabilitation division be responsible for assuring that every worker who could benefit from vocational rehabilitation services be offered services, (d) that the employer or insurance carrier pay all costs of vocational rehabilitation, (e) that special maintenance benefits (above other benefits) be available during the period or rehabilitation, and (f) that second injury funds be established to cover additional expenses resulting from pre-existing impairments.

While each of these recommendations is obviously important, the most critical is that the employer or carrier be "required" to provide suitable vocational rehabilitation services whenever such services are needed for reemployment. It is very difficult to enforce this requirement without a separate unit or division in the workers' compensation agency which at least monitors the medical care and rehabilitation services provided to injured workers. At a minimum, a rehabilitation division should: (a) screen accident reports to identify cases where rehabilitation services may be needed, (b) identify such cases for employers and carriers, (c) monitor the provision of medical and rehabilitation services, (d) investigate rehabilitation service complaints and intervene on behalf of the injured worker whenever necessary, and (e) collect data to evaluate the nature and effectiveness of rehabilitation services. These functions can normally be accomplished through a centralized office located at the state capital. A rehabilitation division can also provide early referral and medical/vocational management services if it has professional staff (i.e., rehabilitation nurses and counselors) dispersed at offices throughout the state. It is important to remember that most injured workers need only timely medical attention to return to their former employment. When this is the case, rehabilitation division field offices can often explain the worker's situation to the employer, and identify and schedule needed medical services far more efficiently than claims personnel. Unfortunately, the majority of states do not presently have rehabilitation divisions capable of performing all or even most of these suggested functions. As of 1981, 20 states did not have rehabilitation divisions within their workers' compensation agency *(Workers' Compensation Rehabilitation Laws and Programs, 1981).*

METHODS OF INSURANCE

Compulsory state workers' compensation laws require employers to insure their work-accident risk, and elective laws, by denying the three common law defenses, accomplish virtually the same end. There are three ways an employer can insure against work-accident risks: (a) purchase a workers' compensation and employers' liability policy from a private insurer, (b) purchase insurance through a state fund set up to provide this coverage, or (c) self-insure.

Private Insurance

Approximately two-thirds of work-accident insurance contracts are written by private insurance companies (Huebner, Black and Cline, 1976). While historically only larger companies were involved in workers' compensation, the trend toward multiple line writing has brought smaller property and liability insurers into the workers' compensation field. Workers' compensation is usually not a highly profitable line of insurance. Most insurance companies provide this coverage in order to offer their customers "full service," and hope that writing workers' compensation policies will lead to other more profitable insurance contracts (Huebner, Black and Cline, 1976).

The standard policy offered by private insurers provides both workers' compensation (Coverage A) and employers' liability (Coverage B) protection (Green and Serbein, 1978). The latter is needed because despite attempts of workers' compensation laws to discourage litigation, employee suits against employers are not infrequent. The limits of Coverage A protection are esentially outlined by each state's workers' compensation law. The basic limit of liability per accident under Coverage B is $25,000, but employers may purchase higher limits if they feel greater protection is necessary (Greene, 1977).

Workers' compensation premiums are essentially determined by: (a) the business activity of the employer, (b) the number of employees in different classes of employment, and (c) the total remuneration paid to employees. State rate sheets exist which indicate the premium amount for each $100 of payroll in different classes of employment. The rate for clerical workers, for example, may be $.25 per $100 of payroll, while the rate for lumberjacks may be $30 per $100 of payroll. Actual premiums paid by employers are frequently modified by flat percentage discounts for premium values above certain dollar amounts or by *experience ratings* (Huebner, Black and Cline, 1976).

State Funds

In the early history of workers' compensation, a number of states established state funds to provide this coverage. These funds were sometimes necessary because commercial insurers were not overly active in the workers' compensation area, or because the state had a large number of high risk industries (e.g., mining industries) which were unattractive to private insurers. State funds are actually quite similar to private insurance. Regular payments are made to the fund which then disperses benefits to injured workers or their dependents. Employers purchase a separate employers' liability policy from a private insurer.

A state fund may be either monopolistic or competitive. States with monopolistic funds require all employers (except self-insurers) to join the fund, and private companies are not allowed to write workers' compensation coverage within the state. Competitive state funds, on the other hand, operate as an alternative to private insurance or self-insurance. The employer may join the state fund, self-insure, or purchase coverage from a private insurer (Vaughan and Elliot, 1978).

It is difficult to compare advantages and disadvantages of state funds versus private insurance. Proponents of state funds argue they provide lower rates because of an absence of profit motivation and less administrative costs. Those favoring private insurance argue that competition reduces rates and leads to better service. One advantage of state funds is that they do provide a readily available means for insuring employers unattractive to private insurers. In state without funds, private insurers must draw and insure undesirable risks from an assigned risk pool.

Self-Insurance

Self-insurance has traditionally been an option available only to large employers with a geographically dispersed work force. A self-insuring employer must provide or make arrangements for adjusting services, and must place on deposit with the state insurance commission securities in some set amount which guarantee the employer's ability to cover workers' compensation obligations. Some states do not allow self-insurance, and in those that do the decision to self-insure is always a difficult one (Guant and McDonald, 1979). The employer may save substantial sums of money if few or no work-accidents occur, but a large number of more serious accidents could eliminate profits or even threaten the solvency of a firm. To protect against excessive workers' compensation losses many self-insurers purchase *stop-loss aggregate* or *specific-excess* contracts from private insurers. The former limits how much the employer will lose in a given year and the latter how much for any single accident.

Rising workers' compensation premiums have made self-insurance an increasingly attractive option (see MacCready, 1980; Pazak, 1981). A large number of self-insurer service organizations have developed to assist employers choosing this option. The service organizations will assume no liability, but will specifically help the employer: (a) set-up the self-insurance account(s), (b) handle loss control and claims processing, and (c) arrange for the purchase of excessive loss contracts from private insurers (Huebner, Black and Cline, 1976). Self-insurer service organizations make self-insurance a realistic option for employers who do not want to find themselves overly involved in the "insurance business."

Regardless of their method of insurance, all employers are interested in having their workers' compensation costs held to a minimum. Rising rates have become a serious nationwide problem, prompting some industries to move from states with high rate schedules to those with lower schedules (Trieschmann and Leverett, 1980). The ultimate cost of workers' compensation in any state is not really determined by the method of insurance, but rather by loss control practices and benefits written into the state's workers' compensation law. Rehabilitation services are an important benefit for injured workers, and an important loss control feature for employers and insurers. The continuing expansion of rehabilitation services in state workers' compensation systems is likely because rehabilitation services benefit employers and carriers, as well as injured workers.

STATE ADMINISTRATION

In most states, workers' compensation laws are administered by a separate state agency. This agency may be known as a commission, board, bureau, division, or any other similar term. A few states still have administration by their courts. The basic tasks of the administrative agency normally involve: (a) creation and dissemination of rules and regulations necessary to operationalize the state law, (b) supervision of employer and carrier compliance with the law, (c) investigations and rulings on disputed claims, (d) supervision of medical and vocational rehabilitation services, (e) management of a second injury fund, and (e) collection of data to evaluate the performance of the state system. While state agencies are primarily administrative, they do have quasi-judicial powers. In the absence of fraud, their rulings on matters of fact are normally final. Appeals can be made through the state's court system on other bases (Bickelhaupt and Magee, 1970).

COVERAGE

While the coverage of state workers' compensation laws is variable and subject to change each time the state legislature convenes, a general pattern of coverage may be outlined. The term "coverage" refers to both workers entitled to receive benefits as well as the risks they are insured against.

Workers Covered

Despite the recommendations of the National Commission, state laws still exempt a significant number of workers. Depending on the state, workers not covered by workers' compensation may include: (a) farm workers, (b) domestics, (c) public employees, (d) employees of charities, (e) professional athletes, (f) employees of small employers, (g) self-employed persons, and (h) casual or incidental workers. When uncovered workers are injured on-the-job they have little alternative other than to sue their employer. If they lose they recover nothing. Even if they win they may bankrupt a small uninsured employer, which usually results in little or no recovery (Green, 1977).

Injuries Covered

Workers' compensation covers all employee injuries, regardless of fault, arising "out of or in the course of employment." Workers' compensation does not cover injuries which occur while employees are at home, or injuries to "visitors" at the work site. In most cases the question of whether an injury is compensable under workers' compensation is relatively clear. When it is not, the claims representative will investigate to determine if the insurer is in fact liable for the injury. In general, injuries that occur while at work are compensable unless they are self-inflicted or result from intoxication. Difficulties often arise when heart attacks, strokes, nervous breakdowns, and the like, occur on-the-job. The compensability of these "injuries" is frequently resolved in litigation (Vaughan and Elliot, 1978).

Occupational Diseases

An occupational disease is a medical condition such as black lung, asbestosis, radiation poisoning, or the like, which normally develops as a result of long-term exposure at the work site to some dangerous agent or substance. Clinical symptoms may not appear until years later, possibly after the worker has changed occupations or even retired. Most workers' compensation laws provide full coverage for occupational diseases, treating them the same as traumatic injuries.

Second Injuries

One of the most important rehabilitation features of a workers' compensation law is that it provide coverage for the interaction effect between an earlier and later injury. When a worker with residual disability from an earlier injury sustains a second work-related injury, the handicapping aspects of the second injury may be magnified because of the first injury. For example, consider a worker who loses the non-dominant arm in an industrial accident. The extent of the employer's liability for this injury is defined solely by the loss of the non-dominant arm. However, for a worker who had earlier lost the dominant arm and in a second injury the non-dominant arm, the handicapping impact of the second injury would be magnified by the earlier injury. If an employer could potentially be held liable for this interaction between the first and second injury, then employers would be reluctant to hire workers with disability residuals. A second injury to these workers could leave them profoundly handicapped or totally unemployable, whereas the same injury to a worker without disability residuals would have less severe consequences.

Second injury funds are state managed and are financed either by a tax on premiums, by a requirement that survivor benefits be paid into the fund when the deceased worker has no dependents, and/or by special appropriations of the state legislature (Huebner, Black and Cline, 1976). The fund makes it possible to fully cover workers for losses from the second injury, even when these losses are not the "direct" result of the second accident. Second injury funds do not create an actual incentive for employers to hire handicapped workers, but they do eliminate any additional liability which the interaction of a preexisting impairment and new injury might impose on the employer.

BENEFITS

There are four broad classes of benefits to which injured workers or their dependents are entitled. These are: (a) survivor benefits, (b) medical benefits, (c) cash benefits, and (d) rehabilitation benefits.

Survivor Benefits

Survivor benefits, also known as death benefits, are payable whenever a worker is killed on-the-job or later succumbs to injuries sustained while working. Two types of payments are made. The first is a burial allowance which may range from $500 to more than $2000. The second is lost income replacement (usually paid weekly) to the surviving spouse or other dependents.

In most states there is no dollar amount or time limit on income replacement benefits. Although the definition of a dependent is somewhat variable, a spouse, child under 18, handicapped child over 18, child over 18 at an accredited institution of higher education, or dependent parent usually qualify. A dependent spouse can normally collect benefits for life or until remarriage. Income replacement benefits are computed at some percentage of the worker's average gross weekly wage, but are not paid in amounts above some percentage of the state's average weekly wage. This often results in a higher percentage replacement of income earned by lower paid workers, and a less adequate replacement of the income earned by higher paid workers.

Medical Benefits

Most states provide full coverage for medical expenses without any total dollar or time limit. Typical medical expenses involve payments to physicians and surgeons, hospital charges, and the cost of prescription drugs. Some states regard rehabilitation services as a medical benefit.

Cash Benefits

Cash benefits are paid to compensate workers for lost wages and/or for the loss (or loss of use) of body members or a percentage of the body as a whole. They are provided under one or more of the following categories: (a) *Temporary Total Disability*, (b) *Temporary Partial Disability*, (c) *Permanent Total Disability*, and (d) *Permanent Partial Disability*.

Temporary Total Disability (TTD). This benefit is for workers who have sustained an injury that will "temporarily" prevent them from working. It is anticipated that they will recover, usually after a period of healing, convalescence, and/or rehabilitation services, and return to work. As an example, consider a bus driver who stumbles climbing up the steps of a bus, falls, and breaks a leg. While the leg is healing the bus driver is totally disabled (meaning no work can be performed), but after the leg heals the bus driver should be able to return to work. Temporary total disability benefits would be paid during the period that the bus driver is unable to work.

The purpose of temporary total disability benefits is to replace a portion of the seriously injured worker's earnings during a period of healing or convalescence. There is normally a two to seven day waiting period before an injured worker is eligible for temporary total disability benefits, with retroactive payment for the waiting period if the disability lasts more than a few weeks. Most workers can cover a short absence from work with sick leave, and the waiting period significantly reduces the number of minor claims and administrative costs.

The benefit provided under temporary total disability is a weekly or periodic check, the amount of which is computed according to state law. Most states compensate injured workers by paying them 66⅔ % of their gross weekly wage during the period of temporary total disability. The period for which temporary total disability benefits are payable may be unlimited or subject to some maximum number of weeks or dollar amount. State laws also specify a maximum weekly benefit (usually defined as some percentage of the state's average weekly wage) which may result in higher paid workers receiving less than 66⅔% of their average weekly wage. States also set a minimum benefit for lower paid workers, and some states adjust benefits based on the number of dependents. Workers' compensation benefits are not taxed so workers who receive 66⅔% of their gross weekly wage find their compensation close to but slightly less than previous net earnings. The temporary total disability benefit is designed to protect the injured worker from serious income disruption, but also to leave an incentive for returning to work.

Temporary Partial Disability (TPD). This benefit is for workers who "temporarily" cannot perform their own work, but who can still work in another less demanding and lower paying capacity. It is expected that the worker will return, after a period of healing or as the result of rehabilitation services, to the same employment or to employment more commensurate with preinjury capacities. An example would be an assembler with a broken arm. The broken arm would preclude assembly work, but perhaps not work in inventory or quality control. The assembler might be reassigned to an entry level position in one of these areas, paid the lower wage appropriate for the new position, and be reassigned to assembly work after the arm healed. Temporary partial disability benefits would compensate the assembler for part of the wage loss resulting from temporary assignment in a lower paying position.

As in TTD cases, state laws specify minimum and maximum payments for temporary partial disability benefits. The benefit time limit is normally the same as that set for TTD benefits. The temporary partial disability benefit replaces a percentage of the difference between pre and post injury wages, preventing serious financial problems but leaving an incentive for injured workers to return to their preinjury employment.

Permanent Total Disability (PTD). An industrial injury may result in a worker being unable to engage in any substantial remunerative activity. In this case, permanent total disability benefits would be paid for life (some states still specify a set number of years or total dollar amount) or until Social Security retirement benefits or private pension plans replaced them. The permanent total disability benefit is normally calculated the same as the TTD benefit, and like TTD the permanent totally disabled worker receives a weekly or periodic check. Maximum and minimum weekly benefits for permanent total disability are specified by the workers' compensation law.

Determining whether a worker is in fact permanently and totally disabled is one of the most interesting and intriguing aspects of workers' compensation. The term "totally disabled" is actually synonomous with "unable to work," meaning that the emphasis is placed on whether the person can work again rather than on the seriousness of the medical condition or degree of physical impairment per se. An uneducated laborer with a low back injury, for example, might be judged permanent totally disabled, while a more educated white collar worker with the same or a more serious back injury is judged to have reemployment potential. Despite the emphasis placed on the reemployment prognosis, most states specify that the loss or loss of use of two major members (i.e., hands, arms, legs, feet or eyes) in any combination constitutes permanent total disability regardless of vocational rehabilitation potential (Vaughan and Elliot, 1978).

In all but the most serious injuries, incapacitated workers will receive TTD benefits before PTD benefits. Rehabilitation services are normally initiated during the TTD benefit period, and in most states the carrier is allowed to continue TTD benefits past the normal ending date if the worker has not reached maximum medical improvement or if there is reason to believe the claimant is making substantial progress toward vocational rehabilitation. If a worker is not reemployed by the end of the TTD benefit period one or more of the following will occur: (a) the worker will be paid PTD benefits, (b) the worker will be cut-off from further cash benefits, or (c) the carrier will make an effort to settle the claim, normally offering a lump sum settlement to compensate the worker for a loss the carrier believes represents partial rather than permanent total disability. PTD recipients are periodically reevaluated by the workers' compensation agency, and if their condition changes their benefit status may change.

Permanent Partial Disability (PPD). This benefit is paid to compensate workers for the loss of a body member (included here would also be fingers, toes, and hearing) as well as other *scheduled injuries* and for *non-scheduled injuries* where the loss is expressed as a percent of disability to the body as a whole (e.g., lower back injuries). There is a great deal of variability in how and to what extent states compensate injured workers for various "impairments" or permanent partial disabilities (Logan, 1972). Payments are usually based on a state schedule of injuries (to reduce litigation) with a specified dollar amount or number of weeks of disability benefits specified for each scheduled injury or percent of impairment to the body as a whole. Payments for PPD may be periodic or in a lump sum, and they normally do not reduce TTD benefits.

Unlike TTD and PTD benefits, compensation for PPD is not directly related to ability to work. Injured workers are entitled to scheduled injury benefits even if they can return to their former employment without a handicap. If an accountant, for example, lost an eye at work through some fluke accident with a pen or pencil, the accountant would be entitled to the scheduled benefit for the loss of one eye, even though the loss did not adversely impact employment or earning potential. In most cases permanent partial disabilities do adversely affect employment or earning potential, but the compensation is nevertheless for the physical rather than economic loss. Some states, such as Florida, are moving away from scheduled injuries and non-scheduled injury impairment ratings (they have not been given up completely) toward *wage-loss* compensation for workers with partial disabilities (see Waters, 1981a; 1981b). Wage-loss benefits are essentially the same as TPD benefits except that the worker has reached maximum medical improvement and has subsequently been reemployed in a lower paying position. A set percentage of the difference between pre and post injury wages is paid for a set number of weeks to reimburse the worker for the actual economic consequences of the partial disability. The wage-loss model reduces litigation over non-scheduled injuries because compensation is based on lost earnings rather than on medical and legal arguments concerning the percent of total body impairment.

Rehabilitation Benefits

Most state workers' compensation laws enumerate both physical and vocational rehabilitation benefits to which injured workers are entitled. Even when these benefits are not fully enumerated, the workers' compensation agency or courts may order their provision to an injured worker. In some states, injured workers receive a special maintenance allowance (above and beyond other benefits) during the period they receive rehabilitation services. This is an important benefit since it compensates injured workers for rehabilitation related costs such as travel and meals away from home, and provides an incentive to accept and actively participate in a rehabilitation program.

When rehabilitation services are provided, they are paid for either from a special state fund established for workers' compensation rehabilitation, or directly by the employer/carrier. State rehabilitation funds may be supported by a one or two percent tax on either the premium or compensation paid by insurers, by requirements that insurers pay the fund or set a dollar amount in death cases where there are no dependents, and/or by various special assessments. When there is no state fund, the employer or carrier must purchase rehabilitation services directly. One advantage of state rehabilitation funds is that they provide the workers' compensation agency with a convenient means for monitoring the frequency and cost of different rehabilitation services.

Physical Rehabilitation. After the acute medical treatment of an injury, natural healing processes take over which bring about the full or partial recovery of the injured worker. Physical rehabilitation services are provided: (a) to maximize the recovery obtained in the healing process, (b) to prevent or correct errors of the healing process, and (c) to maximize the functional value of residual capacities. Physical rehabilitation services typically involve therapeutic exercises, bracing and splinting, and selection and training in the use of various prosthetic devices. While all states provide injured workers with physical rehabilitation services, how easily injured workers access these services and the comprehensiveness of services varies on both a state by state and case by case basis.

Vocational Rehabilitation. In most cases where TTD or TPD benefits are paid, the injured worker will recover sufficiently to return to the same job with the same employer. When an early referral is made to a rehabilitationist, the rehabilitationist will facilitate this process through medical and vocational management services. In some cases, and for a variety of different reasons, injured workers will not be able to return to the same or any other job with their former employer. Unless this results from a truly catastrophic injury, vocational rehabilitation services are usually indicated.

As noted earlier, the provision of vocational rehabilitation services within the state managed workers' compensation system is still highly variable. While many state laws now "mandate" vocational rehabilitation services, some only "support" rehabilitation. State laws are said to mandate rehabilitation if they require the employer/carrier to offer rehabilitation services to workers unable to return to their preinjury position. Under some mandatory laws, rejection of rehabilitation by an injured worker may result in the reduction of cash income benefits, or possibly their cancellation. Laws which support rehabilitation usually state that injured workers are entitled to needed rehabilitation services, but services are provided only if the injured worker requests them. Regardless of the law, carriers will offer rehabilitation services if they seem worthwhile from a cost containment perspective. Medical management services help the carrier control medical costs and hopefully shorten the duration of disability, and vocational rehabilitation reduces carrier exposure under cash benefits. How actively carriers pursue the vocational rehabilitation of their claimants under non-mandatory laws is determined by the potential of rehabilitation to reduce carrier losses.

In order to assure that rehabilitation benefits are provided, state laws should make the provision of these benefits mandatory. To do less leaves rehabilitation a "hit and miss" affair. There should be rehabilitation incentives for the claimant, such as special maintenance payments while rehabilitation services are being provided (Cheit, 1961). A trial work period should also exist for those classified as permanently disabled. There should be rehabilitation incentives for carriers as well. These are provided by adopting workers' compensation laws which: (a) maximize carrier exposure for lost wages, (b) lessen carrier exposure for scheduled and non-scheduled injuries, and (c) reduce the incidence of litigation. Finally, time limits for rehabilitation benefits should be liberalized so that workers who lack transferable skills sufficient for direct placement can be provided with substantial job retraining.

CLAIMS PROCESS

Rehabilitation service providers receive most of their referrals from private insurance companies which have written workers' compensation policies. The referral is made after the injured worker has filed a claim for workers' compensation benefits. While employers are required to report all industrial accidents to the workers' compensation agency regardless of their seriousness, the worker files a claim only when medical expenses or lost work time (beyond that specified as a waiting period) result from the injury. When the claim is filed the claims process begins.

The employees of insurance companies who handle workers' compensation claims are usually called *claims representatives* (the term *adjuster* is more frequently used in other personal injury lines). Because workers' compensation is a unique type of insurance, these insurance company representatives often deal exclusively with workers' compensation cases. The responsibilities of the claims representative involve: (a) determining if the case is compensable, (b) determining what benefits the carrier will need to provide and establishing an appropriate reserve to cover the cost of the benefits, (c) authorizing the provision of benefits, and (d) closing the case at an appropriate time. There is usually a workers' compensation claims supervisor who oversees the work of several claims representatives. There may also be investigators to assist the claims representative in determining facts in a claim, and rehabilitation nurses to coordinate the provision of medical and rehabilitation benefits.

When a claim is filed the first task of the claims representative is to determine the facts in the injury and decide whether the claim is compensable or one that should be controverted. Claims representatives recognize that the purpose of workers' compensation insurance is to promptly provide injured workers with statutory benefits, and that "technical obstructions" and unnecessary delays have no place in the system, and are seldom tolerated by the workers' compensation agency. The essential question which the claims representative must answer is: "Did the injury arise out of or in the course of employment?" With few exceptions, if the injury is work-related the case is compensable. When claims are contested the carrier should have a very solid case. Workers' compensation appeal boards usually give the injured worker the benefit of any doubt.

After a case is determined to be compensable, the claims representative must determine the probable medical and cash benefits for which the carrier will be liable. If the exposure in the case is substantial in either the medical or cash benefit area, the case may be referred to a rehabilitationist for medical management and/or vocational rehabilitation services. The claims representative monitors the case throughout the benefit period, having responsibility for seeing that statutory benefits are provided and that excessive and unnecessary expenses are avoided. When the benefit period expires or when the injured worker returns to employment the case will be closed. In cases where the injured worker has disability residuals and cannot or is not returning to employment, a settlement in the form of a lump sum payment may be negotiated. The dollar amount of this payment is based upon an agreement as to the degree or percent of disability, with each percent corresponding to a set dollar amount defined in the workers' compensation law.

In working with claims representatives it is important that the rehabilitationist view them as "team members" and not as antagonists. The rehabilitationist is actually a limited agent of the carrier and in that respect an extension of the claims representative. The claims representative has a responsibility to avoid unnecessary costs, and it is their job to ask questions and be skeptical. The claims representative must be informed as to what services are needed, why they are needed, and how long they will take. It is their case before it is the rehabilitationist's case, and keeping them advised of progress is essential.

FUTURE OF WORKERS' COMPENSATION

When the National Commission made its report in 1972, it concluded that workers' compensation was a needed institution and one that should be maintained, but also that the state programs, for no justifiable reasons, fell far short of what the system should be. The future of workers' compensation is therefore in the hands of the state legislatures. If they provide adequate programs, workers' compensation will remain a state managed system. If they fail, Congress may set minimum standards for state laws or possibly even federalize the system. While the states have improved their programs in recent years, federally mandated minimum standards may be necessary if even one state should fail to provide an adequate program.

In the task of modifying existing state laws, a number of politically powerful groups with different economic interests in workers' compensation vie for influence. These groups include employers, labor unions, insurers, trial attorneys, physicans, and rehabilitationists — all of whom have access to the law making process. While some compromises between the interests of these different groups is inevitable, states must nevertheless adopt workers' compensation laws that provide adequate benefits for injured workers while at the same time avoiding runaway costs. For most states, this will be accomplished by both: (a) reducing the profitability and thereby the frequency of litigation, and (b) returning injured workers to the labor force. Regardless of the administrative future of workers' compensation, rehabilitation services will be a vital component of the system.

References

Berkowitz, M.: *Workmen's Compensation: The New Jersey Experience.* New Brunswick: Rutgers University Press, 1960.

Bickelhaupt, D.L. and Magee, J.H.: *General Insurance.* Homewood: Richard D. Irwin, 1970.

Cheit, E.F.: *Injury and Recovery in the Course of Employment.* New York: John Wiley and Sons, 1961.

Gaunt, L.D., McDonald, M.E.: *Examining Employers' Financial Capacity to Self-Insure Under Workmen's Compensation.* Publishing Services Division, College of Business Administration, Georgia State University, Atlanta, 1977 (Research Monograph No. 72).

Gordon, M.S.: Industrial injuries insurance in Europe and the British Commonwealth since World War II. In E.F. Cheit and M.S. Gordon (Eds.) *Occupational Disability and Public Policy.* New York: John Wiley and Sons, 1963.

Green, M.R. and Serbein, O.N.: *Risk Management: Text and Cases.* Reston, Virginia: Reston Publishing, 1978.

Huebner, S.S., Black, K. and Cline, R.S.: *Property and Liability Insurance.* Englewood Cliffs: Prentice-Hall, 1976.

Lewin, S.S., Ramseur, J.H. and Sink, J.M.: The role of private rehabilitation: Founder, catalyst, competitor. *Journal of Rehabilitation,* 1979, *45*:16-19.

Logan, J.E.: *An Analysis of Workmen's Compensation: South Carolina and the United States.* Columbia: Vogue Press, 1972.

MacCready, B.B.: Self insuring the worker's compensation risk — A creative approach. *Risk Management,* 1980, *27*:38-42.

Mehr, R.I. and Cammack, E.: *Principles of Insurance.* Homewood: Richard D. Irwin, 1966.

Mehr, R.I. and Hedges, B.A.: *Risk Management: Concepts and Applications.* Homewood: Richard D. Irwin, 1974.

Oberman, C.E.: *A History of Vocational Rehabilitation in America.* Minneapolis: T.S. Denison and Company, 1965.

Pazak, D.: How one Pennsylvania county successfully self insured its workers' comp program. *Risk Management,* 1981, *28*:38-42.

Post, J.E.: *Risk and Response.* Toronoto: Lexington Books, 1976.

Trieschmann, J.S. and Leverett, Jr. E.J.: Answering the question: To self-insure or not to self-insure workers' comp costs. *Risk Management,* 1980, *27*:39-42.

Turnbull, J.G., Williams, C.A., and Cheit, E.F.: *Economic and Social Security.* New York: Ronald Press, 1968.

Vaughan, E.J. and Elliot, C.M.: *Fundamentals of Risk Insurance.* New York: John Wiley and Sons, 1978.

Waters, G.: Florida's unique workers' comp program survives a stormy debut. *Risk Management,* 1981, *28*:18-22. (a).

Waters, G.: Florida's workers' comp rehab program gets results. *Risk Management,* 1981, *28*:21-24. (b).

Workers' Compensation Rehabilitation Laws and Programs: Washington, D.C.: Division of State Workers' Compensation, Office of Workers' Compensation Programs, Employment Standards Administration, U.S. Department of Labor, 1981.

Part II

REHABILITATION CASE MANAGEMENT

CHAPTER IV

EARLY CASE MANAGEMENT SERVICES

WHEN people sustain severe injuries they suddenly find themselves with new and pressing needs (e.g., for pain relief, income replacement, medical or surgical interventions), and because of their reduced physical condition, with less personal resources to apply toward the resolution of their newly acquired problems. The result is a period of disability induced dependency when others, out of necessity, must be relied upon to solve or help solve disability related problems. Early case management services are provided during this period to assist the newly injured individual toward an optimal medical, psychosocial, and vocational recovery. When effectively applied, these services often reduce the disability period, prevent serious financial problems from developing, prevent the loss of employment, and reduce the likelihood of litigation. Early case management services benefit injured individuals by helping them through the disability induced dependency period, and benefit insurance carriers and employers by containing costs.

This discussion of early case management services is written generically. It is applicable to workers' compensation as well as other insurance supported personal injury cases which are referred early or before the claimant reaches maximum medical improvement. The discussion does not take into consideration any specific rules, procedures, or requirements of the various workers' compensation agencies and their rehabilitation bureaus, carriers, or rehabilitation companies.

CARRIER EXPECTATIONS

When a case is referred by a carrier (or self-insuring employer or workers' compensation agency), the first task of the rehabilitationist is to ascertain exactly what services the carrier wants provided. If it is an early referral, the carrier will normally want the rehabilitationist to: (a) contact the client, involved physicans, and employer; (b) report on the status of the claimant medically, financially, and vocationally; and (c) make recommendations as to what services should be provided. If the claimant is being referred after reaching maximum medical improvement the carrier may want a vocational rehabilitation program developed, or if a program was previously developed, assistance with job placement. Referrals may be for "total" rehabilitation services (involving both medical management and vocational planning) or for only one or two limited services.

In addition to determining desired services, the rehabilitationist should request that the carrier provide pertinent information on the claimant. This is normally accomplished with a referral form and through telephone contact with the claims representative. Typical data requested on referral forms include: (a) client name, address, and telephone numbers; (b) age or date of birth; (c) sex; (d) occupation; (e) date of injury; (f) social security number; (g) type of insurance coverage and estimated reserve; (h) current cash income benefits; (i) name of insured party; (j) employer name, address, and telephone number; (k) name, address, and telephone numbers of physicians and hospitals; (l) diagnosis or medical condition; (m) name, address, and telephone number of attorney; (n) name of claims representative or individual referring; (o) insurance company name and account file number; and (p) reason for the referral. Copies of available medical reports should also be provided. After receiving a referral form it is customary to acknowledge the referral with both a telephone call (through which additional information may be collected) and letter.

Most private rehabilitation companies expect their rehabilitationists to contact referred claimants as soon after receiving the referral as possible, normally within 24 hours, 48 hours at the latest. This is very important because the claimant may have medical or financial problems that require prompt attention. It is also a good business practice since it is embarrassing to have a claims representative call several days after having made a referral, and be forced to tell the representative that the client has not been contacted.

Most claimants referred by insurance companies and self-insured employers will not have legal representation. The probability that the claimant will have engaged the services of an attorney increases with elapsed time since the date of the injury. In liability cases the claimant will have an attorney, in workers' compensation cases sometimes, and in LTD cases only occasionally. Whenever the rehabilitationist knows that a claimant has an attorney, the attorney should be contacted before the client, and permission obtained to work with the client. If the existence of legal representation is not discovered until the initial interview, the interview should stop until the attorney can be reached by telephone for permission to interview the client. This is necessary because the carrier has engaged the services of the rehabilitationist, and the rehabilitationist is technically an extension of the carrier, even though services are provided on behalf of the client. While most attorneys will authorize contact with their client and will encourage their client to work toward rehabilitation (Treon, 1979), there are some who will not. If the attorney denies the rehabilitationist permission to see the client this must be immediately reported to the carrier. Some attorneys will want to be present for the first meeting between the rehabilitationist and their client, and the rehabilitationist should not oppose this desire. It is helpful, however, to ask for a first meeting on "neutral ground," such as the client's home or rehabilitationist's office, rather than the attorney's office.

The goals of an initial interview are the same whether an attorney is present or not. If an attorney is present there will usually be input from the attorney on how he or she perceives the problems and needs of the client. The rehabilitationist's goals for the initial interview are normally: (a) to ascertain what the client perceives as his or her problems, needs, and goals; (b) to identify physicians and other medical and social service personnel who should be contacted; (c) to obtain a medical, work, and educational history from the client; and (d) to lay the foundation for a sound working relationship with the client.

After the initial interview, the rehabilitationist normally proceeds with the case by contacting involved physicians, other medical and social service personnel who have had contact with the client, and the employer. In consultation with the rehabilitationist's supervisor and medical consultant a report is prepared for the carrier which identifies relevant medical, financial, psychosocial, and vocational issues. Recommendations are made concerning needed services and how to best proceed with the rehabilitation of the injured claimant.

MAJOR SERVICES

In order to understand early case management services it is helpful to consider each of three major service areas separately. The three principal areas which the rehabilitationist normally addresses with early referrals (i.e., referrals made shortly after the injury) are: (a) medical management, (b) financial management, and (c) vocational management.

Medical Management

Medical management (also known as disability management) is the process of identifying medical problems and issues, and arranging for appropriate medical services or interventions. The basic goal is to bring the client to maximum medical improvement (MMI) as soon as possible. This is normally the first service area that the rehabilitationist addresses since the client may be medically unstable and in need of immediate medical attention, especially if the referral is made immediately after the injury.

At a minimum, medical management of the injured client will normally involve all of the following:

1. Determining the client's current medical condition and diagnosis.
2. Identifying the probable period of hospitalization or convalescence before the client will reach MMI or be released for work.
3. Determining the medical and related interventions that physicans and other health care providers recommend.
4. Identifying probable and later actual physical and/or mental capacities at MMI.
5. Preventing duplicate or unnecessary medical services.
6. Presenting identified medical issues and physician service recommendations to the rehabilitation company's medical consultant, carrier, workers' compensation agency, and client.
7. Scheduling, coordinating, and following-up authorized services.

In addition to these services, medical management may also involve helping the client and family make the transition from a hospital or rehabilitation center to the home, identifying and correcting architectural barriers or transportation problems, teaching the client or family members appropriate home health care practices (including proper body mechanics and the use of prescribed medicines), and checking for the possible development of medical complications or psychological problems (see Branton, 1983).

Medical management is a very demanding service role, and consistently effective service requires that the rehabilitationist have a strong background in state-of-the-art medical procedures and local treatment resources. For this reason, many private rehabilitation companies prefer to have registered nurses provide medical management services, and certified rehabilitation counselors vocational services. Regardless of the rehabilitationist's medical background, continuing education is a must. Continuing medical education can take many forms such as company sponsored in-service training programs, attendance at medically oriented workshops and conferences, and also regular review of select medical journals and rehabilitation literature (e.g., *Archives of Physical Medicine and Rehabilitation, Journal of Bone and Joint Surgery, Rehabilitation Forum*). Most importantly, however, the rehabilitationist should have access to the opinion of a qualified and impartial medical consultant. Every private rehabilitation company should have a medical consultant on staff or under contract.

While medical management issues and procedures will vary on a case by case basis, the process will normally proceed somewhat as follows:

1. Contact the client and family to determine the current medical situation and to identify problems such as physical impairments, pain, restrictions on activities, and what the client and family have been told by attending physicians.
2. Contact involved physicians to obtain information on the client's current medical condition and diagnosis, and recommended medical intervention. By visiting the client first, the rehabilitationist will be able to share the client's perceptions with the physician, and hopefully resolve outstanding medical issues.
3. Present the obtained medical information (including hospital records and physician reports) to the rehabilitation company's medical consultant. The two basic goals of medical consultation are to identify any additional diagnostic evaluations which may be needed, and to obtain the impartial opinion of a medical expert on how to proceed with the resolution of outstanding medical issues.
4. Report findings and make service recommendations to the carrier and client. The carrier is normally contacted first, unless the rehabilitationist believes the client will oppose some of the medical recommendations.
5. Schedule and coordinate authorized medical services.
6. Follow-up medical services and report results to the carrier and physicians. Medical complications or other health issues which arise should also be reported to the appropriate physician and carrier.

When medical management is successful, the injured client receives all necessary medical services, and reaches MMI at the earliest possible date. Moreover, unnecessary, duplicated, and over charged services are avoided. Quality medical management is in the client's best interest since a full and early recovery is facilitated, and in the carrier's interest because medical costs and the disability benefit period are held to a minimum.

Financial Management

One of the main purposes of personal injury insurance is to protect the insured's financial well-being in the event of a temporary or permanent inability to work. Almost every client who loses substantial work time has some anxiety about future finances. When a client's expenses exceed income, the anxiety generated can lead to emotional problems, family problems, and possibly even a slower or less complete physical recovery. The rehabilitationist must therefore consider the client's financial situation during the rehabilitation process.

Income replacement benefits vary by state and by type of insurance. In most cases, however, the rehabilitationist will find that the client is receiving 66⅔ % of pre-injury gross weekly wages. While this benefit is not taxed, most clients will still be receiving less than what they cleared when working. This is especially true for higher salaried workers, and for workers who had a second part-time job or regular overtime employment. Moreover, some clients will have been in a difficult or marginal financial situation before their injury, and will subsequently be in or headed for a financial crisis.

The rehabilitationist will also occasionally encounter clients who, for various reasons, have a post-injury income which is equal to or even higher than their pre-injury income. Assuming they are entitled to all the benefits they are receiving, this situation can negatively impact the client's interest in returning to work. The rehabilitationist should not knowingly contribute to the development of a situation where a client with employment potential is receiving more disability related income benefits than their previous work earnings. If the rehabilitationist believes benefits are being received fraudulently, this must be reported to the benefit source.

The tasks which are involved in financial management normally include the following:

1. Determining the probable length of the disability period (i.e. date the client will likely be released for full or partial resumption of work activities) so that a disability period financial plan can be developed.
2. Identifying other benefits to which the client is entitled (e.g., other insurance benefits, SSDI, SSI, VA benefits, food stamps).
3. Assisting the client in establishing eligibility for other needed benefits.
4. Accurately determining weekly or monthly income for the projected disability period.
5. Identifying general and disability related expenses for the projected disability period.
6. Identifying priority expenses and other expenses which might be eliminated, postponed, or assumed by another party.
7. Determining if any disability related expenses should be paid in advance by the carrier to avoid financial difficulties for the client. This is known in the insur-

ance industry as *advance payment* for covered expenses. While this is something the rehabilitationist may wish to recommend or discuss with a claims representative, *such payments can never be promised to a client.*

8. Construction of a disbility period budget.

The rehabilitationist addresses the above tasks through the counseling process. The role of the rehabilitationist is to assist the client in establishing a financial posture for the disability period. It is important to remember that an unimportant expense, from the perspective of the rehabilitationist, may be a very important expense to the client. The rehabilitationist acts as a financial consultant helping the client identify and match available income and financial reserves with priority expenses. The client and family are ultimately responsible for their own financial well-being.

The tangible product of financial management is often a written disability period budget. While it is not necessary that a budget be constructed with every client, it is highly desirable when income is only slightly greater than expenses, and a necessity when it is less. Most clients and their families are capable of constructing their own budget, as long as they have accurately identified relevant variables (i.e., income, necessary expenses, savings, and probable length of unemployment). It is important that the client and family construct their own budget, because if it is their product, they are more likely to adhere to it. Again, the rehabilitationist's role is that of a financial consultant.

When financial management services are successful clients will: (a) receive all benefits to which they are entitled, but normally not more income replacement benefits than what they could earn from working (the exception here is for clients who are so profoundly injured that reemployment is not feasible), (b) have an adequate income to meet personal and family expenses during the disability period, and (c) experience no financial crisis which interrupts or undercuts rehabilitation efforts.

Vocational Management

The third early case management service is vocational management. As used here, vocational management refers to efforts designed to return the injured worker to the former employer in either the same or different job, and vocational rehabilitation to efforts designed to place the client with a new employer. While making a distinction between vocational management and vocational rehabilitation is somewhat arbitrary, there are private sector placement issues to support such a distinction. As indicated earlier, Welch (1979) noted that private sector placement priorities were sequentially:

1. Return to work — same job — same employer.
2. Return to work — different job — same employer.
3. Return to work — different job — different employer (p. 25).

The private sector rehabilitationist first attempts to actualize priorities one or two through vocational management, and when this proves impossible, priority three through vocational rehabilitation.

Vocational management is therefore largely a "preventive" service. Through vocational management, the rehabilitationist attempts to stop or contain the "spread of disability effects" (see Wright, 1960) into the vocational area. *Vocational rehabilitation,* on the other hand, is a "restorative" service that redresses or corrects the already existing adverse vocational impact of an injury. A rehabilitationist's efforts in vocational management are often directed toward activities such as:

1. Encouraging the employer to replace the client with a temporary rather than permanent employee until an accurate determination can be made as to whether the client will be medically able to return to the old job or a modified version of the old job.
2. Identifying other jobs in the employer's business that the client might do at MMI, and encouraging the employer to hold any present or future openings in these positions for the recovering client.
3. Identifying existing jobs or work activities in the employer's business that the client might perform while recovering from the injury, thereby changing the TTD period into a TPD period.
4. Determining and advocating job modifications that would allow the client to resume the pre-injury position at MMI.
5. Determining major work activities in the employer's business that might be reassigned between jobs, thereby creating a new work position that the client could perform at MMI.

While the exact sequence of activities performed in vocational management is variable, the rehabilitationist normally first interviews the client to:

1. Determine the present medical difficulties and physical limitations the client is experiencing.
2. Learn the general nature and work responsibilities of the client's pre-injury job, including client perceptions of physical demands and working conditions.
3. Determine whether a positive, negative, or neutral relationship exists between the client and employer.
4. Identify the past work experiences of the client (i.e. obtain a work history).
5. Identify transferable skills based upon the client's past work experiences, educational history, avocational activities, and personal qualities which might be relevant in the job placement process.

After interviewing the client, the rehabilitationist schedules an interview with the employer and/or supervisor in order to explain the rehabilitationist's role, and bring them up to date on the client's medical status as it pertains to work (to the extent this information is known). Other goals for the employer interview are to:

1. Obtain permission to do a job analysis on the client's pre-injury job.
2. Learn if the employer is receptive to having the worker return to his or her former job (when and if it is medically feasible) or to a new position with the firm, and what jobs might be open in the future.
3. Learn the employer's and/or supervisor's perceptions of minimum physical requirements for performing the client's pre-injury job and other jobs in the firm.

4. Obtain permission to study jobs in the firm (i.e. to do job analyses and talk to workers).
5. Learn the employer's and/or supervisor's opinion of the client as a worker.

If the employer is at all receptive to having the client return to work, it is imperative that the rehabilitationist obtain a job analysis for the client's position and other less physically demanding jobs at the work site. Illustration 4-1 presents a *Job Analysis Form*, which in the author's experience is adequate for describing most positions. The reason for conducting a job analysis is to ascertain the specific work activities, physical demands, and working conditions associated with a job (Wright, 1980). This information is subsequently presented to the primary physician and/or medical consultant for a determination of the post-injury suitability of the job. Readers interested in a more detailed discussion of job analysis should consult the *Handbook For Analyzing Jobs* (1972).

Illustration 4-1

JOB ANALYSIS FORM

General Information

(1) Job Title (used by company): ________________

(2) D.O.T. Job Title and Code: ________________

(3) Company Name, Address, and Telephone Number: ________________

____

____

____

(4) Contact Person at Company: ________________

(5) Nature of Company's Business: ________________

____

____

____

Job Description

(6) Hiring Requirements (e.g., education, licenses, work experience, special training, test scores, union card): ________________

____

____

____

____

(7) Working Hours (Shifts): ________________

(8) Salary (Wage): ________________

(9) Brief Description of Job: ____

____

____

____

____

(10) Tools Utilized (e.g., hand tools, office equipment, machinery): ____________

____

____

____

____

(11) Job Components or Tasks (After each letter write one sentence, beginning with an action verb, that describes a specific job activity or duty): ____________

(a) ____

(b) ____

(c) ____

(d) ____

(e) ____

(f) ____

(g) ____

(h) ____

(i) ____

(j) ____

(k) ____

(l) ____

(m) ____

(n) ____

(o) ____

(p) ____

(q) ____

(r) ____

(s) ____

(t) ____

(u) ____

(v) ____

(w) ____

(x) ____

(y) ______________________________

(z) ______________________________

(12) Physical Demands:

(a) Characteristic Lifting and/or Carrying Requirements (Check one):

______ Sedentary (10 lb maximum)

______ Light (20 lb maximum and 10 lb frequently)

______ Medium (50 lb maximum and 25 lb frequently)

______ Heavy (100 lb maximum and 50 lb frequently)

______ Very Heavy (More than 100 lb maximum and 50 lb frequently)

(b) Pushing and/or Pulling Requirements: ______________________________

(c) Climbing and/or Balancing Requirements: ______________________________

(d) Stooping, Kneeling, Crouching, and/or Crawling Requirements: ______________________________

(e) Reaching, Handling, Fingering, and/or Feeling Requirements: ______________________________

(f) Talking and/or Hearing Requirements: ______________________________

(g) Vision Requirements (e.g., acuity, depth perception, field of vision, accommodation, color vision): ______________________________

(h) Daily Standing Requirements (Hours): ______________________________

(i) Daily Sitting Requirements (Hours): ______________________________

(j) Daily Walking Requirements (Distance): ______________________________

(13) Working Conditions:

(a) Location (Check one):

______ Indoor

______ Outdoor

______ Both

(b) Exposure to Cold and/or Heat: ______________________________

(c) Exposure to Wet and/or Humid Conditions: ______________________________

(d) Exposure to Noise and/or Vibration: ______________________________

(e) Hazards (Check any that apply):

______ Moving Machinery

______ Fixed Machinery

_______ Chemicals
_______ Explosives
_______ Electrical Devices
_______ Other (Explain) ____

____

(f) Exposure to Fumes and/or Odors: ______________________________________

____

(g) Architectural Barriers (Describe any present on or in accessing premises):

____

____

____

When vocational management is successful, the client returns to the former employer in the same, modified, or new position at the earliest possible time. The impact of the injury on the vocational sphere of the client's life is accordingly kept to a minimum.

WORKING WITH CLIENTS

Although the rehabilitationist characteristically works with many parties in the rehabilitation process, the relationship developed with the client is the most critical to success. For this reason, it is usually best to meet the client before contacting physicians and the employer. A good working relationship is something that does not develop automatically, and is instead dependent upon the listening and communication skills of the rehabilitationist. In addition to the importance of giving first priority to building a good working relationship with the client, the rehabilitationist needs to understand the client's perspective in order to effectively interact with all other parties in the rehabilitation process. This does not occur unless the rehabilitationist takes the time to really know the client.

Contacting the Client

After receiving a referral, the rehabilitationist telephones the client to schedule a personal interview. While the first meeting may be scheduled in the rehabilitationist's office, it is often helpful and more convenient for the newly injured client if the first interview is scheduled in the client's home. The time invested in traveling to the client's home is more than offset by the fact that the rehabilitationist is able to see how and where the client actually lives. The distance the client must travel to the pre-injury employer, and businesses or industries in proximity to the client's home can also be noted.

When contacting the client by telephone the rehabilitationist should first state his or her name, the name of his or her employer, explain who referred the client (e.g., the workers' compensation agency, insurance carrier for their employer) and the general reason for the referral (i.e., to monitor and assist in their recovery/rehabilitation). An appointment should then be scheduled to see the client at the earliest possible date. Immediately after ending the conversation, a letter confirming the appointment should be dictated, typed, and mailed to the client. It is also advisable to send a copy of this letter to the claims representative to indicate that the client has been contacted, and rehabilitation case management initiated.

With a tactful and reassuring approach the rehabilitationist will normally encounter no difficulty in scheduling an appointment with the client. Even when a case is in litigation the client's attorney will usually advise the client to cooperate with rehabilitation efforts. If a client is adamant in his or her refusal to see the rehabilitationist, this information must be immediately shared with the referral source.

Initial Interview

As indicated earlier, an important objective for the initial interview is to ascertain what the client perceives as his or her problems, needs, and goals. While this is often easily accomplished with more self-expressive or verbal clients, at other times it requires considerable skills in facilitating communication. After a brief introduction and statement of the rehabilitationist's role, the emphasis should shift toward listening to what the client has to say. Careful listening is the indispensable foundation of effective communication. It is only by listening that the rehabilitationist develops empathy with the client, and only through communicating that he or she has listened that a good working relationship can develop.

The initial interview is a critical junction in the rehabilitation process. The rehabilitationist must characteristically obtain relevant medical, vocational, educational, and socioeconomic data from the client, and at the same time lay the foundation for a good working relationship in the future. It does not profit the rehabilitationist to come away from the initial interview with an excellent "assessment" of the client's situation, if the process of obtaining that assessment damages the relationship with the client. Although the rehabilitationist must have an agenda for the interview (i.e., specific information to be collected, questions to be answered), the agenda may need to be partially or even fully subordinated to the interest of developing a good working relationship. Both listening and the communication of having listened are often (not necessarily always) accomplished by restating and/or summarizing what the client has been saying (see Benjamin, 1981). For example, the rehabilitationist would occasionally begin a statement as follows:

1. "Let me see if I understand what you've told me so far."
2. "I'm hearing you say..."
3. "You're telling me..."
4. "If I'm understanding you right, you're saying..."

It is important to remember that it is only through restating or summarizing what a client has said that listening is clearly communicated. Questions, advice, interpretations, reassurance, and similar responses do not clearly communicate listening or understanding. As listening is practiced and communicated, empathy develops, making it possible for the rehabilitationist to identify and respond to the client's true feelings and needs (see Roessler and Rubin, 1982; Rubin and Roessler, 1978).

Although an interview agenda should not be allowed to undercut the development of a working relationship, an agenda is nevertheless necessary. The interview agenda is simply the information and questions which a rehabilitationist must collect and answer to begin serving the client. While some of this information may be necessary for only reporting or file requirements, most of the interview should be focused on substantive issues. As indicated earlier, the rehabilitationist will primarily explore medical, financial, and vocational issues as they relate to the client's disability. In order to do this effectively and efficiently, it is helpful to have some general questions which serve as a starting point for exploring each of these three areas.

In relation to medical implications of the disability, the rehabilitationist may wish to answer questions such as:

1. Who are the physicians and other health care personnel who have seen or are working with the client?
2. What has the client been told about his or her medical condition?
3. Have any medical procedures been recommended or scheduled, and by whom?
4. What physical limitations have been imposed by the injury and how have these restricted the client's activities?
5. Is the client in pain, and if so where is the pain located, and when and how often does it occur?
6. What medications is the client taking and who prescribed them?
7. Are there any secondary disabilities from earlier injuries or pre-injury medical conditions?
8. What is the overall health and past medical history of the client?

In the financial area, the rehabilitationist should always identify what disability benefits the client is receiving or expecting to receive. The rehabilitationist should also ask if the client is encountering or anticipating any significant financial difficulties from the disability. If the answer to this second question is affirmative, then the rehabilitationist will need to collect detailed information on the client's financial status, and will possibly need to assist the client in constructing a disability period budget. Financial counseling essentially involves determining through what avenues income might be increased (e.g., a spouse returning to the work force, borrowing money from family members, taking a second mortgage on the house, establishing eligibility for other insurance or social welfare benefits) and where expenses might be decreased or postponed.

In early case management services, vocational issues center around returning the client to employment with the former employer in either the same, modified, or a new position. The rehabilitationist therefore needs to develop a sound understanding of the client's pre-injury job as well as the nature of the employer's business and jobs performed there. The rehabilitationist should have the client fully explain his or her job including scheduled or regular job tasks as well as unscheduled job demands (e.g., periodically helping out in another part of the plant when someone is sick or a "bottleneck" develops). The *Job Analysis Form* indicates areas the rehabilitationist would normally address.

In addition to a detailed investigation of the pre-injury job, it is important to get a work and educational history from the client (Deutsch and Raffa, 1982). When clients cannot return to their former position at MMI, their past work and educational experiences become very relevant in identifying other jobs with their present employer that they might also perform. Collecting a good work/educational history can take a considerable amount of time, especially if the client has held many different jobs, and it is therefore sometimes advisable to seek only a general understanding of the client's past work and educational experiences during the initial interview, and obtain a complete work and educational history later. A *Work and Education Survey Form* (see Illustration 4-2) can be given to the client during the initial interview with instructions that it be completed and mailed to the rehabilitationist. In addition to saving time, such a procedure provides an early indication of how well and promptly a client will follow through with an assigned task, and reviewing the form with the client provides the rationale and starting point for a subsequent interview.

Illustration 4-2

WORK AND EDUCATION SURVEY

General Information

Directions: Please answer the following questions to the best of your ability.

1. Name: ______________________________
2. Address: ______________________________
3. Telephone: ______________________________
4. Highest Grade Completed (Circle): 1 2 3 4 5 6 7 8 9 10 11 12
5. What high school did you attend and where is it located? ______________________________

   ____
6. Did you ever attend college or graduate school (Circle): Yes No
7. If so, where did you attend, what was your major, and what degrees were conferred? ______________________________

   ____

   ____

   ____

   ____

   ____
8. Have you ever enrolled in a vocational, technical, or trade school (Circle):
   Yes No

9. If so, what did you study, for how long, and what diplomas or certificates were received? ______________________________

10. Are you a veteran? (Circle): Yes No
11. If so, did you receive any specialized training in the armed forces and what was its nature? ______________________________

12. What types of jobs did you do in the armed services and for how long? ______________________________

13. Is there any other specialized training you have received or self-taught knowledge and skills you have developed (e.g., home carpentry, amateur radio, arts and crafts)? ______________________________

Work History

Directions: Begin with your most recent (last or present) employment and work backwards. Please provide the following information for each position: (1) employer, (2) address of employer, (3) telephone number, (4) last supervisor, (5) your job title, (6) dates of employment, (7) salary or wage, (8) average number of hours worked weekly, (9) description of job duties, and (10) the reason you left. You may not remember all of the above, but please be as complete as possible. If you worked in more than one position for the same employer, please list these separately.

I. MOST RECENT EMPLOYMENT

A. Employer: ______________________________

B. Address: ______________________________

C. Telephone: ______________________________

D. Supervisor: ______________________________

E. Job Title: ______________________________

F. Dates of Employment: From ______________ To ______________

G. Salary or Wage: ______________________________

H. Average Hours Worked Weekly: ______________________________

I. Job Duties: ______________________________

____

____

____

____

____

J. Reason Left: ______________________________

II. PREVIOUS POSITION

A. Employer: ______________________________

B. Address: ______________________________

C. Telephone: ______________________________

D. Supervisor: ______________________________

E. Job Title: ______________________________

F. Dates of Employment: From ______________ To ______________

G. Salary or Wage: ______________________________

H. Average Hours Worked Weekly: ______________________________

I. Job Duties: ______________________________

____

____

____

____

____

J. Reason Left: ______________________________

III. PREVIOUS POSITION

A. Employer: ______________________________

B. Address: ______________________________

C. Telephone: ______________________________

D. Supervisor: ______________________________

E. Job Title: ______________________________

F. Dates of Employment: From ______________ To ______________

G. Salary or Wage: ______________________________

H. Average Hours Worked Weekly: ______________________________

I. Job Duties: ______________________________

____

____

____

____

____

J. Reason Left: ______________________________

Note: The form should continue in this fashion to allow the client to list up to eight or nine positions.

Although the vocational management of disability is a critical service, the rehabilitationist should remember that in early referrals immediate medical and financial issues are often more pressing concerns. It is often very difficult, and even at times inappropriate, to conduct a detailed exploration of work issues with a client who is medically unstable or personally overwrought with the immediate impact of the disability. In such situations, the rehabilitationist must first attend to the issues immediately presenting themselves, deferring vocational issues to subsequent interviews.

Subsequent Client Contacts

After the initial interview, the rehabilitationist will normally communicate with involved physicians, the employer, and claims representative before recontacting the client. By the second contact, the rehabilitationist will usually have identified needed medical diagnostics or treatments, and will have authorization from the claims representative to schedule and coordinate these in the client's behalf. The rehabilitationist will also follow-up on the results of medical interventions. The rehabilitationist is responsible for rehabilitation case management, and in this capacity will serve as a liaison between the client and other involved parties.

As indicated earlier, in order to work effectively with clients in the immediate aftermath of an injury, when they may be medically unstable, emotionally distraught, or even hospitalized, the rehabilitationist must have excellent listening and communication skills, and the capacity to develop empathy with the client. The automatic continuation of a good working relationship with the client can never be taken for granted, and in each subsequent telephone contact or personal interview the rehabilitationist should attend to the working relationship. A positive relationship is primarily maintained by carefully listening to what the client says, and by communicating to the client that his or her concerns have indeed been heard and understood.

THE EMPLOYER

After interviewing the client, the rehabilitationist will normally visit the employer. Depending on the nature and size of the business, the contacted "employer" may be an owner, manager, or personnel director. The rehabilitationist may also wish to personally contact the direct supervisor and union steward. This is because the opinion and support of these individuals is often critical in the employer's decision to keep or rehire the injured worker. If the firm has a company physician or nurse this individual should also be contacted. In many larger firms, the injured worker will need medical approval from the company physician before returning to work.

The rehabilitationist must contact the employer to obtain permission to do a job analysis of the client's preinjury position, and to ascertain the employer's plan for the client's job during the expected disability period. The rehabilitationist should also become familiar with the nature of the employer's business and other jobs existing within the firm. Moreover, the rehabilitationist should develop an overall picture of the work activities and tasks which are performed in the business, independent of the specific jobs they are currently assigned to. This familiarity with the work tasks of the business often allows the rehabilitationist to identify how tasks might be reassigned between currently separate jobs, thereby creating a less physically demanding job that might be suitable for a handicapped worker.

In addition to the above, it is very important that the rehabilitationist assess the relationship between the employer and client, especially regarding the employer's opinion of the client as an employee. Rather than asking if there have been problems, it is best to make a more neutral and open-ended inquiry such as, "How is Mr. Jones as a worker?" If there have been past difficulties, the rehabilitationist should ascertain their nature and make a mental note of them as they may be very relevant to subsequent evaluation and job placement efforts.

Beyond the identification and evaluation of factors that will affect whether the client can return to work with the employer, the rehabilitationist will want to complete an *Employer Survey Form* on the contacted firm (see Illustration 4-3). This is because the collection and filing of data on different businesses will greatly assist the rehabilitationist and his or her co-workers in placing present and future clients. Over a period of years, such a local employer data bank can easily become an invaluable placement resource. For each contacted firm, the rehabilitationist will normally want to identify factors such as:

1. The person responsible for hiring.
2. The nature of the business and its products or services.
3. Specific jobs existing in the firm and the number of employees in each.
4. Salary or wage levels for different jobs.
5. Work hours or shifts.
6. Present or anticipated vacancies and employee turnover.
7. General and specific job hiring requirements.

Illustration 4-3

EMPLOYER SURVEY FORM

(1) Company ____________________ (2) Date of Report: ________________

(3) Company Address: ____

____

(4) Contact Person (Responsible for hiring): _______________________

(5) Telephone: ____

(6) Total Number of Employees: ___________________________________

(7) Nature of Business: ____

____

____

____

(8) General Hiring Requirements (If any): __________________________

____

(9) General Working Hours or Shifts: ______________________________

(10) Specific Jobs (For each job indicate number of employees, approximate salary or wage, and probable strength requirement by letter V, H, M, L, or S):

(a) ____

(b) ____

(c) ____

(d) ____

(e) ____

(f) ____

(g) ____

(h) ____

(11) Comments: (e.g., turnover rates, present or anticipated vacancies, attitudes of personnel manager or owner) __________________________________

____

____

____

WORKING WITH PHYSICIANS

In relation to the provision of medical services, the rehabilitationist's goal is to bring the client to MMI at the earliest possible date and at the lowest possible cost. This requires that the rehabilitationist identify pertinent medical issues and subsequently arrange for their resolution. The process begins with a careful review of the client's file, especially medical reports provided by the carrier. Subsequently the rehabilitationist contacts involved physicians, and with the approval of the carrier arranges for additional diagnostics and/or recommended medical treatments.

The identification and resolution of medical problems requires the development and maintenance of good working relationships with physicians. The first step in working with physicians is to learn medical terminology. Without a strong foundation in medical terminology, the physician will have difficulty communicating with the rehabilitationist, and will be prone to view the rehabilitationist as more of a lay than professional person. Every rehabilitationist needs a good medical dictionary, *Physician's Desk Reference* (for information on medications), and anatomy text. While there is no way to master medical terminology without repeated exposure to it, the new rehabilitationist should be advised that learning a few hundred Latin (and to some extent Greek) prefixes and suffixes is the key to developing a basic competency. Since many private sector cases involve low back and other orthopedic injuries, the rehabilitationist should become especially familiar with medical issues and terminology pertaining to such injuries (see McMahon and Matkin, 1983).

The rehabilitationist will normally contact physicians involved with the case after first speaking with the client and employer. Physicians should always be approached professionally and the rehabilitationist should seek a personal meeting with involved physicians rather than simply a telephone discussion of the case. In some instances the physicians may want to bill the carrier for this consultation, and approval for such billings must be obtained in advance. The rationale for meeting with the client before the physician is that this enables the rehabilitationist to formulate more pertinent questions and specifically address client concerns. The rationale for first seeing the employer is to obtain a job analysis on the client's position for the physician to review.

It is important for the rehabilitationist to remember that it is the physician who determines whether the client can return to the previous position, and if the client can return, the actual date of return. In order to help the physician accurately make these determinations the rehabilitationist should provide the physician with a job analysis of the client's pre-injury job, and should be prepared to discuss possible job modifications that would make the position less physically demanding. If the client cannot return to the former job, the rehabilitationist will need, at some point, job analyses or the equivalent information on new jobs that would be considered. There must be medical approval of all job objectives, and the physician cannot accurately determine the suitability of a job objective without knowledge of its physical demands and actual working conditions.

Sometimes a problem develops in medical care coordination in that different physicians make incompatible assessments of the client's present or projected physical status at MMI, or make different treatment recommendations. While this can occur in any case, it is especially common for cases in litigation where physicians known to generally have more conservative or liberal opinions regarding the impact or management of different injuries have been engaged by one side or the other. Whenever the rehabilitationist encounters incompatible assessments or treatment recommendations, the opinion of the rehabilitation company's medical consultant should be used as the basis for recommending a rehabilitation plan.

When the rehabilitationist must consider job modifications or a new job for the client, having the primary physician provide a physical capacities assessment often proves to be an invaluable aid. The *Physical Capacities Form* (see Illustration 4-4) can be used for this purpose. In a physical capacities assessment the physician identifies the maximum physical abilities and work tolerances of the client. This information is then used to determine whether modifications to the former job would be sufficient to allow the client to safely return to it, or if other new job openings would be suitable. Some physicians may be reluctant to complete a written form, especially if the case is in litigation, but sufficient information can usually be obtained simply by asking questions which address the issues covered by the form.

Illustration 4-4

PHYSICAL CAPACITIES FORM

Patient's Name: ______________________________

Physician Completing Form: ______________________________

Diagnosis: ______________________________

Date Completed: ______________________________

Anticipated date of maximum medical improvement: ______________________________

Probable date patient could resume work activities: ______________________________

Directions: Based upon your present knowledge of the patient's situation, please check all areas where there is a restriction of the patient's capacities. Briefly explain each restriction.

(1) *Strength* (lifting, carrying, pushing, and/or pulling)
Check maximum job strength requirement
_______ More than 100 lbs. maximum and 50 lbs. frequently
_______ 100 lbs. maximum and 50 lbs. frequently
_______ 50 lbs. maximum and 25 lbs. frequently
_______ 20 lbs. maximum and 10 lbs. frequently
_______ 10 lbs. maximum

(2) _______ Climbing and/or Balancing ______________________________
____

(3) _______ Stooping, Kneeling, Crouching, and/or Crawling ______________________________
____

(4) _______ Reaching, Handling, Fingering, and/or Feeling ______________________________
____

(5) ______ Talking and/or Hearing ______________________________

____

(6) ______ Seeing (acuity, depth perception, field of vision, accommodation) ____

____

(7) Patient can work: Indoors only __________
Outdoors __________
Both __________

(8) Patient should not be in work settings where there would be exposure to:
______ Cold temperature (below freezing)
______ High temperature
______ Abrupt temperature changes
______ Wet conditions (contact with water or other liquids)
______ Humid conditions
______ Loud noise
______ Vibration
______ Potentially hazardous situations (e.g., moving machinery, explosives)
______ Fumes
______ Odors
______ Toxic substances
______ Dust
______ Poor ventilation

(9) Can the patient work at a job where he/she would stand all day (with relief at work breaks)? ______________________________

(10) Can patient work at a job where he/she would sit all day (with relief at work breaks)? ______________________________

(11) Can the patient tolerate an 8 hour work day in a job where he/she could stand or sit intermittently? __________
If not, how many hours could the patient tolerate? ______________

(12) Maximum distance patient can walk in a day (explain restriction): ________

____

(13) Other comments on patient's condition: ______________________

____
____
____
____
____
____

Finally, in working with physicians, the rehabilitationist should always behave in both a highly professional and cordial manner. It is important to remember that the rehabilitationist's client is also the physician's patient, and that the treatment of outstanding medical issues is the physician's and not the rehabilitationist's area of expertise. Clients must be medically stable before serious vocational planning can begin, and in early referrals, where the client may even be seen while still hospitalized, this is often not the case. The rehabilitationist's ability to function as an effective liaison between physicians, the carrier, and client is often a critical variable in the rate and extent of medical recovery achieved by the client.

REPORTING REQUIREMENTS

Every workers' compensation jurisdiction and insurance company has different reporting requirements (or reporting expectations) for rehabilitation service providers. In some instances reporting requirements are quite explicit or structured, while in others there is considerable latitude. Each rehabilitation company develops its own reporting, case recording, and service documentation procedures based upon its own needs, rehabilitation bureau requirements, and customer expectations.

In relation to report preparation, the rehabilitationist synthesizes pertinent information obtained from the client, employer, physicians, and other sources, into a case study or initial case report. This report normally serves as the narrative justification for the rehabilitation plan. The rehabilitation plan is sent to the carrier for approval, and in industrial injuries also to the rehabilitation bureau. When approved, services called for by the plan may be initiated. It should be noted, however, that the rehabilitationist can often obtain telephone authorization from the claims representative and proceed with necessary or emergency services before presenting a written rehabilitation plan.

The rehabilitation plan is normally developed as soon as possible, with modifications or additions made as necessary. In early referrals it may be impossible to determine if the client will be able to return to the former employer as his or her physical status at MMI is as yet unknown. This does not preclude the rehabilitationist, however, from developing a plan that is as complete as possible with currently available data. Such plans usually call for a return to the former job as medically feasible, and for a further evaluation of residual vocational capabilities if this proves unrealistic.

Although the format for rehabilitation plans may vary somewhat between workers' compensation jurisdictions and different rehabilitation companies, there are several areas which must be addressed. These are:

1. The identification of a vocational objective (albeit a preliminary objective during the early stages of recovery).
2. The identification of needed services (e.g., medical examinations, surgery, vocational testing, job training).
3. The cost of services.

4. Time line for services.
5. Recommended service providers.

In addition to preparing an initial report of findings and a rehabilitation plan, the rehabilitationist is also required to submit updated case service reports at time intervals designated by the rehabilitation bureau or carrier. Such periodic reporting necessitates case reviews, helping to assure that clients are not forgotten and that systematic monitoring of rehabilitation progress occurs (for an example of state workers' compensation rehabilitation service rules and reporting requirements, see Sanchez, Workman, Morris, Millier and Edelstein, 1981).

The private sector rehabilitationist is also responsible for recording the amount of time he or she spends working on each case and the specific services provided (see Deneen and Hessellund, 1981). This is normally accomplished by using a daily schedule that breaks the day into billable time units. For example, if a six minute time interval is used, then each hour is broken into 10 separately billable units. If professional time is $50 per hour and the rehabilitationist spends half an hour reviewing the file on Client X, 12 minutes talking on the telephone to Client Y about job leads, and 18 minutes doing a labor market survey for job objectives being considered for Client Z; then 50% of the hour ($25) is billed to Client X, 20% ($10) to Client Y, and 30% ($15) to Client Z. On a billing form, different codes are used to show the specific services provided for each case.

It is obvious that managing and billing time in units as small as six minutes requires careful attention to scheduling and time management. In practice it is not as difficult as it might first seem, the key being to schedule the next day's activities at the end of each work day. By reserving the last part of each day for next day planning, the rehabilitationist can avoid lost hours that result from a slow morning start, casual mental processing of issues in various cases, or simply pondering what to do next.

SUMMARY

Early case management services normally focus on maximizing the physical recovery of the client, and on minimizing the spread of disability effects. Goals are to bring the client to MMI at the earliest possible date and at the lowest possible cost, and to preserve employment with the former employer in the same, modified, or new job, whenever this is medically feasible. These objectives are accomplished by building a strong working relationship with the client, by identifying unresolved problems and needs, by recommending appropriate interventions, and by scheduling and coordinating authorized client services.

References

Benjamin, A.: *The Helping Interview.* Boston: Houghton Mifflin, 1981.

Branton, H.M.: Medical care coordination: Process and issues. *Rehabilitation Forum,* 1983, *10*:17-20.

Deneen, L.J. and Hessellund, T.A.: *Vocational Rehabilitation of the Injured Worker.* San Francisco: Rehab Publications, 1981.

Deutsch, P.M. and Raffa, F.A.: *Damages in Tort Actions* (Volume 8). New York: Matthew Bender, 1982.

Handbook for Analyzing Jobs, Materials Development Center, Stout Vocational Rehabilitation Institute, University of Wisconsin-Stout, 1972.

McMahon, B.T. and Matkin, R.E.: Preservice graduate education for private sector rehabilitation counselors. *Rehabilitation Counseling Bulletin,* 1983, *27*:54-60.

Roessler, R.T. and Rubin, S.E.: *Case Management and Rehabilitation Counseling.* Baltimore: University Park Press, 1982.

Rubin, S.E. and Roessler, R.T.: *Foundations of the Vocational Rehabilitation Process.* Baltimore: University Park Press, 1978.

Sanchez, I., Workman, E.L., Morris, G.M., Miller, J. and Edelstein, M.: *The California Workers' Compensation Rehabilitation System.* New York: Macmillian, 1981.

Treon, R.T.: Private rehabilitation of injured persons: A plaintiff-lawyer's perspective. *Journal of Rehabilitation,* 1979, *45(3)*:34-36.

Welch, G.T.: The relationship of rehabilitation with industry. *Journal of Rehabilitation,* 1979, *45*:24-25.

Wright, B.A.: *Physical Disability — A Psychological Approach.* New York: Harper and Row, 1960.

Wright, G.N.: *Total Rehabilitation,* Boston: Little, Brown and Company, 1980.

CHAPTER V

DEVELOPING THE VOCATIONAL REHABILITATION PLAN

IN Chapter IV a distinction was made between vocational management and vocational rehabilitation. Vocational management is largely a preventive service, designed to preserve employment with the present employer, while vocational rehabilitation involves finding a new job and a new employer. Although no national statistics are available, most private sector rehabilitation cases currently involve reversing the adverse vocational impact of disability (i.e., vocational rehabilitation) rather than the containment or minimization of vocational effects (i.e., vocational management). This is because workers' compensation statutes generally fail to assure a prompt evaluation of the rehabilitation needs of workers missing more than a few weeks of work, and because claims representatives appreciate the remedial more than the preventive value of referral to a rehabilitationist. As these situations change, private sector practitioners will see fewer cases where early neglect has compounded vocational problems.

It is important to emphasize that regardless of any vocational management/ rehabilitation distinction, early case management services (e.g., financial counseling, medical management) are provided whenever they are appropriate or needed. A "total" rehabilitation program involves bringing the client to MMI, minimizing the disability's adverse impact upon employment and other areas of life, and when employment is lost, affecting vocational rehabilitation. While the focus of this chapter is on the "vocational" aspects of a rehabilitation program, it is important to remember that in a total rehabilitation program the vocational components discussed here are integrated with those "nonvocational" components discussed earlier in Chapter IV.

ORGANIZATION OF THE PLAN AND CASE REPORTING

As noted in Chapter IV, a vocational rehabilitation plan indicates: (a) vocational objective, (b) needed services, (c) cost of services, (d) time line for service delivery, and (e) service providers. The plan is always developed with client participation and consent. When completed, it is written on a special form and submitted to the carrier (and in most states the workers' compensation agency) for review and approval. The rehabilitation plan is always written at the conclusion of the diagnostic and assessment process. Using evaluative data, the plan delineates the services that are necessary for rehabilitation.

In some instances, the carrier or agency may deny a plan, or may insist that it be modified in some substantial way. This usually occurs for one of two reasons. First, there may be a question as to whether the proposed services are capable of achieving the vocational objective, or if the vocational objective is even realistic. Second, there may be a question as to whether the requested services are needed or compensable, or whether a more cost-effective vocational rehabilitation is possible. In order to prevent both situations from occurring, the rehabilitationist must be professionally competent, must follow private sector placement priorities, and must be familiar with benefit provisions of the applicable workers' compensation law or insurance contract.

After the rehabilitation plan is accepted and services initiated, the rehabilitationist must keep the claims representative and any supervising agency regularly informed of case activities and progress. This is normally accomplished through telephone calls, billings, and monthly written case activity/progress reports. Because of the ever present possibility of litigation occurring between the claimant and insurance company, all case records and reports should be objective and factual. There is no need to present subjective assessments of the client (i.e., "This person does not really want to work") in either written reports or oral discussions. When opinions are presented, they should be clearly noted as such.

THE VOCATIONAL GOAL

In developing a vocational rehabilitation plan, the first objective is to identify a realistic vocational goal. This requires the assessment and integration of two separate areas of information. The first of these is information about the client, and the second information about the world of work as it exists in the client's community. Successful vocational rehabilitation always involves a careful assessment and integration of pertinent data from both areas.

In relation to the client, the rehabilitationist must know: (a) physical capacities and work tolerances, (b) existing work skills and other work relevant attributes (i.e., transferable skills), (c) work related needs, aptitudes, and interests, and (d) job seeking and job maintenance competencies. Work environment factors which the rehabilitationist must consider include: (a) the industrial/commercial base of the community and resulting labor market, (b) the requirements and demands of various jobs, and (c) available job openings. When this information is appropriately integrated with client characteristics, the identification of a realistic vocational goal is possible.

CLIENT CHARACTERISTICS

Physical Capacities and Work Tolerances

Illustration 4-4 presented the physical capacities information which the rehabilitationist utilizes in vocational planning. Specifically, the rehabilitationist must know the strength of the client, any restrictions of motion or limitations in perception, working conditions the client should not be exposed to, and daily activity tolerances. This information is normally obtained from the primary physician, and is then compared with data obtained from job analyses. For a vocational goal to be realistic there can be no inconsistencies between the requirements of a job as delineated by the job analysis, and the capabilities of the client as reported by physicians. Assuming the client is at MMI and the medical report and job analysis incompatible, then the rehabilitationist's choices are to: (a) modify or redesign the job bringing it or some new version of it into compliance with the client's physical capacities (this includes providing the client with a prosthesis or some other device that makes the job easier), or (b) acknowledging that the job objective is unrealistic and looking for other less demanding choices. Possibly the greatest error that a rehabilitationist can make is to support or encourage a client toward a job objective that is incompatible with his or her residual physical capacities. Such errors not only result in failed or unsuccessful placement, but can also result in further injury.

Although the reported physical capacities of a client must be compared with an actual job analysis of the position being considered in order to be sure the job is suitable, many rehabilitationists utilize published data on the typical or average demands of different jobs as an aid in the evaluation of job suitability. Two excellent publications in this area are *The Classification of Jobs According to Worker Trait Factors* (1982) and *Selected Characteristics of Occupations Defined in the Dictionary of Occupational Titles* (1981). This information on typical job demands is also available through various software packages (e.g., *Choices, Ability Information Systems*).

While the rehabilitationist must utilize the physician's assessment of physical capacities in vocational planning, the client's assessment of his or her physical capacities must also be given careful consideration. In some instances the client will believe he or she can do more, and in other instances less. An effective way to resolve such discrepancies is for the rehabilitationist to arrange a conference with the client and physician. A second medical opinion might also be sought. However, when discrepancies remain between the assessment of the medical expert(s) and client, the rehabilitationist must rely on the expert medical opinion.

Existing Skills and Work-Relevant Attributes

As indicated earlier, in private sector rehabilitation transferable skills are carefully evaluated to identify suitable job objectives. When a realistic job objective cannot be identified through the assessment of transferable skills and the comparison of those skills with opportunities in the local labor market, then the rehabilitationist must consider some form of training (retraining) or self-employment. Transferable skills are utilized first because the liability of an insurance carrier is to restore the claimant to suitable employment, and not to actualize never before realized vocational potentials.

A transferable skill is any client attribute which is relevant to the performance of some job. The process of their assessment begins with a detailed collection of the client's past education and work history (see Illustration 4-2). In addition, the rehabilitationist considers personal qualities of the client (e.g., ability to relate well to people, preference for a structured work routine) and the possible vocational relevance of client avocational activities (e.g., woodworking, gardening, sewing).

One way to systematically approach the assessment of transferable skills from past employments is to use the Vocational Diagnosis and Assessment of Residual Employability (VDARE) process as developed by McCroskey, Wattenbarger, Field and Sink (see *VDARE Training Manual*, 1979). This method uses nationally available information on physical demands, working conditions, general educational development, specific vocational preparation time, aptitudes, interests, and temperaments associated with "average" job/worker situations to construct transferable skills profiles based upon past client work experiences. Profiles are then adjusted in relation to the impact of the disability and other factors, and the suitability of new jobs are judged by comparing their profiles with adjusted client profiles.

VDARE profiles are constructed from data printed in *The Classification of Jobs According to Worker Trait Factors*. Specific information on different jobs include:

1. *Dictionary of Occupational Titles* (D.O.T.) code.
2. *Guide for Occupational Exploration* (G.O.E.) code.
3. Physical demands in terms of strength, climbing and balancing, stooping and bending, reaching and handling, talking and hearing, and vision
4. Working conditions in relation to indoor/outdoor setting; and exposure to cold, heat, wet/humid conditions, noise/vibrations, hazards, and fumes/dust/odors.
5. General educational development in terms of reasoning, math, and language.
6. Specific vocational preparation which is the usual time required to prepare for or learn a job and reach average worker performance.
7. Vocationally relevant aptitudes including intelligence or general learning ability, verbal ability, numerical ability, spatial perception, form perception, clerical perception, motor coordination, finger dexterity, manual dexterity, eye-hand-foot coordination, and color discrimination.
8. Interests in relation to opposing preferences for activities dealing with: (a) things and objects versus the communication of data, (b) business contact with people versus scientific and technical activities, (c) routine, concrete, and organized activities versus abstract and creative activities, (d) activities involving working for the good of people versus activities in relation to processes, machines, and techniques, and (e) activities resulting in prestige and esteem versus tangible and productive satisfaction.

9. Temperaments or personal traits required of a worker including: (a) accepting responsibility and planning, (b) dealing with feelings and personal views of others, (c) influencing people, (d) making evaluations or decisions based upon sensory or judgemental criteria, (e) making evaluations or decisions based upon measurable or verifiable criteria, (f) dealing with people beyond giving or receiving instructions, (g) adaptability to performing repetitive work, (h) adaptability to working under stress, (i) dealing with precise tolerances or standards, and (j) adaptability to performing varied duties.

In summary, the VDARE process allows the rehabilitationist to compare a disability adjusted residual employability profile for the client with profiles for previously held employments and new job objectives of interest to the client. While the VDARE process is an excellent method for assessing "average worker" transferable skills, the rehabilitationist must remember that the data is based upon the "central tendency" demands and requirements of listed jobs, and not upon specific job analyses of a client's past employments. A detailed work history which delineates actual job tasks and elements of previous employments is therefore indispensable in transferable skills assessment. A detailed work and avocational history can also identify many work relevant attributes such as machine skills (e.g., keypunching, typing, forklift operation), language skills, artistic skills, possible aptitudes, and leadership qualities.

Vocational Testing

Although placements are usually arranged on the basis of identified transferable skills, at times the psychometric testing of vocational aptitudes, educational development, and vocational interests helps to clarify reemployment issues. This testing data is especially useful when there is a limited work history (as is often the case with younger workers), when educational records are absent or incomplete, and with clients who are nonverbal (i.e., have difficulty expressing themselves).

Cronbach (1970) defined an aptitude test as a test designed to predict success in some occupation or training course. The testing of vocational aptitudes can be very helpful in determining if a job objective is realistic, especially when the job objective can only be actualized through a vocational school or on-the-job training program. There are a wide variety of specific aptitude tests (for measuring clerical aptitude, mechanical comprehension, etc.) as well as aptitude test batteries which offer a broader assessment of vocational potentials (e.g., Differential Aptitude Tests).

Space does not allow for a discussion of the many different aptitude tests currently on the market. However, it should be noted that the most widely used (outside of public school settings) and most extensively normed of all aptitude tests is the United States Employment Service's General Aptitude Test Battery (GATB). This instrument reports nine vocationally relevant aptitudes (the same as utilized in the VDARE process except for eye-hand-foot coordination and color discrimination) and testing is normally available free of charge from State Employment Service offices. The great utility of the GATB stems from the fact that normative data is available for different Occupational Aptitude Patterns (OAP) and for specific occupations within those patterns, and minimum scores on critical aptitudes for each OAP are identified. A Spanish language version of the GATB and Nonreading Aptitude Test Battery (NATB) are also available (Botterbusch, 1978; Droege and Mugaas, 1976).

The assessment of achievement is similar to aptitude assessment, the basic difference being that past learning is being measured rather than learning potentials. Aptitude tests generally have problem-solving items and achievement tests items that require the demonstration of previously learned materials, and thus achievement tests emphasize recall, recognition, and other memory functions (Parker and Hansen, 1976).

The area of educational development is where achievement tests are most commonly used. It is helpful to obtain educational development measures when client language skills appear minimal or when occupations are being considered where language, arithmetic, or reading skills are important. Educational development measures may also be helpful in determining if a client is suitable for a specific job training program. For example, if a vocational school is using a text with a 10th grade reading level, a client testing at a 6th grade reading level may have an inordinate amount of difficulty in the course.

As in the case of aptitude tests, there are a number of achievement tests currently on the market. A popular short screening test (20 to 30 minutes testing time) for general educational development is the Wide Range Achievement Test (WRAT) which provides measures of spelling, arithmetic, and reading ability. However, for a thorough assessment of educational development a longer and multilevel test such as the Adult Basic Learning Examination (ABLE) or Tests of Adult Basic Education (TABE) is recommended (see Buros, 1972).

Vocational interest inventories differ from aptitude and achievement tests in that in the former there are no right or wrong answers, only individual preferences. Interest inventories are often normed for different occupations in relation to the likes and dislikes of satisfied workers. The rationale is that if the subject indicates preferences similar to satisfied workers in a given occupation, he or she might also be satisfied with that occupational choice. It should always be remembered, however, that "liking" an occupation does not mean a person can "do" the job.

Probably the most widely utilized interest inventory is the Strong - Campbell Interest Inventory (SCII). This instrument reports scores for: (a) six General Occupational Themes based on the Holland (1973) typology of work environments and personality types, (b) 23 Basic Interest Scales, and (c) 124 Occupational Scales. Other popular interest inventories are the Kuder Occupational Interest Survey and the Minnesota Vocational Interest Inventory (MVII). The Kuder reports scores for 114 occupations and 48 college majors, and the MVII has 29 Occupational Activity scales and nine Area scales. While all of these instruments can be used with rehabilitation clients, the MVII, because of its norms, is a good choice for measuring nonprofessional interests of males. Unlike the MVII, the SCII and Kuder can be used with both males and females, and are better choices for measuring professional and academic interests (see Harmon, Sharma and Trotter, 1976).

Vocational Evaluation

Rehabilitationists in both the public and private sectors work with many clients who have substantial vocational handicaps, and if employability potential could only be evaluated through the administration of aptitude and achievement tests, results from such tests alone would certainly lead to the conclusion that many rehabilitation clients are unemployable. In order to identify realistic vocational goals and work adjustment problems, what is needed is a comprehensive assessment process that evaluates work-relevant attitudes, behaviors, and skills from a "screening in" rather than "screening out" perspective. In the field of rehabilitation, *vocational evaluation* is the term which denotes this comprehensive assessment service.

Numerous definitions have been offered for vocational evaluation. The Tenth Institute on Rehabilitation Services (1972) defined vocational evaluation as a comprehensive process that systematically utilizes work, real or simulated, as a focal point for vocational assessment and exploration, the purpose of which is to assist individuals in their vocational development. More recently, Gunnaway and Wattenburger (1979) defined vocational evaluation as "...a process of assessment of potential, especially with respect to an individual's optimum potential for vocational functioning, arrived at through a variety of sources, but characteristically through the observation of an individual's behavior in work-related or work-like activities" (p. 50). Both definitions indicate the vocational development or "actualizing" aspect of vocational evaluation services, and that client behaviors in real or simulated work activities figure prominently in the evaluation process. While the psychometric testing of vocational aptitudes and interests are part of the vocational evaluation process, the observation and recording of client behaviors on real-work activities and work samples carries the evaluation process beyond psychometrics into an analysis of specific client behaviors and behavioral patterns.

Due to its more comprehensive and observational nature, vocational evaluation, unlike psychometric testing, is a service which cannot be provided in the rehabilitationist's office. The client must be referred to a rehabilitation center or sheltered workshop offering vocational evaluation services. Such facilities usually have a variety of psychometric tests, work sample batteries (e.g., J.E.V.S., Valpar, Singer, Micro-Tower, etc.), work stations, and sheltered employment situations that may be utilized in the evaluation process.

Depending upon a client's employability problems and the evaluation procedures used, a vocational evaluation may take as little as two weeks (Rasch and Rasch, 1978) or as long as several months. In general, clients require more time for vocational evaluation when they have work adjustment problems (e.g., problems with punctuality, attendance, accepting supervision, relating to co-workers, staying on task, obeying rules and regulations, etc.). When significant work adjustment problems are present, any final evaluation of a client's employment potential must take into consideration whether the work adjustment problems are correctable or not. This usually requires the provision of work adjustment training. If the client responds favorably to this training (i.e., problems are reduced or eliminated) there is more employment potential than if the response is poor.

If there is any single key to using vocational evaluation services effectively, it is to carefully formulate pertinent questions before referring a client for evaluation services. When the vocational evaluator knows what questions the rehabilitationist needs answered, it is then possible for the evaluator to tailor assessment activities toward answering specific questions. In the absence of this structure, the evaluator is left to proceed as best he or she can, and the final report may not fully address all pertinent case planning issues.

When the vocational evaluation process ends, the rehabilitationist should have answered all relevant questions involving client work functioning, tolerance, aptitudes and abilities, and vocational interests. It should be possible to identify job objectives for which the client is physically and mentally suited, and any services necessary to prepare the client for those jobs. However, before the rehabilitationist and client can develop a rehabilitation plan, they must integrate evaluative data on the client with information on local labor market needs and characteristics.

LABOR MARKET CHARACTERISTICS

In the development of rehabilitation plans considerable emphasis is given to determining what clients are mentally and physically capable of doing. While this is essential for vocational planning, it is also necessary to know what jobs exist in the local economy, the demands of those jobs, and whether there are reasonable opportunities for employment. When local labor market information is not considered in the development of the rehabilitation plan, clients may be counseled and trained for jobs that do not exist, or for jobs where they will be noncompetitive with the current pool of job applicants. It is not enough to know that a client could physically and mentally do *Job A*. The rehabilitationist must also know that the client has a realistic chance of being hired for *Job A*.

Industrial and Commercial Base of Communities

In order to deliver effective services, rehabilitationists need to be familiar with the industrial and commercial base of the communities in which they work. This knowledge is necessary for rehabilitation plan development, and later for placement activities.

The best place to start learning about the industrial and commercial base of a community is the local Chamber of Commerce. This is because it is usually possible to obtain a publication from the Chamber of Commerce that identifies all major employers including address and telephone number, nature of the business, number of employees, and even types of jobs. If this information cannot be obtained through a local Chamber of Commerce, the rehabilitationist should contact the state Chamber of Commerce for a statewide listing (which usually lists employers by county).

After obtaining a listing of the major employers in the community, the next step is to meet the personnel directors (or company presidents or owners whenever possible) to explain your services and how they can benefit large employers. The rehabilitationist should first become familiar with the large employers in a community because they have the greatest personnel needs, most circumscribed jobs, and are more likely to come under Affirmative Action requirements.

The most important way rehabilitationists can assist large employers is by becoming a placement resource for them. To fill this role, the rehabilitationist must be familiar with the products or services, and with the personnel needs and job requirements of the company. The rehabilitationist's goal is to build a good working relationship with the personnel director, and to have that individual call the rehabilitationist when a sedentary or light job becomes available. The idea is for the rehabilitationist to have the first chance to fill the position, before it is advertised or turned over to a placement service.

Another source of local labor market information is the State Employment Service. In addition to being an important resource for job placement, local State Employment Service offices have information on the hiring requirements of different employers, job analyses, and employment trends in the community. The counselors in the State Employment Service have daily contact with new job orders and job applicants, and they know not only who is hiring, but also what types of training and work experience are in demand, and equally important, what types are not.

While the Chamber of Commerce and State Employment Service are probably the two best sources of information, the rehabilitationist will also find the local newspaper and telephone book useful in understanding the industrial and commercial base of a community. In addition to job advertisements in the classified section, newspapers publish stories that indicate what businesses are coming into or leaving an area, political developments that might affect local business, and who important business and civic leaders are. The yellow pages of the telephone book list all local retailers and service establishments, and this listing is useful in labor market surveying.

In addition to local sources of labor market information, the rehabilitationist may find occupational projection data (usually available from the state's Department of Labor) and certain federal publications such as the *Occupational Outlook Quarterly* and *Occupational Outlook Handbook* helpful. Also, the Bureau of Labor Statistics of the U.S. Department of Labor conducts wage surveys for select occupations in different Standard Metropolitan Statistical Areas, and this information is useful in predicting entry level and maximum earnings for different jobs.

Requirements and Demands of Local Jobs

In addition to knowing principal employers and jobs existing in the local economy, the rehabilitationist must know the hiring requirements and on-site demands of specific jobs. Publications (discussed earlier) such as *The Classification of Jobs According to Worker Trait Factors* (1982) and *Selected Characteristics of Occupations Defined in the Dictionary of Occupational Titles* (1981) provide "central tendency" data, but local job demands may be somewhat different. Moreover, the rehabilitationist cannot be a placement resource to the employer unless he or she understands the jobs the employer needs filled and what successful worker performance entails. It is not enough to know only the capabilities and limitations of the client. The rehabilitationist must know the on-site demands of the jobs as well.

The rehabilitationist learns about actual job demands primarily by conducting on-site job analyses. Although there are no substantive differences in how job analyses are conducted, they are usually more detailed when part of vocational management/rehabilitation efforts for a specific client then when conducted for general job bank development. In a typical job analysis, the rehabilitationist identifies job elements and tasks, tools utilized, physical demands, and working conditions (see Illustration 4-1). When talking to a personnel director, the rehabilitationist should explain that being an effective placement resource requires familiarity with jobs existing in the company. Permission should then be sought to spend several hours (less or more time depending on the number of jobs) talking to employees and supervisors, and observing on-going work activities. Data collected through this process should be kept in a separate file for each company. The rehabilitationist can then refer to it when calling back to check for anticipated job openings, or for a quick evaluation of the suitability of a job for a given client. Before placing a client, however, it is advisable to do a second job analysis on the position, updating the original data while having a specific client in mind.

REALISTIC AND UNREALISTIC VOCATIONAL GOALS

One of the most difficult problems faced by rehabilitationists is dealing with clients who have unrealistic vocational expectations. This problem is fairly common and helping clients identify realistic vocational goals is an early objective of rehabilitation services. A realistic vocational choice has certain attributes: (a) the job exists in the client's community, (b) there are job vacancies or real opportunities for employment, (c) the job is compatible with the client's aptitudes, abilities, and residual physical capacities, and (d) the client meets or can be reasonably brought to minimum standards for the job in terms of education, training, and/or work experience requirements. It is unfortunate that clients make post injury vocational choices where one or more of the preceding elements is absent. When this occurs, it is the responsibility of the rehabilitationist to counsel the client toward a more realistic vocational goal.

Clients may embrace unrealistic vocational goals for a number of reasons. These include: (a) limited or inaccurate occupational information, (b) inaccurate perceptions of personal aptitudes, abilities, or residual physical capacities, (c) financial needs, (d) secondary disability gains, and (e) the absence of appealing vocational alternatives (Salamone and McKenna, 1982). When a client makes an unrealistic vocational choice one or more of the preceding elements is usually present. The first task of the rehabilitationist is to identify which elements contribute to the unrealistic choice. The second is to provide vocational counseling and related services which address each identified problem. The problems which contribute to an unrealistic vocational choice are often interrelated, and the rehabilitationist must frequently work on two or more problem areas simultaneously.

Limited or Inaccurate Occupational Information

Many clients have a limited or inaccurate knowledge of the world of work, especially as it exists in their community. In order to make realistic vocational choices clients must have information on: (a) the types of jobs which exist in their community, (b) availability of job openings, (c) minimum hiring requirements in terms of education, training, and work experience requirements, (d) characteristic working conditions, (e) physical and mental demands, and (f) salary or wage levels. Absent or inaccurate information in any of these areas can result in unrealistic vocational goals. The rehabilitationist can evaluate whether adequate or inadequate job information underlies a vocational choice by assessing client knowledge in each of the preceding areas. To do this the rehabilitationist will, of course, need to have accurate occupational information on the specific job or jobs in question. This knowledge is usually obtained by contacting local employers by telephone to obtain labor market surveys, or in person for job analyses.

When an unrealistic vocational choice stems totally from absent or inaccurate occupational information, the rehabilitationist's sharing of occupational knowledge and sources of that knowledge normally dissuades the client from the unrealistic choice. This sharing of occupational information also helps direct the client toward other vocational alternatives. When a client remains committed to an unrealistic vocational goal despite knowledge of local occupational information which argues against successful placement (e.g., strenuous physical demands, unemployment of currently trained or experienced workers) other issues almost certainly contribute to the client's unrealistic choice.

Inaccurate Perceptions of Aptitudes, Abilities, or Residual Physical Capacities

Clients may have accurate job knowledge, but poor knowledge of personal aptitudes, abilities, or residual physical capacities. In order to make realistic vocational choices clients must relate information about themselves to information about jobs. This requires introspection and honesty.

Clients with self-knowledge problems are frequently helped toward accurate self-evaluations by the rehabilitationist's collection and interpretation of evaluative data (e.g., results of vocational tests, work evaluations, medical examinations). The rehabilitationist must be careful to present evaluative data to clients in ways that are professional and tactful. Clients often need time to assimilate new information about themselves, especially when the new information is inconsistent with their previous beliefs or self-concept. It is critical that evaluative data be presented in a manner which allows the client to initially reject or question it without a corresponding rejection of the rehabilitationist (Rubin and Roessler, 1978). By emphasizing capabilities over limitations, and by relating capabilities to the local labor market, the rehabilitationist can help direct clients toward new and realistic vocational choices.

Financial Needs

Clients also choose unrealistic vocational goals because of expectations or pressing needs for high remuneration. Poorly conceived vocational goals are especially common when clients are preoccupied with thoughts about their future economic security. When a vocational choice has been overly influenced by financial considerations the client will characteristically show a marked reluctance or actual hostility toward discussing other variables (e.g., necessary aptitudes, physical requirements). The defense mechanism of denial is readily apparent.

Some of the more difficult cases where expectations of high post-injury work earnings occur are those that involve workers with histories of high remuneration for medium, heavy, or very heavy work. After sustaining a serious injury many of these workers become suitable for only sedentary or light employment. The transition of such workers into sedentary or light employment often results in an initial reduction in earnings, and clients frequently find this wage loss very difficult to accept from both self-concept and economic perspectives. They may continue to insist upon work which involves unacceptable physical demands, or choose less physically demanding but high remunerative work for which they cannot qualify.

When financial needs underlie an unrealistic vocational choice the rehabilitationist must provide financial counseling services. The economic security issues immediately impacting upon the client must be addressed before vocational choice variables can be processed. Financial counseling, as indicated earlier may involve any or all of the following: (a) determining the disability period income and financial reserves of the client, (b) identifying other benefits for which the client is entitled – other insurance benefits, SSDI, SSI, VA benefits, food stamps, etc., (c) assisting the client in establishing eligibility for other benefits, (d) determining general and disability related expenses, (e) identifying priority expenses and other expenses which might be eliminated, postponed, or assumed by another party, and (f) constructing a disability period budget. It is often necessary to bring some form of closure to immediate financial concerns before it is possible to realistically process the other variables which impact vocational choice.

Secondary Gains

It is not uncommon for rehabilitationists to meet clients who have strong secondary gains from the disability process. Although secondary gains come in many forms (e.g., release from family and work responsibilities, sympathy, attention) the most difficult secondary gains, from a vocational rehabilitation perspective, are economic. When clients have an effective post-injury income which approximates or exceeds their pre-injury income they may be very reluctant to explore new vocational objectives (assuming they will not be able to return to their former job) as these might adversely affect their post-injury economic gains. One client reaction (which may be conscious or unconscious) is to embrace an unrealistic vocational goal. This unrealistic goal may be presented to the rehabilitationist as a specific job, as an outline of idealistic work activities, or as high post-injury earning requirements.

When unrealistic vocational goals are related to secondary economic gains (which may be real or anticipated) the rehabilitationist faces a difficult task. It is far easier to prevent this situation from developing (through early and substantial post-injury client contact with a rehabilitationist) then to correct it once it exists. In addressing the problem the rehabilitationist must provide counseling services. The nature of these services are largely determined by whether the client's unrealistic vocational goals are conscious (deliberate) or unconscious (unintentional) obstructions to vocational rehabilitation.

When unrealistic vocational goals are unconscious or semi-conscious obstructions it is characteristically possible for the rehabilitationist to develop a counseling relationship with the client. It is important to remember that the client is essentially ambivalent about the personal desirability of post injury vocational activity. The rehabilitationist must be prepared to address a variety of personal/vocational issues in counseling (e.g., fear of failure or re-injury, attitudes toward employment held by a spouse or other family members, intrinsic rewards of working). In the absence of psychopathology, it is generally best for the rehabilitationist to personally provide counseling services to vocationally ambivalent clients. Referral to professional psychotherapists may result in a loss of focus on the essential decision which the client must make — namely that of utilizing or not utilizing remaining vocational potential. When a choice on this critical issue is delayed the inertia of unemployment often results in a decision (by indecision) not to work again.

Another type of client with secondary economic gains is the hostile client. This client has made a conscious decision not to utilize residual vocational capacities and often views the rehabilitationist overtly or covertly as an antagonist. The first goal with such clients is to recognize and differentiate them from ambivalent clients. The rehabilitationist subsequently attempts to counsel them toward a more ambivalent work position and then toward a realistic vocational goal. This is a difficult task and it sometimes proves to be impossible. The rehabilitationist then documents the case services provided, their lack of impact, and possibly even or the actual obstruction of services by the client.

Appealing Vocational Alternatives

Most clients are motivated to return to work. However, when they cannot return to their former employment they may pick a vocational goal which is well suited to their interests, but not their capabilities or the local labor market. For maximum effectiveness, the rehabilitationist must be able to direct clients toward both realistic and appealing vocational alternatives. Many rehabilitationists recommend vocational interest testing as a means to identify appealing alternatives. Although this is an effective method, a more efficient alternative is frequently applicable.

Perhaps one of the best and least utilized resources for identifying appealing vocational alternatives is the *Guide for Occupational Exploration (GOE)*. The *GOE* is a relatively new U.S. Department of Labor publication which sequentially organizes jobs according to: (a) 12 broad occupational interest areas, (b) 66 work groups, and (c) 348 subgroups. Each *GOE* work group has a discussion of the nature of the work, skills and abilities needed, how individuals prepare to enter the work, etc. Every job referenced under one of the 348 subgroups has a six digit *GOE* code cross referenced to the nine digit *DOT* code.

The *GOE* is an invaluable resource for identifying jobs that a client may be interested in. If a client, for example, indicates a strong preference for Jobs X and Y (but for some reason is unable to enter those jobs) the rehabilitationist can use the six digit *GOE* codes for Jobs X and Y to identify other job titles with similar interest patterns. These can then be evaluated in terms of other suitability factors (e.g., working conditions, GATB score, existence in the local community). Clients are usually receptive to secondary choices generated by the *GOE* since they are related, by interest commonalities, to their original choices.

TO TRAIN OR NOT TO TRAIN

A major feature distinguishing the public and private sectors of rehabilitation is the emphasis given to training (retraining) in the public sector and to placement on the basis of transferable skills in the private sector. The public sector currently emphasizes training for a number of historical reasons (see Oberman, 1965) and because: (a) many public sector clients are young or developmentally disabled and lack both job skills and work experience, (b) severely disabled individuals (the priority service population) frequently need to develop new vocational skills for reemployment, and (c) the existence of a public sector rehabilitation philosophy that calls for "actualizing" as well as "restoring" vocational activity (Diamond and Petkas, 1979). The private sector, on the other hand, provides rehabilitation services that address the statutory provisions of workers' compensation laws and liability issues in third party funded rehabilitation. This has resulted in an emphasis on placing the claimant with the former or new employer on the basis of transferable skills whenever possible. However, the fact that placement opportunities are first explored from a transferable skills perspective does not mean that job training is inappropriate, or even unusual in private sector rehabilitation.

Whenever a rehabilitationist encounters a client who has reached MMI and cannot return to the former employer or be placed with a new employer on the basis of transferable skills, consideration should be given to whether job training would lead to reemployment. In order to determine whether training is appropriate or feasible, a number of factors must be evaluated. These include: (a) the statutory provisions of the applicable workers' compensation law (if an industrial injury) and third party liability for the replacement of lost income, (b) characteristics of the client, (c) alternative methods of training, and (d) local employment opportunities.

Statutory Provisions and Third Party Liability

One of the most perplexing issues in industrial rehabilitation is the uniqueness of each state workers' compensation law. While the states have been revising their laws to make them more consistent with the 1972 recommendations of the National Commission (see Workers' Compensation Rehabilitation Laws and Programs, 1981; Analysis of Workers' Compensation Laws, 1984), some states still make no statutory provision for vocational rehabilitation, although it may be ordered in individual cases by the administrative agency. In other states rehabilitation is mandatory, and a claimant's benefits may be reduced or even forfeited if rehabilitation is refused or obstructed. Moreover, some states specify that vocational rehabilitation services (often referred to as retraining) may be provided for a maximum of one or two years, and authorize additional cash benefits (maintenance) during this period. Finally, carrier financial exposure under temporary and permanent disability provisions vary not only on a case by case basis, but also on a state by state basis for identical injuries.

In order to know when it is feasible to write retraining into a rehabilitation plan the rehabilitationist must be thoroughly familiar with the benefit provisions of the applicable workers' compensation law. Without this familiarity, there is no way the rehabilitationist can predict carrier or employer receptivity to a particular training plan, or advocate effectively in support of a job training program. If the law, for example, specifies a maximum retraining period of 26 weeks with one 26 week extension, recommending a two year training program is inappropriate, unless there are truly special circumstances and the rehabilitationist is prepared to take on a strong advocacy role. In general, when the employer's or carrier's liability for income replacement is high, as is generally the case under more adequate laws and with younger workers, substantial retraining efforts are more easily justified.

In nonindustrial injuries (LTD, auto no-fault, auto liability, and general liability cases) exposure for lost income will largely determine the carrier's receptivity to rehabilitation plans that call for job training. It is not only the cost of vocational training that the carrier must consider (e.g., tuition, books and supplies), but also the benefits that would continue during the training period, the possible delay of a settlement, and the impact on litigation that an unsuccessful retraining program might produce. As in industrial disability, when the carrier's exposure for lost income is high, rehabilitation plans which call for job training are easier to justify from a loss reduction perspective.

Regardless of statutory provisions or loss adjustment issues, when a claimant cannot be placed on the basis of transferable skills, the rehabilitationist has a professional responsibility to inform the employer or carrier of any job training option that the rehabilitationist believes would result in reemployment. When a truly realistic vocational goal has been identified that can only be actualized through job training, the employer or carrier will often authorize the recommended training. It is frequently not so much the cost or time period of training that the rehabilitationist must justify, but rather that there is a high probability of reemployment after the job training program is completed.

Characteristics of the Client

It is obvious that no client should be recommended for a job training program without first ascertaining that the client's aptitudes and physical capacities are adequate for completion of the training program, and for the actual work to be performed after placement. These issues are addressed through vocational testing/evaluation, by on-site visits to schools and potential employers, and through consultation with physicians. It is also helpful to use interest inventories or actual hands-on experiences (e.g., work samples) to assess vocational interests.

Although the rehabilitationist must evaluate aptitudes, physical capacities, and interests; the most critical factor in recommending job training is the client's motivation for reemployment. Motivation for reemployment is not necessarily the same as motivation for job training. Clients who were cooperative earlier in the rehabilitation process (i.e., when the rehabilitationist was trying to arrange a placement on the basis of transferable skills) are almost always better candidates for job training than previously uncooperative clients. Positive client indicators for job training are: (a) good pre-injury work history, (b) willingness to seriously consider a number of training options rather than fixation on only one, (c) absence of excessive somatic complaints or over restriction of post injury activities, (d) verbal statements suggesting the client has internalized the work ethic, (e) the support of significant others for training and subsequent reemployment, (f) willingness to relocate if necessary for employment, and (g) reliable transportation. If formal schooling is to be the method of training, the client's performance in high school, college, and other earlier school experiences should be considered.

Alternative Methods of Training

There are basically two methods to teach clients the specific vocational skills necessary for a job: (a) on-the-job training (OJT), and (b) formal vocational schooling. While an OJT may be arranged a number of ways, it is essentially an agreement where an employer trains a new worker in lieu of certain financial considerations. Formal vocational schooling, on the other hand, occurs primarily in a classroom setting, but also involves hands-on experiences on real or simulated work projects. It is important to emphasize that both methods of job training are used for teaching new vocational skills, and not for redressing work adjustment problems or prevocational skill deficits (which are often resolved through work adjustment training in a rehabilitation facility or sheltered workshop). These later problems should be dealt with before the client is placed in a job training program.

In relation to OJT's, the most typical arrangement is where the carrier and training employer share the salary expense of the client/worker for a set number of weeks or months. The salary should generally be consistent with what would be paid to an entry level worker, the shared salary ratio the most favorable that the rehabilitationist can negotiate, and the training period adequate to teach necessary job skills. While it is possible to arrange an OJT where the client is not an employee of the training employer, which is often done to avoid unemployment compensation if the client does not work out, such OJT's should be avoided whenever possible. When necessary, the unemployed status of the client should usually last no more than several weeks, although the actual OJT may run much longer. If an employer is unwilling to hire a client after several weeks of work, there is a good possibility that the employer is in some way not fully satisfied with the client, or simply does not need another worker. It is important to remember that the most successful OJT's are usually arranged with employers in growing businesses. It is generally better for the client to receive less adequate training from an employer who will hire, than better training from one who will not.

Once an OJT is arranged, it is important for the rehabilitationist to visit the client on-the-job and maintain contact with the employer on a regular basis, especially during the early weeks of the OJT. One very important issue that the rehabilitationist must be sensitive to is whether the client/worker is being treated as a trainee or apprentice. A trainee is a worker who receives daily hands-on instruction and supervision in the performance of skilled acts, while an apprentice performs the unskilled aspects of the on-going work activity (often even menial work), learning by observation and with some training and supervision in skilled work, often for as long as several years. While there is nothing wrong with an apprenticeship per se (it is the normal route toward skilled employment in many industries), physically handicapped individuals can often function adequately only in the skilled employment for which they are ostensibly trained, and not in what is often a more physically demanding apprentice role. In negotiating an OJT, the rehabilitationist should remember that many employers equate training with an apprenticeship. If the OJT is to be a partially supported apprenticeship, then the employer should definitely hire the client.

The alternative to an OJT program is formal vocational training through a private school or the public vocational education system. Training times are variable (usually determined more by the job objective than school), but relatively few training programs last less than six months or more than two years. Advantages of the public system frequently include lower tuition and certified instructors. These may be somewhat offset, however, by long waiting lists for popular programs, and by out-of-date equipment for rapidly evolving industries (where the greatest job demand for newly trained workers frequently exists). Private vocational schools should always be carefully investigated, and this investigation should include requesting and then contacting student and employer references. Although public and private vendors characteristically offer placement assistance, the rehabilitationist should never rely on the school's placement service.

Although it is difficult to compare OJT programs and formal schooling in terms of relative advantages and disadvantages, several issues should be kept in mind when developing the rehabilitation plan. First, the completion of a vocational school training program does not in itself guarantee employment. Many individuals have certificates, diplomas, and even degrees in fields where they could not hope to secure employment. Second, while both formal schooling and OJT's produce job skills, OJT's also provide marketable work experience. Clients with both skills and work experience are usually more placeable than clients with only skills. In general, the rehabilitationist will find that when an employment objective requires a certificate or diploma, as is usually the case in jobs where the public is served by state licensed practitioners, formal schooling is often the only available training method. For other job objectives, if an employer can be found who will hire the client at the beginning or at several weeks into a successful

OJT, this is usually the preferred training method. It is better to make an extensive search for such an employer than to opt for a more readily available vocational school training program.

Local Employment Opportunities

As indicated earlier, the most important issue in the rehabilitationist's decision to recommend job training is normally not the cost or time necessary for training, but rather the probability that the client will successfully complete training, and that training will result in reemployment. For a high probability that training will lead to reemployment, the client must be motivated to work again, the job objective must be physically and mentally realistic, and there must be a local labor market demand for the job skills the client will acquire through training. Evaluating whether there is a local demand for the job objective requires that the rehabilitationist conduct a pre-training labor market survey. The question which the rehabilitationist must answer is: "If the client currently possessed the skills and credentials which could be acquired through the job training program, which employer(s) would hire the client today?" Although it is never possible to predict a labor market with 100% accuracy two years or even six months into the future, if a trained client could presently be placed, then there is a high probability that the successfully completed training program will result in reemployment.

SELF EMPLOYMENT

In some cases it is impossible, even with extensive retraining, to reemploy a client with the former or new employer. These cases generally involve severe disability, and are characterized by substantial mobility restrictions. The client may be unable, for example, to transfer to or from the wheelchair or to move the wheelchair with his or her upper extremities. The client may also be only partially independent in activities of daily living (e.g., dressing, bathing, preparing meals), and what activities are performed may take inordinate amounts of time. While mobility and self-care restrictions do not preclude employment outside the home, when these restrictions are severe, homebound employment should be considered.

Wright (1980) discussed three types of homebound employment: (a) handicraft programs, (b) subcontract work, and (c) self-employment. In a handicraft program, the client produces an "arts and crafts" product which is sold through a retail outlet in the community. In subcontract work, the client usually assembles or packages a product in their home. In some instances, an employer may be willing to consider the client's home as his or her full-time work station. In self-employment, the client personally manages a small business enterprise.

In the literature on homebound employment, most authors have stressed that it should be considered only as a last resort (e.g., Rusalem and Cohen, 1975; Towne, 1972). This is primarily because employment in the community offers more psychosocial benefits, and a homebound worker can feel very isolated, and can eventually be forgotten.

When considering homebound employment, the private sector rehabilitationist should remember that handicraft programs seldom provide substantial earnings, and that business enterprises are very difficult to successfully establish and subsequently manage. In most instances, subcontract work or a homebound work station will be the more viable alternative.

SUMMARY

The vocational rehabilitation plan is formulated with the client at the end of the diagnostic and assessment process. It identifies a vocational objective, the services necessary to actualize the objective, the cost of services, service providers, and a time line for service delivery. The plan is submitted to the carrier and in industrial injuries to the rehabilitation bureau of the workers' compensation agency for approval. When approved, the rehabilitationist delivers the authorized services.

Private sector vocational rehabilitation plans emphasize job placement on the basis of transferable skills. When this is not possible, retraining and self-employment options are considered. Job placement is the most strongly emphasized private sector vocational service. It is so strongly emphasized that some have questioned whether private sector rehabilitation companies need to be licensed as private employment agencies (see Matkin, 1982).

References

Analysis of Workers' Compensation Laws. Washington, D.C.: U.S. Chamber of Commerce, 1984.

Botterbusch, K.F.: *Psychological Testing in Vocational Evaluation.* Stout: Materials Development Center, University of Wisconsin — Stout, 1978.

Buros, O.: *The Seventh Mental Measurements Yearbook.* Highland Park: Gryphon Press, 1972.

Cronbach, L.J.: *Essentials of Psychological Testing.* New York: Harper and Row, 1970.

Diamond, C.R. and Petkas, E.J.: A state agency's view of private for profit rehabilitation. *Journal of Rehabilitation,* 1979, *45*:30-31.

Dictionary of Occupational Titles (4th edition). Washington, D.C.: U.S. Government Printing Office (Stock No. 910-013-00079-9), 1977.

Droege, R.C. and Mugaas, H.D.: The USES testing program. In B. Bolton (Ed.), *Handbook of Measurement and Evaluation in Rehabilitation.* Baltimore: University Park Press, 1976.

Guide for Occupational Exploration. Washington, D.C.: U.S. Government Printing Office (Stock No. 029-013-00080-2), 1979.

Gunnaway, T.W. and Wattenbarger, W.: The relationship of vocational evaluation and vocational placement functions in vocational rehabilitation. In D. Vandergoot and J. Worral (Eds.), *Placement in Rehabilitation: A Career Development Perspective.* Baltimore: University Park Press, 1979.

Harmon, L.W., Sharma, V. and Trotter, A.B.: Vocational inventories. In B. Bolton (Ed.), *Handbook of Measurement and Evaluation in Rehabilitation.* Baltimore: University Park Press, 1976.

Holland, J.L.: *Making Vocational Choices: A Theory of Careers.* Englewood Cliffs: Prentice Hall, 1973.

Matkin, R.: Rehabilitation placement services: Unlicensed placement agencies or something else. *Journal of Applied Rehabilitation Counseling,* 1982, *13*:24-33.

Oberman, C.E.: *A History of Vocational Rehabilitation in America.* Minneapolis: T.S. Denison and Company, 1965.

Parker, R.M. and Hansen, C.E.: Aptitude and achievement tests. In B. Bolton (Ed.), *Handbook of Measurement and Evaluation in Rehabilitation.* Baltimore: University Park Press, 1978.

Rasch, C.A. and Rasch, J.D.: A model for comprehensive short-term assessment. *Rehabilitation Counseling Bulletin,* 1978, *22*:78-80.

Rubin, S. and Roessler, R.: *Foundations of the Vocational Rehabilitation Process.* Baltimore: University Park Press, 1978.

Rusalem, H. and Cohen, M.: Alternatives to homebound rehabilitation. In K. Mallik, S. Yuspeh and J. Mueller (Eds.), *Comprehensive Vocational Rehabilitation for Severely Handicapped Persons.* Washington, D.C.: Job Development Laboratory, George Washington University Medical Center, 1975.

Salamone, P. and McKenna, P.: Difficult career counseling cases: I-Unrealistic vocational aspirations. *Personnel and Guidance Journal,* 1982, *60*:283-286.

Selected Characteristics of Occupations Defined in the Dictionary of Occupational Titles. Washington, D.C.: U.S. Government Printing Office, 1981.

Towne, A.: Homecraft: Source of homebound employment. *Rehabilitation Record,* 1972, January/February, 7-10.

VDARE Service Bureau: *VDARE Training Manual.* Athens: Author, 1979.

Workers' Compensation Rehabilitation Laws and Programs. Washington, D.C.: Division of State Workers' Compensation, Office of Workers' Compensation Programs, Employment Standards Administration, U.S. Department of Labor, 1981.

Wright, G.: *Total Rehabilitation.* Boston: Little, Brown and Company, 1980.

CHAPTER VI

JOB PLACEMENT

DURING the last decade, a great deal has been written on placement services for disabled persons. In addition to several rehabilitation texts that deal exclusively with job placement (e.g., Bowman and Graves, 1976; Geist and Calzaretta, 1982; Vandergoot and Worrall, 1979), there have been major sections or chapters devoted to job placement in other rehabilitation books (e.g., Roessler and Rubin, 1982; Wright, 1980), federally supported studies of placement issues (e.g., Ninth Institute on Rehabilitation Issues, 1982), and a rapidly growing journal literature (see recent issues of the *Journal of Applied Rehabilitation Counseling, Journal of Rehabilitation,* and *Rehabilitation Counseling Bulletin*). The *Rehabilitation Counseling Bulletin,* for example, devoted a special issue to job placement in 1978 (vol. 21, No. 2). Perhaps the best reflection, however, of the increased importance attached to placement services is their training and research emphasis within the Rehabilitation Services Administration and National Institute of Handicapped Research.

Although a considerable literature is now being generated on job placement services for handicapped individuals, there are some philosophical questions about job placement which remain unanswered. For example, is job placement an "event" that occurs after the client is job ready, or is placement a "process"? If it is a process, when does it begin and how is it different from the rehabilitation process? Is job placement, as some have suggested (Welch, 1982), what the rehabilitation process is all about? Are private-for-profit rehabilitation companies really unlicensed employment agencies catering to physically handicapped clientele who have insurance that will pay for placement services, or are they more than specialized employment agencies (Matkin, 1982)? Having long under valued placement as a rehabilitation service, have we now over emphasized it at the expense of the client's "total" rehabilitation needs? There are, of course, no ready answers to any of these questions, or least no answers that would be accepted by everyone. One fact is nevertheless clear, and that is that job placement is a major rehabilitation service, especially in the private sector.

JOB PLACEMENT APPROACHES

Although there are many service issues in job placement, certainly one of the most fundamental is how much placement responsibility the rehabilitationist and client should each accept. For example, should the rehabilitationist arrange the placement, taking responsibility for activities such as identifying employers with job openings, scheduling interviews, providing transportation for the client to and from the interview; or should the client have these responsibilities? This fundamental placement issue is known in the literature as the client-centered versus selective placement controversy (see Geist and Calzaretta, 1982; Salomone and Usdane, 1977; Zandy and James, 1976).

Client-Centered Placement

Client-centered placement was defined by Salomone (1971) as an approach to job placement based upon client responsibility and counselor direction. Salomone argued that clients needed to develop their own job-seeking skills for maximum independence, and that the counselor's (rehabilitationist's) role was to assist and guide this development. In addition to facilitating longterm client independence, Salomone argued that a client-centered approach to placement reduced the likelihood of an unhealthy dependency relationship developing.

Since Salomone's 1971 article, a number of authors have pointed out that many clients need a more directed placement program than a client-centered approach seemed to provide (e.g., Brolin and Kokaska, 1974; Zandy and James, 1976). How, for example, does a rehabilitationist prepare an educable mentally retarded client to perform impressively in a job interview? Even if it is possible to bring such a client to a truly adequate interviewing skill level, is it not more efficient for the rehabilitationist to schedule and accompany the client to the interview, answering employer questions that the client cannot? While it is certainly desirable for clients to have good job-seeking skills and the motivation and self-confidence to accept responsibility for their own placement, it can be argued that this is an ideal which can only be partially actualized in the real world.

Salomone, however, pointed out (Salomone and Usdane, 1977) that the client-centered approach to placement does not view a successful job placement as what the rehabilitation process is all about. Rather, Salomone saw client independence as the primary goal of the rehabilitation process. A client-centered approach to placement facilitates client independence, and although the rehabilitationist may need to assume more placement responsibility with some clients than others, a client-centered approach to placement should not be abandoned simply because it may be less efficient than selective placement. Salomone argued that to abandon a client-centered placement approach simply for efficiency was to lose sight of what the rehabilitation process was all about.

Selective Placement

Selective placement is characterized by the rehabilitationist and client working together in an active and cooperative relationship toward the objective of job placement (Geist and Calzaretta, 1982). Both are involved in planning and implementing the placement strategy, which may or may not include job-seeking skills training. Although the rehabilitationist does not seek to accept more responsibility for placement than necessary, the rehabilitationist recognizes that a suitable job placement is ultimately his or her professional responsibility. In other words, the client contributes what he or she can to the placement process (the rehabilitationist attempts to maximize this contribution) and the rehabilitationist adds whatever else is necessary to effect a suitable placement. In some cases the client will do most of the placement work, and in other cases the rehabilitationist will do most of the work. In the final analysis, however, placement is the responsibility of the rehabilitationist.

It is probably fair to say that the selective placement approach views reemployment as what the vocational rehabilitation process is all about. Rehabilitation services are provided to effect a suitable job placement. It is through reemployment that the client regains lost independence, and how a suitable placement is arrived at (i.e., by primarily rehabilitationist or client efforts) is of no real importance in itself.

In selective placement the rehabilitationist may be involved, to varying degrees, in any of the following activities:

1. Calling employers to identify job openings or follow-up job leads.
2. Obtaining and helping the client complete job application forms.
3. Drafting introductory and interview follow-up letters for clients to send to prospective employers.
4. Assisting clients in resume development.
5. Teaching job interviewing skills, including proper dress and demeanor.
6. Scheduling job interviews.
7. Arranging transportation for clients to and from job interviews.
8. Arranging, when deemed necessary, to be actually present with the client during the job interview.
9. Following-up interviews to learn how the client did and to encourage the employer to hire the client.

Placement Approach in Private Sector Rehabilitation

Because suitable placement is the paramount issue in all private sector vocational rehabilitation cases, it is difficult to see how a successful practitioner could work from other than a selective placement perspective. This does not mean, however, that bringing the client to a point where he or she becomes an independent job seeker should be totally subjugated in the name of placement efficiency. The interpersonal skills and self-confidence which may be developed through attention to job-seeking skill development will, in some cases, generalize to other life areas, creating greater overall client independence. The rehabilitationist, however should be prepared to offer all services necessary to obtain a suitable placement for the client. The client should be encouraged and taught to do as much in this process as is reasonably possible. In this way neither placement efficiency or client development are sacrificed.

PLACEMENT READINESS

One of the hardest issues for some non-rehabilitationists to understand is that a claimant cannot be suitably placed until he or she is "placement ready." The concept of placement readiness includes many elements. First, the client must have reached MMI, or at least be medically stable and free of incapacitating pain. Second, a realistic vocational objective must have been identified. Third, the client must have at least some minimum of job seeking skills, such as being able to present a reasonably positive picture of self in an employment interview. Finally, the client must have a desire to work and have the behavioral competencies necessary to maintain the placement.

In evaluating placement readiness the rehabilitationist must consider pertinent medical, psychosocial, economic, and familial issues (see Chapters IV, V, and VII). Three vocational areas which must also be considered are: (a) the reasonableness of the client's job objective, (b) the adequacy of client job-seeking skills, and (c) motivation to work and job maintenance behaviors. Job objective issues were discussed in Chapter V. The remainder of this section focuses on job-seeking skills and job-maintenance issues.

Job-Seeking Skills

Zandy and James (1977) noted that the process of securing employment is in many respects routine, and therefore clients can be trained to be more successful job seekers. Being able to identify suitable job openings and present oneself effectively is what job-seeking skills are all about. Job-seeking skills training is the cornerstone of client-centered placement. Even in selective placement where the rehabilitationist locates the job openings, the client must still present him or herself effectively in an employment interview.

Job-seeking skills may be taught to clients individually, but the more common and efficient method is to teach these skills in a small group setting. Two to five days of instruction is usually sufficient (Zandy and James, 1977). Areas emphasized in such programs include: (a) sources for job leads; (b) what employers look for in job applicants; (c) how to complete employment applications, construct resumes, and write letters of introduction; (d) appropriate dress and demeanor during the job search and while interviewing; (e) role play rehearsal for employment interviews; and (f) development of appropriate answers to difficult interview questions. Programs may also involve instruction on issues such as the use of public transportation (Lake, 1975). One very successful model is the Job Club approach of Azrin and Besalel (1980) which, in addition to teaching job-seeking skills, emphasizes groups cohension and cooperation in the actual job search (see Azrin, Besalel, Wisotzek and Bechtel, 1982; Azrin and Phillip, 1979; Kauss and Sota, 1981).

Being able to identify suitable job openings is certainly the most important aspect of an independent job search. If the client cannot find job openings, effective interviewing skills are useless. Most programs emphasize the value of canvassing (i.e., contacting and submitting applications to firms without announced vacancies) and the use of informal networks (i.e., identifying current or anticipated job openings by talking with relatives, friends and acquaintances). Research studies have collectively suggested that these methods contribute 50 to 75 percent of all successful job leads (Zandy and James, 1978). Although want ads and employment agencies are also useful for job leads, Zandy and James (1978) reported that want ads accounted for no more than 10 percent of obtained jobs, private employment agencies for less than 5 percent, and public employment agencies for about 12 percent. Other sources for job leads that are occasionally productive include unions (Mallik and Moretti, 1982), civil service bulletins, trade and professional publications, and announcements of new business openings.

Once a suitable job opening is identified, the client must then make an effective presentation of self. To do this requires at least some appreciation of what employers look for in job applicants. The rehabilitationist usually addresses this area by lecturing and facilitating a class discussion of the topic. It is also helpful to arrange for a personnel director or business owner to speak to the group on what they personally look for in job applicants. Such presentations may, with permission, be videotaped for future use.

Having a general knowledge of what employers look for is important, but it is not the same as having the skills that allow for a positive presentation of self. One of the most basic skills is being able to appropriately complete a job application form. Fortunately, job application forms are very similar and solicit essentially the same information, making it feasible for even poor readers to complete them. Clients should know or have readily available all the information which is usually necessary to complete a job application form such as social security number; education and work history; names, addresses, and telephone numbers of references; etc. This may be accomplished by having the client complete a sample job application form that covers probable items (see Illustration 6-1). When needed, a job seeking skills program will also have clients develop resumes and introductory letters to employers (see Illustration 6-2 and 6-3).

Illustration 6-1

JOB APPLICATION FORM

Date of application ____________

Name ______________________________ Social Security # ____________
(Last Name, First Name; Middle Initial)

Address ______________________________
(Street and apartment #)

____
(City) (State) (Zip code)

Home Telephone ( )- ______________________

Business Telephone ( )- ______________________

Birthdate ____________ Sex ____________ Marital Status ____________

Number of dependents ________ U.S. Citizen? ______ Yes ______ No
If not, specify ________________

Racial/Ethnic Data (optional)
______ Hispanic ______ Asian or Pacific Islander ______Black ______White
______ American Indian or Alaskan Native ______Other (specify)__________

List any disabilities you have (optional) ________________________

____

Have you ever been convicted of a felony? ______ Yes ______ No
If yes, explain:____

Military History

Have you ever been in the military? ______ Yes ______ No
If yes, what branch ________ highest rank ________ dates ________

Educational Data

Circle last year completed: Grade school 1 2 3 4 5 6 7 8
High school 9 10 11 12 College 1 2 3 4 5 6 7 8

List all schools attended, their addresses, dates attended, and degrees or diplomas earned.

School or college	Address	Dates Starting	Dates Ending	Did you graduate?	Degree/Major

Employment Data

Beginning with your most recent job, describe duties and responsibilites, including periods of self-employment and military service. Use additional pages, if needed.

1. Name and address of present or last employer: ________________

____

Supervisor's name and title: ________________________

Your job title: ________________________________

Dates employed from: ________ (mo./yr.) until: ________ (mo./yr.) Hours per week ________

Starting salary: ________ Ending salary: ________

Specific duties and responsibilities: ______________________________

____

____

____

Reason for leaving: ______________________________

2. Name and address of next previous employer: ______________________________

____

Supervisor's name and title: ______________________________

Your job title: ______________________________

Dates employed from: __________ until: __________ Hours per week __________
mo./yr. mo./yr.

Starting salary: __________ Ending salary: __________

Specific duties and responsibilities: ______________________________

____

____

____

Reason for leaving: ______________________________

3. Name and address of next previous employer: ______________________________

____

Supervisor's name and title: ______________________________

Your job title: ______________________________

Dates employed from: __________ until: __________ Hours per week __________
mo./yr. mo./yr.

Starting salary: __________ Ending salary: __________

Specific duties and responsibilities: ______________________________

____

____

____

Reason for leaving: ______________________________

Do you object to your present employer being contacted? ______ Yes ______ No

Do you have any relatives employed by this company? ______ Yes ______ No

If yes, specify ______________________________

Have you ever been employed by this company before? ______ Yes ______ No

If yes, when? ______________________________

What position are you applying for? ______________________________

What are your salary requirements? ______________________________

Available starting date ______________

Do you prefer full or part time employment? ______________

Please list names, addresses, and occupations of three references. Do *not* list relatives or former employers.

____

____

____

____

____

____

Please list any professional or occupational licensure, registration or certification you currently hold. Also include special skills (e.g., typing, shorthand, machine operation, etc.). ____________________________________

____

____

____

I hereby certify that all statements made on this application are true. I understand that any misstatement of facts herein may invalidate my employment application.

Signature ____________________________ Date ____________

Illustration 6-2

SAMPLE RESUME

Resume for John Doe

Address:	17549 Fowler Avenue Tampa, FL 33548
Telephone:	(813) 949-2685
Personal Data:	Age 45, Married, Two Children, U.S. Citizen
Vocational Objective:	Automobile or Truck Sales
Educational History:	Certified Automobile Mechanic Autotech Vocational School 1420 West Kennedy, Tampa, FL (May, 1976)
	Associate of Arts Degree Hillsborough Community College 245 Tampa Boulevard, Tampa, FL (September, 1963)

	High School Diploma, King High School, 447 Busch Boulevard, Tampa, FL (June, 1960)
Work History:	Automobile Mechanic Hawthorn Service Center 5251 Terrace Lane, Tampa, FL (1974 - 1984)
	Automobile Mechanic Gulfside Service 225 Bay to Bay Avenue, Tampa, FL (1967 - 1974)
	Service Station Attendant Hannon's Garage 1215 N.W. 56th Street, Tampa, FL (1962 - 1967)
References:	Available upon request.

Illustration 6-3

LETTER OF INTRODUCTION

John Doe
17705 Hanna Road
Tampa, FL 33548

June 15, 1984

Mr. Robert Harper
Personnel Manager
Hoyt Ford
954 Sunrise Avenue
Tampa, FL 33640

Dear Mr. Harper:

I would like to apply for the new car sales position recently advertised in the *Tampa Times*. I have enclosed a copy of my resume for your review.

To briefly summarize my credentials, I would like to note that I am a graduate of King High School and a lifetime resident of Tampa. I am also a certified automobile mechanic with fifteen years of work experience.

I am looking for a position in new car sales because I want more people contact in my work, and believe I can sell effectively. My knowledge of automobile mechanics will be a valuable aid when customers want to discuss the construction or maintenance of a vehicle. I am available for immediate employment, and hope you will give my application serious consideration.

Sincerely,

John Doe

After the client has applied for a job, the next step is to make an effective presentation of self in the employment interview. Preparation for employment interviews is a major component of job-seeking skills training because even when the rehabilitationist finds a job lead, the client must still earn the position through an employment interview. The employment interview may be conviently approached in relation to three component parts: (a) scheduling, (b) preparation, and (c) execution.

Although job applicants must be prepared for the possibility of impromptu interviews (as might occur while canvassing), in most cases the applicant will schedule an interview for some time in the near future. When scheduling interviews applicants should always make a written note of: (a) the store or business where they are to interview, (b) directions to the interview site, (c) the name of the interviewer, (d) date and time of the interview, and (e) position they are interviewing for. This is especially important for applicants contacting a large number of employers and arranging multiple interviews within a relatively short span of time. The applicant should also be prepared to interview at the employer's convenience (i.e., the job search should have top priority) and have reliable transportation. Because scheduling and keeping interview appointments is not as simple as it might seem, many private sector rehabilitationists prefer to make interview arrangements for their clients.

After an interview is scheduled, the client must prepare to present him or herself effectively. This involves two aspects: (a) grooming and dress, and (b) content to discuss.

Although many clients know proper grooming and dress for employment interviews, there are many who do not. If the client has groomed and dressed appropriately for interviews with the rehabilitationist, the client will probably do likewise for employment interviews. The basics of grooming and dress include: (a) getting a haircut, if needed; (b) bathing and washing hair the night before the interview; (c) cleaning and repairing fingernails; and (d) selecting clothing that is appropriate, clean, and in good repair. It is far better for a client to over dress or over groom for an interview than to fall short in these areas.

Preparing for the content discussion of an interview is very important (Geist and Calzaretta, 1982). The interviewee's task is to convince the interviewer that he or she would be an excellent choice for the job. To do this the client must organize his or her thoughts about the job, employer, and self. Ideas and points to be communicated should be identified as well as those areas or issues the client would like to avoid. Although there are many questions typically asked in employment interviews (see Tesolowski, 1979), at a minimum, the client should be prepared to answer such basic interview questions as:

1. "Why do you want this job?"
2. "Why should I hire you?"
3. "How do I know you will stay with our company and not quit?"
4. "How does your disability affect your ability to work?"
5. "What are your salary or wage requirements?"

In preparing clients for interviews it is often helpful for them to complete an *Interview Preparation Form* (see Illustration 6-4). Completing such a form can help the client organize his or her thoughts, and may make the difference between a successful and unsuccessful interview.

Illustration 6-4

INTERVIEW PREPARATION FORM

Position: ______________________________

Company: ______________________________

1. What do you know about this company or business?

____
____
____
____
____

2. What do you know about this position?

____
____
____
____
____

3. What are the requirements to successfully fill this position and how can you show the employer that you fill each of these requirements (e.g., through past training, work experience, ability to learn, other personal qualities)?

Position Requirements:	How You Meet Them:
______________	______________
______________	______________
______________	______________
______________	______________

4. Why should the employer hire you?

5. What difficult questions might the employer ask and how would you answer them?

Difficult Questions: Answers:

6. What questions would you like to ask the employer if he or she does not answer them first?

In conducting an actual interview, clients are taught to pay attention to their entrance, the interview proper, the exit. There are many fine points of interview behavior (e.g., a firm handshake, eye contact, clear speech, waiting for a cue to sit) which are best learned through role play rehearsal with small group and videotape feedback. The *Role Play Evaluation Form* (see Illustration 6-5) delineates important areas of interview behavior. The trainer and client role play an interview, and the other group members evaluate and comment on the client's performance using the *Role Play Evaluation Form* as a guide.

Illustration 6-5

ROLE PLAY EVALUATION FORM

Name: ______________________ Date: ______________________

Behavior	Yes	No	Comments
Entrance:			
1. Stands straight			
2. Smiles appropriately			
3. Walks to employer			
4. Eye contact			
5. Hand shake			
6. Introduces self			
7. Clear speech			
8. Waits to sit			
9. Lets employer begin			
Actual Interview:			
1. Sits still			
2. Sits straight			
3. Eye contact			
4. Smiles appropriately			
5. Clear speech			
6. Lets employer ask questions			
7. Answers appropriately			
8. Positive self-presentation			
9. Asks appropriate questions			
Exit:			
1. Recognizes cue to stand			
2. Asks when decision will be made			
3. Asks permission to call back			
4. Smiles appropriately			
5. Stands straight			
6. Hand shake			

Strongest Interview Areas:

Areas Needing Improvement:

When playing the role of an employer in a simulated interview, it is very important for the rehabilitationist to remember that the difficulty of the questions asked must be tailored to the skill level of the client. Through repeated role plays, the client gradually builds the skills and needed confidence to handle more difficult questions or a "hard nosed" interviewer. The role play interview should be a successful and positive experience for both the client and those who observe. Anyone can play a difficult interviewer and defeat the client, but this serves no useful purpose and is actually counter productive. Moreover, when the rehabilitationist and group give the client feedback, the positive aspects of the client's performance should receive attention as well as areas needing improvement.

In summary, successful job-seeking involves the ability to find good job leads and the effective presentation of oneself. Job-seeking skills can be developed and refined, and they are an important component of placement readiness. The fact that a client can secure employment, however, does not mean that the client can keep it. In order to be placement ready, a client must also be able to maintain the placement.

Job Maintenance

As indicated earlier, job maintenance involves many issues. For example, the client must be medically stable, free of debilitating pain, and the placement must be consistent with physical capacities. Neff (1968) noted that the successful worker must also: (a) have at least some motivation to work, (b) possess a necessary minimum of work relevant aptitudes and skills, (c) conform to work-site rules and regulations, (d) meet minimum standards for work productivity and quality, (e) look and act like a worker, and (f) relate appropriately to different types of people (e.g., supervisors, co-workers, customers). Unlike the roles of spouse, parent, or family member, the role of worker (employee) may be terminated very rapidly for poor performance in any area. The maintenance of employment, even in the most menial of positions, requires daily performance consistent with expectations and standards existing at the work-site.

Motivation to work is certainly a critical aspect of job maintenance. If the client does not want to work, or is dissatisfied with the placement, the continuation of employment is often short lived. In order to be motivated to work there must be work-related reinforces for the client. These may be extrinsic or intrinsic. In discussing why people work, Neff (1968) noted five basic needs met through vocational activity:

1. *Material Needs* — such as food, shelter, clothing, and everything else money can buy.
2. *Self-Esteem Needs* — a sense of identity, autonomy, and pride from successfully functioning as a worker.
3. *Social-Esteem Needs* — the respect and social status others ascribe to successful workers.
4. *Activity Needs* — such as avoiding boredom, isolation, and filling up the day with meaningful things to do.
5. *Creativity Needs* — such as bringing something unique into existance, or achieving or producing something.

Although any of Neff's five areas might be a sufficient motivator for some people to work, most people think of work first as an economic activity, and second as an activity with other values. This is especially true in occupations outside the professional, managerial, and technical category (*D. O. T.* codes 0 and 1) where there may be less opportunities to meet creativity, social, and self-esteem needs. Indeed, there are few people who would work for long at any job if they were not paid for their time and effort.

Work is primarily an economic activity, and a number of authors have discussed disincentives to vocational rehabilitation inherent when there are third party disability payments (e.g., Lamb and Rogawski, 1978; Walls, Masson and Werner, 1977; Schlenoff, 1979). Walls (1982), for example, reported results of a research study which showed that as total cash or in-kind benefits increased, the probability of successful rehabilitation decreased. In private sector rehabilitation, the rehabilitationist usually works with an insurance claimant receiving a substantial income replacement benefit. The client often believes this benefit will last throughout whatever he or she perceives as the period of disability, possibly terminating with a substantial lump sum payment based upon the severity of the disability (Eaton, 1979). For some clients, especially those who never found many non-monetary rewards in their work role, this may introduce a serious motivational problem in returning to work. If they are unable to work the benefit continues, and as work is perceived as offering no rewards other than monetary ones, and is perhaps even seen as an aversive or punishing activity, there is little motivation to resume the work role. Disability also offers a socially and personally acceptable justification for not working, protecting the social and self-esteem of the individual. If the individual can also fill what was formerly work time with more personally rewarding activities, then an even stronger disincentive to resuming work exists.

There are a number of ways to approach motivational problems. For example, counseling might be provided to help the individual recognize nonmonetary rewards and other needs met through work activity. The client might also be counseled and/or trained for a new occupation offering more nonmonetary or intrinsic rewards. A trial work period might be provided where the client can keep full earnings and part of the disability benefit, thereby reintroducing a monetary incentive to work. Finally, the client can be threatened by the carrier with the reduction or termination of benefits if a "good faith" or successful job search is not conducted.

The first three motivational methods are usually effective with clients who have some secondary gains from their disability, but who are essentially ambivalent in their desire to work or are fearful of reinjury. With counseling, an opportunity for retraining (when necessary), and a temporary economic incentive; reestablishing suitable employment is usually feasible. In cases where there is malingering, after several warnings, benefit reductions are appropriate. Usually the carrier will engage the services of a private investigating firm and place the claimant under surveillance to determine if malingering is involved. Unfortunately, it is often hard to distinguish a malingerer from a pain debilitated, depressed, or otherwise marginally employable person. While the threat of benefit reductions has certainly induced some capable workers to return to the labor force, it has also caused unconscionable hardships on other deserving beneficiaries. The issue of whether a claimant can or cannot work must often be resolved in a hearing before a workers' compensation commissioner or administrative law judge (Grossman, 1979).

Being motivated to work is necessary for job maintenance, but the client must also know and practice appropriate job maintenance behaviors. In summarizing the literature on job retention, Wright (1980) noted that most jobs are lost because of problems in the areas of: (a) job attendance and punctuality, (b) quantity and quality of work produced, and (c) interpersonal relationships.

In relation to job attendance and punctuality, the client must have reliable transportation, and if small children are present, dependable day care arrangements. It is also advisable for the client to have a back-up plan for transportation and day-care if their primary method fails. The client must also have a reliable alarm clock and habitually retire at a reasonable hour on nights which precede work days. The client must also know the acceptable excuses for being late or tardy to work, the limits of these excuses, and the importance of promptly calling the employer (supervisor) when late or absent.

When a client does not produce work of acceptable quality or quantity, a question naturally arises as to whether the placement is truly suitable (i.e., within the physical and mental capabilities of the worker). If it is not, an attempt should be made to modify the job before abandoning it. When the problem stems from a poor work attitude or underdeveloped job skills, counseling and job coaching may be effective interventions.

More jobs are probably lost because of interpersonal difficulties than because of any other reason. Even if a client is having frequent transportation problems which result in tardiness or absence, or difficulty producing goods or services at an average worker level; if interpersonal relationships are good, the employer may be willing to give the worker more chances. The client must relate appropriately not only with supervisors, but also with co-workers, and on some jobs with customers. With supervisors the client must relate in a non-arrogant and non-threatening way, stay on task, follow instructions, and appropriately handle praise and criticism. With co-workers a non-competitive and friendly relationship should develop which does not interfere with, but rather supports on-going work activities. Customers must be treated cordially and courteously.

There are many important job maintenance behaviors, and even though most private sector clients are industrially injured and therefore have had at least some enculturation in the work role, the rehabilitationist should never overlook this area. Reasons given for previous job terminations and interviews with former employers may alert the rehabilitationist to possible problems. Serious job maintenance skill deficits are best addressed in a rehabilitation facility offering work adjustment services. There are many techniques in work adjustment training, but most are best performed near or around a worksite (see Gregory, Whitlow, Levine and Wasmuth, 1982).

Tesolowski (1979, pp. 67 and 71) summarized behaviors conducive to both the maintenance and loss of employment (see Illustration 6-6). When a client is motivated to work, is suitably placed, and knows appropriate and inappropriate work-site behaviors; job maintenance is usually assured.

Illustration 6-6

JOB MAINTENANCE BEHAVIORS

Appropriate Job Behaviors

1. Always arrive 15 minutes before you are expected to begin your job.
2. Attend work on a regular basis.
3. Promptly return to your job after the lunch period has ended.
4. Promptly return to your job after your break or rest period has ended.
5. Carefully listen to instructions given by your supervisor or co-workers.
6. Ask well thought out questions when you do not understand (especially if you must question your supervisor).
7. Maintain good grooming habits.
8. Getting plenty of rest will better enable you to be active and friendly on the job.
9. Look for additional work.
10. Remain at your work station.
11. Keep busy.
12. Exhibit patience.
13. Inform your supervisor of your progress.
14. Systematically conduct your work tasks.
15. Plan ahead and know what tasks you are going to do before you get to work.
16. Learn company policies and rules.
17. Constantly do the best job possible.
18. Do more work than is expected of you.
19. Refer to your supervisor and co-workers by name.
20. Be as agreeable as possible when talking to your supervisors or co-workers.
21. Observe how co-workers perform tasks which you are doing.
22. Exhibit friendly, cheerful, and courteous behaviors.
23. Be sensitive and understand your co-workers' feelings.
24. Be concerned about the quality of your work.
25. Be concerned about the amount of work which you are producing.
26. Respect your supervisor.

Inappropriate Job Behaviors

1. Frequently missing work.
2. Arriving late for your job.
3. Being extremely friendly with your supervisor.
4. Being extremely aggressive with your supervisor or co-workers.
5. Talking to your supervisor or co-workers when they do not want to be bothered.
6. Expressing anger when your work is constructively critized.
7. Allowing your emotions to affect your work.
8. Treating co-workers unfairly.
9. Taking full credit for a group effort.
10. Breaking company rules and policies.
11. Always trying to be the first person out of the building after work.
12. Expressing superiority to your supervisor or co-workers.
13. Allowing comments or criticisms about your work to become personal.
14. Indicating that you are more important than anyone or anything else concerned with your job.
15. Always trying to gain personal advantages.
16. Asking your supervisor a lot of unnecessary questions.
17. Verbally or non-verbally telling your supervisors or co-workers that you are smarter or have a better education than they have.
18. Taking problems to higher management than your immediate supervisor.
19. Being extremely sensitive to comments made by your supervisor or co-workers.
20. Always making excuses when problems arise.
21. Continually complaining and finding faults with everything.
22. Blaming co-workers for your mistakes.
23. Doing personal tasks during work hours, such as reading magazines or writing letters.
24. Being extremely critical of your supervisor, co-workers, or the company you work for.
25. Trying to learn co-worker's jobs before you know your own.
26. Constantly complaining about anything associated with your job.
27. Constantly watching the clock while working.
28. Frequently being unhappy while working.
29. Ignoring safety rules.

Reprinted from: *Job Readiness Training Curriculum* by Dennis G. Tesolowski, Materials Development Center, Stout Vocational Rehabilitation Institute, University of Wisconsin-Stout, Menomonie, Wisconsin, 1979 (pp. 67 and 71).

JOB DEVELOPMENT

Job development is the process of finding or arranging a suitable placement for the client. The term should be clearly differentiated from *vocational development*, which is an individual human development process resulting in a vocational choice (i.e., selection of an occupation). In public and especially private sector rehabilitation, job development is considered a major responsibility of the rehabilitationist. So much attention is now being focused on this area that a new professional role of job development and placement specialist is emerging (Crimando, 1982).

In Chapter V it was noted that the rehabilitation plan targets a certain job objective for the client. This objective is usually a specific job existing within some type of business or industry. However, when the rehabilitationist begins contacting potential employers, other jobs currently open and suitable for the client may be identified. At times there will be limited opportunities for employment in the client's first choice occupation, and waiting several months for a possible job opening when the client is placement ready is often unwise. When job openings are identified for which the client is physically and mentally qualified, interviewing for these positions should be seriously discussed with the client. Accepting a job does not mean one will work there for a lifetime or until retirement. It is understood in the work world that employees may choose to better their employment situations (i.e., take a higher status, easier, or better paying job) when and if an opportunity presents itself. Moreover, working always involves certain tradeoffs, such as balancing what one would ideally like to do with what one can make a living at, and the presence of a disability does not change this reality. A job consistent with client physical and mental capabilities, but not personal interests, is considerably better than no job at all.

In job development, the rehabilitationist may use many different sources to identify job leads (e.g., friends and relatives, state employment agencies, unions, trade and civil service publications, newspaper want ads). However, the essence of job development is reaching employers and identifying job leads before they are publicly announced. According to Salomone and Rubin (1979), the value of exclusive information about job openings cannot be over emphasized. This is because once a job opening is publicized, the job applicant pool (especially for good positions) becomes substantial.

In the following discussion of job development, four areas are highlighted: (a) contacting employers to identify job openings, (b) presenting clients to prospective employers, (c) dealing with employer objections to hiring handicapped individuals, and (d) scheduling interviews and follow-up. These areas represent the major job development responsibilities of the private sector rehabilitationist. Readers interested in a more comprehensive discussion of job development should consult *Marketing: An Approach to Placement* (Ninth Institute on Rehabilitation Issues, 1982).

Contacting Employers

The first step in contacting employers is to identify them. As indicated earlier, the local and state Chamber of Commerce publish a business and industry directory, and this is an invaluable aid in identifying employers who are not directly involved with the public. Businesses that interface with the public are almost always listed in the telephone book's yellow pages.

Once the rehabilitationist has a listing of local employers, the next question is which employers should be contacted early in job development efforts. The literature on job development suggests that larger employers are better prospects than smaller employers, apparently because larger employers have more specialized work forces, while smaller employers need more versatile employees. Manufacturers also appear to hire more handicapped persons than nonmanufacturers, but this may also be related to the fact that manufacturers tend to have larger work forces (see "Enhancing Employer Receptivity to Hiring Disabled Workers," 1979). It would seem that the ideal target for job development efforts is a large employer having mostly sedentary or light work positions. It is certainly desirable to single-out such employers for special and highly personalized job development efforts.

Regardless of the employer, there are certain precontact activities that should be considered. According to Minton (1977), for maximum placement success, prior to contacting a company the rehabilitationist should:

1. Determine the kind of business the company operates, the products it makes or the service it delivers, the number and types of jobs in the work force, and any seasonal trends in employment.
2. Ascertain if the company is covered under Affirmative Action for handicapped individuals, i.e., if it has a contract with the federal government totalling more than $2,500 or is the recipient of federal grant funds.
3. Try to determine if the employer has hired handicapped individuals in the past.
4. Identify the person in the company who has the real authority to hire and fire — it may not be the personnel director.
5. Ascertain the entry level job requirements and career ladders in the company and whether they are established and controlled through a union contract.
6. Evaluate whether or not the company is accessible to handicapped individuals and, if not, how difficult and costly it would be to make it accessible (pp. 144-145).

The literature on job development indicates three direct ways for initially contacting employers: (a) by letter and/or mailed survey, (b) through an unscheduled face-to-face meeting, and (c) over the telephone (see Roessler and Hiett, 1983). There are other more indirect ways of meeting employers, such as through civic, fraternal, and religious organizations, shared sporting or recreational activities, and the like; but the discussion here is limited to direct approaches.

A sometimes used and widely researched method for initially contacting employers is to send a letter and job survey form. The letter introduces the rehabilitation company and its business, tells how the rehabilitation company can help the employer (e.g., serving as a placement resource), and requests that any current or anticipated job openings be noted on the survey form and returned in the envelope provided. While this approach will produce some job leads, most studies have shown that employer response to such inquiries are generally poor (Cates, 1981; Vandergoot, 1976). Moreover, large scale mailings are costly because of postage, stationery, and word processing charges. Mailing approaches are probably best utilized by rehabilitation companies that offer several services (e.g., employee assistance programs, affirmative action plan development, staff development and training seminars, personnel testing) as these can be efficiently announced in a brochure, and with multiple service offerings, there are multiple chances of presenting a service the employer is interested in.

Another widely used method of job development is to travel to prospective employers for an unscheduled face-to-face contact. Unlike a mailed survey, this method allows two way communication, and also the opportunity to discuss specific clients with the employer (Roessler and Hiett, 1983). It is also a powerful method of job development since it is more difficult to say "no" to someone in person than to ignore a letter or end a telephone call.

In the author's opinion, unscheduled face-to-face contacts are best utilized when a client is limited geographically and must work within a certain area or not at all (e.g., lives in a small town, must use public transportation). The rehabilitationist identifies the target geographical area, and in one trip to the area contacts many employers. It is a good idea to have the client present during this canvassing if larger businesses or industries are to be contacted that likely take walk-in applications. If only smaller employers are being contacted, it is probably better to first find the job openings, and then bring the client in for job interviews.

Although unscheduled face-to-face contacts are powerful and effective, they are less efficient then the third direct method, telephone canvassing. For an equal investment of time, it is possible to contact far more employers by telephone than in person. Also, there is no expense incurred from a telephone call (unless it is long distance), whereas driving to an employer's place of business involves car expenses.

Telephone canvassing is a widely used method of job development in private sector rehabilitation. It is also widely used by private employment agencies. The presentation over the telephone should be non-aggressive and professional. The fact that the rehabilitationist can serve as a placement resource, now and in the future, should be emphasized. When job openings are found, face-to-face meetings or actual job interviews may be scheduled. In addition to initial contacts, the telephone is a convenient means of recontacting employers with whom a relationship was previously developed to see if any recent job openings have occurred.

Presenting the Client

Before contacting an employer, the rehabilitationist must thoroughly know the abilities and limitations of the client he or she is planning to present. This is critical, for without this knowledge the rehabilitationist cannot evaluate the suitability of identified openings, and will come across to the employer as poorly prepared or unprofessional. Although in job development efforts it is desirable to build relationships with persons as high in the company's hierarchy as possible (Hedley, Smart and Young, 1982), when presenting a specific client the rehabilitationist normally talks with the person responsible for hiring.

In order to present clients effectively, the rehabilitationist should be familiar with affirmative action and tax credits for employing handicapped individuals, and whether these would apply in the employer/client situation being considered. At the time of this writing, any employer doing business with the federal government under a contract of $2,500 or more must take affirmative action to hire handicapped persons, and any institution receiving federal financial assistance (e.g., schools, hospitals, human service agencies) must assure that handicapped individuals are not discriminated against (see Section 503 and 504 of the Rehabilitation Act of 1973). According to the President's Committee on Employment of the Handicapped (1979) some 3,000,000 businesses fall under affirmative action guidelines. For financial incentives to employ the handicapped, at the time of this writing, tax deductions of up to $25,000 per year were available for the removal of architectural barriers (see Tax Reform Act of 1976). Moreover, the Targeted Jobs Tax Credit (TJTC) replaced up to $3,000 of first year and $1,500 of second year salary payments to eligible handicapped workers.

In the author's experience, one issue that many rehabilitationists find difficult in presenting clients is that they are uncomfortable with what they perceive as a "selling" role. Shell (1976) correctly pointed out that selling means nothing more than to persuade and convince. Being able to present clients effectively is more a matter of interpersonal skills than anything else, and as with all skills, they are developed and refined by practice. In order to be comfortable talking to employers, the rehabilitationist must believe in the suitability of the client they are presenting, and should see their role with the employer as primarily that of a placement resource.

According to Minton (1977), the following are important points the rehabilitationist or counselor should address when presenting clients to employers:

1. Avoid the use of rehabilitation jargon. Be sure to talk with employers using terms they understand. Wherever possible, when discussing specific clients, try to describe the clients' abilities in behavioral terms. Remember that the primary focus with the employer should be upon the individual's ability to handle the job.
2. Under Affirmative Action legislation employers are required to seek out appropriate agencies in the community for information and for recruiting handicapped individuals. Thus, the counselor can be of assistance to the employer in meeting Affirmative Action regulations. But the counselor must have a thorough knowledge of the law and what the employer is required to do.
3. The counselor should explain what vocational rehabilitation is, what the vocational rehabilitation process involves, and how rehabilitation can be of assistance to the employer in the hiring and upgrading of handicapped individuals. The counselor must also explain to the employer what vocational rehabilitation cannot do.
4. The counselor should be prepared to deal with the employer's concerns regarding insurance, workmen's compensation, pensions, the union contract, and the Occupational Safety and Health Administration (OSHA). There is evidence that qualified handicapped individuals who are properly placed in employment have better safety and performance records than nonhandicapped individuals.
5. The counselor will have to allay any fears the employer may have regarding the dependency of handicapped individuals. Employers need to know that they are not any more responsible for the well being of handicapped individuals than they are for any other employee.
6. Employers have a tendency to focus on the disability of the individual, primarily because they have no clear understanding of what the disability involves. The counselor should try to steer the conversation away from the disability and focus on how the disability impacts upon the world of work. It is the individual's skills which should be considered, not the disability (pp. 145-146).

Dealing With Hiring Objections

As indicated by Minton (1977), the rehabilitationist must be prepared to allay common employer concerns or fears regarding hiring handicapped workers. These include incorrect beliefs that:

1. Workers' compensation costs will increase.
2. Insurance companies oppose the hiring of handicapped workers.
3. Handicapped workers create safety hazards and are more likely to be involved in accidents.
4. Handicapped workers require special work arrangements or troublesome privileges.
5. Job attendance and punctuality is less than average.
6. Overall job performance and productivity is less than average.
7. Other workers will not accept handicapped workers.

In relation to workers' compensation rates, it is well-established that hiring handicapped workers does not increase the employer's cost (American Mutual Insurance Alliance, undated; President's Committee, 1979). These rates, as indicated in Chapter III, are determined by the employer's business and the past safety record of the employer. It is also important to remember that second injury funds protect the employer from any interaction effect between earlier and subsequent injuries. The idea that insurers are not interested in the reemployment of handicapped individuals is a misnomer inconsistent with economic and statutory realities. The insurance industry is, in fact, the financial foundation of private sector rehabilitation.

In relation to the other objections, U.S. Department of Labor surveys have shown that handicapped workers have fewer serious and approximately the same number of minor injuries as other workers exposed to the same hazards (see American Mutual Insurance Alliance, undated). Moreover, the 1973 E.D. Du Pont de Nemours and Company studies of 1,452 handicapped employees (out of a total work force of 110,000) found:

1. No increase in workers' compensation costs or lost time for injuries.
2. Most handicapped employees required no special work accommodations.
3. In relation to safety, 96% of handicapped employees were rated average or better both on and off the job.
4. In relation to job performance, 91% rated average - or - better.
5. In relation to job attendance, 79% rated average - or - better.
6. No significant problems in other workers accepting handicapped employees (see American Mutual Insurance Alliance, undated; Geist and Calzaretta, 1982).

Although the evidence indicates that as a group, handicapped workers make good employees, employer attitudes toward hiring handicapped workers are not always positive (see Schroedel, 1978; Schroedel and Jacobsen, 1978). In dealing with objections, the rehabilitationist needs to know the capabilities and limitations of the client, the demands of the job(s) under consideration, and general facts about handicapped workers (as indicated above). There is also no substitute for good interpersonal or communicative skills.

In relation to interpersonal or communicative skills, a critical ability is to be able to moderate an employer's objections without becoming involved in an argument or confrontation. A very useful technique is to meet the objection with an "admit/deny" response. This is a response that normally begins with the word "While" or "Although," initially agrees with the employer's objection, and then in the same sentence denies the essential validity of the objection. Examples are:

Employer: "Handicapped workers don't mix well with other workers."
Rehabilitationist: "Although some workers may initially feel uncomfortable around a handicapped worker, this normally lasts for no more than a few weeks, and then the handicapped worker is usually accepted very well."

Employer: "On this job a worker sometimes needs to lift 20 lb. bags from the floor to the bench, and with that low back injury Mr. Harper won't be able to do that."
Rehabilitationist: "While it is true that many people with low back injuries have substantial lifting restrictions, Mr. Harper has been taught proper lifting mechanics, and has been released by Dr. Smith for occasional lifting of objects weighing up to 25 lbs."

Employer: "A handicapped worker could not perform this job at a fast enough pace."
Rehabilitationist: "Although this job is at a pace that would be too fast for many of my clients, Mr. Smith has done this type of work before, and his disability will not be a work limiting factor."

Scheduling Interviews and Follow-Up

When presenting a client (potential employee) to an employer, the rehabilitationist's goal should be to come away from the discussion with an interview time. As indicated earlier, interviews should be arranged at the employer's convenience. When contacting employers to place a job ready client, it is helpful to have earlier established weekly times (usually full or half days) which the client will keep free for possible interviews. This greatly simplifies the process of negotiating and confirming appointments.

In some cases, the rehabilitationist can simply advise the client of the position which is open, the associated job duties, the name and address of the employer, and time of the interview; knowing that the client will be able to follow through appropriately. It is more common, however, to discuss the job duties and upcoming interview in far more detail with the client (possibly even role play to rehearse for the interview), and to arrange to personally transport the client to and from the interview. Whether the rehabilitationist should attempt to be present in the actual employer/client interview is best determined in consideration of the employment motivation and interviewing skills of the client. When employment motivation or interviewing skills are poor, it may be advantageous to be present in the interview.

Interviews should be followed-up by first contacting the client, and then, when appropriate, the employer. In contacting the client, the rehabilitationist should learn how the interview went, whether the client was hired (and if so when employment starts), and when a decision on employment is expected. When a client is vague about an interview or cannot describe how it went, it is advisable to contact the employer. How and if an interview is followed-up with an employer should be determined by each individual situation. The rehabilitationist must balance the need to know and encourage a positive decision with relationship and independence issues.

When a client begins work, the rehabilitationist must notify the carrier of this fact. The rehabilitationist should follow-up with both the client and employer to make sure the placement is truly suitable, and that there are no work-related problems. One method for catching problems early is to call the client during the evening after his or her first day of work, and the employer the next day. The rehabilitationist should also plan to visit the client and employer sometime during the first two weeks of employment. Unlike the public sector where clients must be employed for 60 days before their case is closed, in the private sector there is no uniform standard. When the client is placed and the employer, client, and carrier are satisfied, the client may be considered successfully rehabilitated.

References

American Mutual Insurance Alliance. *Hiring the Handicapped: Myths and Facts,* Chicago, Illinois, undated.

Azrin, N., and Besalel, V.: *Job Club Counselor's Manual.* Baltimore: University Park Press, 1980.

Azrin, N., Besalel, V., Wisotzek, I., McMorrow, M. and Bechtel, R., Behavioral supervision versus informational counseling of job seeking in the Job Club. *Rehabilitation Counseling Bulletin,* 1982, *25*:212-218.

Azrin, N. and Philip, R.: The Job Club method for the job handicapped: A comparative outcome study. *Rehabilitation Counseling Bulletin,* 1979, *23*:144-155.

Bowman, J. and Graves, W.: *Placement Services and Techniques.* Champaign: Stipes Publishing Company, 1976.

Brolin, D. and Kokaska, C.: Critical issues in job placement of the educable mentally retarded. *Rehabilitation Literature,* 1974, *35*:174-177.

Cates, C.: A comparison of three matching approaches to solicit job opportunities for handicapped persons. *Rehabilitation Counseling Bulletin,* 1981, *24*:362-365.

Crimando, W.: The job development and placement specialist: An emerging role for rehabilitation practice. *Journal of Rehabilitation,* 1982, *48*:20-24.

Eaton, M.W.: Obstacles to the vocational rehabilitation of individuals receiving workers' compensation. *Journal of Rehabilitation,* 1979, *45*:59-63.

Enhancing Employer Receptivity to Hiring Disabled Workers. *Rehab Brief,* Rehabilitation Research Institute, University of Florida, Vol. 2, No. 8, September 24, 1979.

Geist, C.S. and Calzaretta, W.A.: *A Placement Handbook for Counseling Disabled Persons.* Springfield: Charles C Thomas, 1982.

Gregory, R.J., Whitlow, C.B., Levine, M. and Wasmuth, W.: The techniques of work adjustment. *Vocational Evaluation and Work Adjustment Bulletin,* 1982, *15*:5-10.

Grossman, H.I.: A new concept of disability. *Journal of Rehabilitation,* 1979, *45*:41-49, 71.

Hedley, E., Smart, L. and Young, J.: Employment research: Working with business and industry. *Rehabilitation Counseling Bulletin,* 1982, *26*:101-109.

Kauss, P. and Sota, M.: Job Club and transferable skills: Models for placement of severely handicapped. *American Rehabilitation,* 1981, *6*:7-11.

Lake, J.B.: Specific training for job placement. *Journal of Rehabilitation,* 1975, *44*:20-41.

Lamb, R. and Rogawski, A.: Supplemental security income and the sick role. *American Journal of Psychiatry,* 1978, *135*:1221-1224.

Mallik, K. and Moretti, V.: Unions as a resource in job placement. *Journal of Rehabilitation,* 1982, *48*:20-24.

Matkin, R.: Rehabilitation placement services: Unlicensed placement agencies or something else. *Journal of Applied Rehabilitation Counseling,* 1982, *13*:24-33.

Minton, E.B.: Job placement: strategies and techniques. *Rehabilitation Counseling Bulletin,* 1977, *21*:141-149.

Neff, W.S.: *Work and Human Behavior.* New York: Atherton Press, 1968.

Ninth Institute on Rehabilitation Issues. *Marketing: An Approach to Placement.* Research and Training Center, University of Wisconsin-Stout, Menomonic, Wisconsin, 1982.

President's Committee on Employment of the Handicapped, *Dear Employer.* Washington, D.C., U.S. Government Printing Office, 1979.

Roessler, R.T. and Hiett, A.: A comparison of job development strategies in rehabilitation. *Journal of Rehabilitation,* 1983, *49*:65-69.

Roessler, R.T. and Rubin, S.E.: *Case Management and Rehabilitation Counseling: Procedures and Techniques.* Baltimore: University Park Press, 1982.

Salomone, P.R. and Rubin, D.C.: Job placement: New tactics for securing job leads. *Rehabilitation Counseling Bulletin,* 1979, *22*:338-346.

Salomone, P.R. and Usdane, W.M.: Client-centered placement revisted: A dialogue on placement philosophy. *Rehabilitation Counseling Bulletin,* 1977, *21*:85-91, 176.

Schlenoff, D.: Obstacles to the rehabilitation of disability benefits recipients. *Journal of Rehabilitation,* 1975, *45*:56-58.

Schroedel, J.: *Attitudes Toward Persons with Disabilities: A Compendium of Related Literature.* Human Resources Center, Albertson, Long Island, New York, 1978.

Schroedel, J. and Jacobsen, R.: *Employer Attitudes Toward Hiring Persons with Disabilities.* Human Resources Center, Albertson, Long Island, New York, 1978.

Shell, C.I.: Selling: Another role for the placement counselor. In J.T. Bowman and W.H. Graves (Eds.), *Placement Services and Techniques.* Champaign: Stripes Publishing Company, 1976.

Tesolowski, D.G.: *Job Readiness Training Curriculum.* Stout: Materials Development Center, 1979.

Vandergout, D.A.: A comparison of two mailing approaches attempting to generate the participation of businessmen in rehabilitation. *Rehabilitation Counseling Bulletin,* 1976, *20*:73-75.

Vandergout, D.A. and Worrall, J.D.: *Placement in Rehabilitation: A Career Development Perspective.* Baltimore: University Park Press, 1979.

Walls, R.T.: Disincentives in vocational rehabilitation: Cash and in-kind benefits from other programs. *Rehabilitation Counseling Bulletin,* 1982, *26*:37-45.

Walls, R., Masson, C. and Werner, T.: Negative incentives to vocational rehabilitation. *Rehabilitation Literature,* 1977, *38*:143-150.

Welch, G.: Private and public rehabilitation. In J. Rubin (Ed.) *Alternatives in Rehabilitating the Handicapped.* New York: Human Sciences Press, 1982.

Wright, G.N.: *Total Rehabilitation.* Boston: Little, Brown and Company, 1980.

Zandy, J.J. and James, L.F.: A review of research in job placement. *Rehabilitation Counseling Bulletin,* 1977, *21*:150-158.

Zandy, J.J. and James, L.F.: A survey of job search patterns among state vocational rehabilitation clients. *Rehabilitation Counseling Bulletin,* 1978, *21*:60-65.

Zandy, J. and James L.: *Another View on Placement: State of the Art 1976.* Portland, Oregon: Regional Rehabilitation Research Institute, Portland State College, 1976.

Part III

SPECIAL PRIVATE SECTOR ISSUES

CHAPTER VII

CHRONIC PAIN AND LOW BACK INJURIES

THIS chapter overviews two problems frequently encountered in the caseloads of private sector rehabilitationists – chronic pain and low back injury. The problem of chronic or recurrent pain is common in many injuries, including low back injuries, where MMI is not always synonomous with a full or complete recovery. Tissues have been damaged, and there is residual pain that may vary in severity from a mild and occassional annoyance to intolerable agony. In low back injuries chronic pain is a major problem (Lynch, 1978), and these injuries are especially important to review in that they are the most frequently seen disability in private sector caseloads (Ross, 1976).

CHRONIC PAIN

Physiology of Pain

Before discussing the problem of chronic pain, it will be helpful to briefly overview some current ideas and lines of research which address the physiological basis of pain. Despite the importance of pain as a human problem, and considerable research on the topic, our understanding of the physiology of this phenomenon is still far from complete. This is likely to remain so for the foreseeable future, not simply because pain is a complex and multifaceted phenomenon, but also because pain is, in the final analysis, the subjective perception of each individual.

One of the oldest theories that attempts to explain the nature of pain is the *specificity theory.* This theory holds that the degree of experienced pain is directly proportional to the intensity and duration of the pain stimulus. Nociceptors (nerve endings in the upper layers of the skin) are receptive to different stimuli (e.g., warmth, cold, touch) which are projected through separate pathways in the spinal cord to different thalamic centers (Melzack, 1973). Large myelinated A fibers rapidly conduct impulses into the cord which are subsequently experienced in the thalamus as "sharp" pain, while small unmyelinated C fibers carry slower impulses which are interpreted as "dull" pain. Although the specificity theory offers a straightforward and reasonable physiological explanation for pain, it totally disregards perceptual factors which are known to play a major role in the actual experience of pain.

Probably the most widely accepted and studied pain theory is the *gate theory* postulated by Melzack and Wall (1965). This theory holds that a neural mechanism in the dorsal horns of the spinal cord acts like a gate, increasing or decreasing the flow of impulses from the peripheral to the central nervous system, and thereby influencing pain perceptions. The pain experience is modulated by inhibitory A fibers and facilitory C fibers, and by descending impulses from the brain (Beaudet, 1984). When the gate is open, peripheral nerve impulses are readily transmitted to the brain where they may be perceived as pain. Conversely, when the gate is fully or partially closed, pain perceptions are blocked or moderated. Unlike the specificity theory, the gate theory offers at least a partial explanation for the role of perceptual factors in the experience of pain.

In addition to the specificity and gate theories, there are biochemical explanations of pain. Luce, Thompson and Byyng (1979) postulated that substances released from injured tissues, such as histamine and prostaglandin, lower the excitation threshold of nociceptors, and consequently pain perceptions. One of the newest biochemical lines of research emphasizes the importance of brain opiate receptors and the peptides (such as the enkephalins) which act on them, moderating not only pain sensations, but also emotional responses to pain (Snyder, 1977).

While most pain has a physiological basis, it is important to remember that the actual experience of pain in moderated by perceptual and emotional factors. Pain may also be psychogenic, meaning that it originates in the mind rather than from the excitation of neurons in the peripheral nervous system. Psychogenic pain is usually viewed as serving underlying psychological needs (such as dependency needs) or as symptomatic of a psychiatric disorder (e.g., hypochondriasis, hysteria, depression). From a learning theory perspective, psychogenic pain results from reinforcement and conditioning.

Acute vs. Chronic Pain

When pain operates as nature intended it to, it serves as a signal to the organism that tissues are being damaged or destroyed. The focused or circumscribed quality of the stimulus allows the organism to identify the location of the damage, and the aversive nature of the stimulus encourages action to end it. Pain that protects the organism in this manner is usually called acute pain. It alerts the organism that is experiencing it to the fact that something is wrong (Maltbie, Cavenar, Hammett and Sullivan, 1978).

Although acute pain may be very intense, it is normally considered to end when tissues are no longer being damaged and have healed. The other type of pain, chronic pain, which is frequently a rehabilitation problem, may then set in. Individuals are often considered to be suffering from chronic rather than acute pain if their pain continues more than six months after the original injury (Deutsch and Raffa, 1982). While chronic pain may also signal that tissues are being further damaged by reinjury or long term illness, it is usually better to conceptualize chronic pain as a by-product of damage previously done.

Social and Personality Factors

Chronic pain is a major social problem. It has been estimated that about 75 million

Americans experience it to some degree (Report of the Panel on Pain, 1979), and that the total cost to society for hospitalization, medical treatment, lost income, disability payments, and litigation is between $40 and $50 billion annually (see "Chronic Pain," 1982). Beyond the social cost, it is a personal tragedy for the individuals and families that must endure it, all too often destroying their plans and hopes for the future.

Because chronic pain can almost always be traced to some identifiable injury or illness, it is considered a symptom rather than a diagnosis (Maltbie et al., 1978). Pain is a symptom, however, that no one can directly see or measure, and its severity can only be inferred from the subjective report of the individual and from observed pain behaviors. More importantly, over time this symptom can take on an existance that is partially or even fully disassociated from any underlying pathology. This is possible because the symptom is manifested only in the verbalizations and behaviors of the individual, and these may be reinforced by others. When this occurs, the pain symptomatic verbalizations and behaviors may obtain an independent social basis for continuance.

A great deal has been written on the personality characteristics of chronic pain sufferers. It has been suggested that pain symptomatology may be more readily magnified and maintained by individuals who are angry and hostile (overtly or covertly), anxious, dependent, guilt ridden, depressed, sexually inhibited, or in some other way emotionally disturbed (see Merskey, 1978; Pilowsky, 1978; Sparks and Clark, 1981). Merskey and Boyd (1978) pointed out that in addition to this psychosomatic relationship, there is a strong somatopsychological relationship as well. Although certain personalities may be more at risk to develop chronic pain problems (i.e., the psychosomatic relationship), the experience of chronic pain can also result in personality changes (i.e., the somatopsychological relationship).

Because of the ever present potential for an interaction between personality factors and chronic pain, it is important to overview variables that may increase or serve to maintain a chronic pain problem. Using the terminology of learning theory, these may be conceptualized as reinforcers of pain behavior.

Reinforcers of Chronic Pain

Attention can be a major positive reinforcer of chronic pain (Cairns, Thomas, Mooney and Pace, 1976). When someone is hurting the natural human response is to go to them offering comfort and assistance. Attention to their needs is intended to reduce their pain and suffering, and to make life more bearable for them. However, in the case of chronic pain, some of which a person must usually learn to live with, attention can occasionally make the pain worse. This is because the attention, which is valued in itself, is linked to the reoccurance of the pain. The person must literally "hurt more" to continue to receive the valued attention (Huneke, 1982).

It is very easy for a spouse and other family members to make the mistake of over attending to the hurting member's needs and complaints. When attention, sympathy, concern, and the like are obtained after pain behaviors, the probability of further pain behaviors increases. Physicians and clinic or hospital staff may also reinforce pain symptomatology by paying little attention to the patient when not hurting, and providing great amounts of attention when the patient is in pain. When the pain problem is chronic, essentially benign, and not fully resolvable through medical interventions; over attending to it is inappropriate, and can lead to greater disability and dependency. What is often necessary is to extinguish or ignore pain behaviors, and concurrently reinforce "well" behaviors which are incompatible with pain, disability, and helpless dependency (Cairns and Pasino, 1977).

Drugs can also be a major reinforcer of chronic pain complaints, especially when they are prescribed on an as-needed basis (Fordyce, 1976). This is because the more the person hurts, the more drugs he or she receives. Drugs can be especially powerful reinforcers because they are primary (physiological) rather than secondary (social) in nature, and because they may have both positive and negative reinforcing elements. The negative reinforcer is that the aversive stimulus of pain is removed or reduced, and the positive reinforcer is that a pleasant feeling or state of mind is introduced (especially when the drug is a narcotic). The person must continue to keep the pain in order to receive the drugs that bring good feelings.

Another potential reinforcer of chronic pain is the release from responsibilities associated with the assumption of the "sick role." When someone is sick or hurting they are normally not expected to work, help care for children, clean house, take care of the yard, shop for groceries, and the like. This release from responsibilities or unpleasant activities is negative reinforcement for pain behavior, and as with the positive reinforcement of attention, it increases the probability that pain behaviors will continue.

In discussing release from responsibilities, Aronoff and Wilson (1979) noted that for some people, chronic pain can actually be used as a substitute for social skills, removing the burden of all or most social responsibilities. The person essentially assumes the role of a suffering victim, and is from then on taken care of by others. Although this role may at first seem highly undesirable, it does provide a lasting identity and an excuse for avoiding any unpleasant activity or responsibility. In effect, passive dependency is embraced as a simple solution to life's complex problems.

One of the most widely discussed reinforcers of chronic pain is the disability payment system (see Block, Kremer and Gaylor, 1980; Hammonds, Brena and Unikel, 1978; Huneke, 1982; Singer, 1961). It is not uncommon to find individuals suffering from chronic pain who receive disability payments of one type or another that are roughly equal to or even higher than their preinjury wage or salary. When a client perceives monetary compensation as the only substantial reinforcement for work activity, and perceives work as essentially a punishing activity, being able to obtain roughly equivalent compensation through the "sick role" can be a powerful reinforcer for remaining disabled.

In research on the relationship of compensation factors to medical improvement, Krusen and Ford (1958) reported that of 509 patients treated for low back injuries at Boston University Hospital, only 55.8% of the 272 patients receiving compensation were rated as "improved" when discharged, compared with 88.5% of the 237 patients not receiving compensation. More recently, Hammonds, Brena and Unikel (1978) reported that for 61 persons treated at the Emory University Pain Control Center, significant increases in functional performance were obtained by 43% of the 35 patients receiving compensation, and by 69% of the 26 patients receiving no compensation. Although much has been written about how compensation factors sometimes contribute to the maintenance of disability, this is an area that needs more carefully controlled research (Sparks and Clark, 1981).

Methods of Alleviating Pain

Whenever a patient is in pain, acute or chronic, part of the medical intervention process must be directed toward the elimination or reduction of this symptom. There are essentially two ways to go about this. One is to cure or improve the underlying pathology, thereby eliminating or reducing pain, and the other is to address the symptom directly. When pain is of an acute nature, the thrust of medical intervention will be toward improving the pathological situation that creates pain. When pain is chronic and the underlying pathology cannot be substantially improved, then the thrust of medical inervention must address the symptom itself.

There are a number of ways physicians can correct or improve pathological conditions, thereby eliminating or reducing the pain associated with them. The two most common ways involve prescribing medications that address the underlying disease process and performing surgical procedures. Other methods include radiation therapy; dietary control; realignment, immobilization, and support of the body parts (e.g., traction, casts, braces and corsets, etc.); bed rest and exercise. When the experience of pain declines through these methods it is essentially because there has been some improvement in the pathological condition that created it.

Although it is certainly best to cure or improve the underlying pathology, this is of course not always possible. Even with acute pain, some immediate relief from the symptom is often necessary. Medicine has historically sought to control patient pain through the prescription of analgesics. Today there are a host of analgesics and other drugs on the market that may be prescribed for patients needing relief from acute or chronic pain. As the chronicity of pain increases, so does the probabilty of complications, abuse, or addiction to one or more of these substances (see Illustration 7-1).

In addition to medications, other procedures sometimes employed to directly reduce pain symptomotology include: (a) acupuncture — which creates a competing nerve signal to block the pain signal, (b) biofeedback — which can be used to induce mental and local muscle relaxation, and in some cases vasodilation, (c) hypnosis and self-hypnosis — which can be used for relaxation and to distract or alter the person's perception of the pain stimulus, (d) relaxation training — which reduces anxiety through mental and muscle relaxation, and (e) transcutaneous nerve stimutators — which like acupuncture set-up a competing neurological signal. Psychotherapy and behavior modification programs may also be helpful in reducing pain symptomotology.

Illustration 7-1

OVERVIEW OF MEDICATIONS COMMONLY USED IN PAIN TREATMENT

Definitions

Analgesics Medications which release pain by acting on centers in the nervous system to affect one's response to painful stimuli. Analgesics don't take pain away, they reduce the response produced ("felt") by the pain. These drugs are classified by the severity of pain for which they are effective:

- *Mild Analgesics* - relieve mild to moderate pain
- *Strong Analgesics* - relieve severe pain

Controlled Analgesics Strong analgesics which can be secured only through prescription from licensed physicians. Regulation of their procurement is required due to their potency and the potential for addiction. This group includes all narcotic and some non-narcotic pain relief medications.

Barbiturates A group of organic compounds which act as Central Nervous System depressants. They are used as sedatives, hypnotics and antispasmodics. Due to their potency and potential for addiction, they can only be secured through prescription from licensed physicians.

Anti-Anxiety Drugs Minor tranquilizers which relieve or prevent feelings and manifestations of anxiety by acting on the centers of the brain which are involved with emotion.

Anti-depressants Medications which relieve or prevent the symptoms of depression. These drugs do not cure depression, but do allow one to deal more effectively with one's problems.

Anti-flammatory Medications which relieve pain and/or increase mobility by counteracting or diminishing inflammation or its effects.

Anti-arthritic Medications which relieve the pain and mobility limitations resultant from arthritic conditions. This relief is achieved through the anti-inflammatory and/or analgesic actions of the medications.

	Indication/Uses	Contraindications	Precautions
Analgesics			
Mild Analgesics			
Aspirin	Short and/or long term therapy for relief of mild-moderate pain from such things as headaches, muscle aches, arthritis, sprains, strains, etc.	Allergy/Hypersensitivity History of peptic ulcer, some bleeding disorders	*Concurrent administration of Anti-coagulants, some Antidiabetics, Benemid, some Diuretics, Alcohol
Tylenol (acetaminophen)	As above, when administration of aspirin is contraindicated or not desired by physician	Allergy/Hypersensitivity	
Darvon	Short term therapy for relief of pain as detailed above	Allergy/Hypersensitivity Head injury History of addiction or suicide attempts	Long Term Therapy *Concurrent administration of Tranquilizers, Sedatives, Hypnotics, Narcotics, Alcohol

	Indication/Uses	Contraindications	Precautions
Strong Analgesics			
Tylenol #3 Demerol Percodan Talwin Codeine Fiorinal Morphine	Short term therapy for relief of moderate-severe pain	Allergy/Hypersensitivity Head Injury History of addiction or suicide attempts	Long Term Therapy History of asthma or other respiratory problems *Concurrent administration of Tranquilizers, Barbiturates, Hypnotics, Alcohol
Anti-Depressants			
Elavil Tofranil Ascendin	Relief or prevention of the symptoms of depression, when same are manifested as physical symptoms (i.e., pain)	Allergy/Hypersensitivity History of heart disease, convulsive disorders, glaucoma, thyroid disease	*Concurrent administration of MAO Inhibitors, Barbiturates, Tranquilizers, CNS Depressants, some Anti-hypertensives, Thyroid Medication, Alcohol
Anti-Anxiety/Muscle Relaxants			
Valium	Relief of symptoms of anxiety, tension, fatigue, or agitation	Severe depression or psychotic syndromes History of narrow angle glaucoma	Long Term Therapy *Concurrent administration of MAO Inhibitors, Tranquilizers, Narcotics, Sleeping pills
Barbiturates			
Phenobarbital Nembutal Seconal	To achieve daytime sedation or as a sleeping medication	History of addiction or suicide attempts	Long Term Therapy *Concurrent administration of Tranquilizers, Other Sedatives, Alcohol, Muscle Relaxants, Strong Analgesics, Anticoagulants
Anti-Arthritic, Anti-Inflammatory			
Butazolidan Indocin Motrin Naprosyn Tolectin Feldane	Relief of pain and inflammation of joints and muscles; such conditions as arthritis, gout, rheumatoid arthritis, osteoarthritis, bursitis	History of ulcers, bleeding disorders, hypersensitivity to aspirin	Long Term Therapy *Concurrent administration of Sulfa Drugs, Blood thinners, some Anti-diabetics

* Concurrent administration of certain medications is an area to question or explore, particularly if progress towards recovery is not being attained and/or "new" symptoms and problems are developing. Concurrent administration can be therapeutic if same is under the direction of a qualified physician who is aware of *all types and dosages* of drugs being taken.

Chart prepared by Carol Eshelman, R.N., Associate Director of Service, IRA. Reprinted with permission of IRA.

To effectively treat a chronic pain problem it is often necessary to place the sufferer in a multi-disciplinary and comprehensive intervention program. Toward this end, pain clinics have developed throughout the country where professionals from different disciplines evaluate medical, psychological, vocational, and social aspects of the pain problem for each referred client; and subsequently develop a comprehensive treatment program. Such clinics essentially attempt to improve the pain problem through improved medical management, and by teaching the client to tolerate and live with the chronic pain problem, minimizing its adverse consequences on life functioning.

Learning to Live With Pain

Many private sector rehabilitation clients must learn to live with some chronic or recurrent pain. It is important to carry on as full and normal a life as possible despite the presence of pain. There are a number of services that can help a patient learn to live with pain, and these services will be discussed as they might be provided through a multidisciplinary pain clinic or pain management program. This is not to say that some of these services cannot be provided outside of such a center, but when the pain problem is severe and long term, the comprehensive program of a reputable pain clinic is usually indicated.

Although pain clinics vary somewhat in their treatment methods, their goal is to help clients again take responsibility for their own lives and health care, and to become productive and functional members of our society (Aronoff and Wilson, 1978). Pain clinics may be run on an in-patient or out-patient basis, and although the latter are less expensive, in-patient programs are generally more effective (Deutsch and Raffa, 1982). Regardless of whether they are run on an in-patient or out-patient basis, pain clinics are multidisciplinary treatment efforts that create a therapeutic milieu in which attitudinal and behavioral changes may occur (Newman, Painter and Seres, 1978).

One of the major focuses of pain centers is to reduce client dependence on prescription medications as a means of controlling pain. Most patients entering pain clinics are overly dependent upon analgesics, and may be taking large doses of prescription medications on an "as-needed" basis. An early goal is to shift medication usage from an as-needed basis to a fixed schedule of usage, and then to subsequently reduce the dosages of prescribed analgesics (Block, 1982). This is important because when analgesics are taken as needed (i.e., when pain is severe) patients readily learn to rely on their medications as their principal method for controlling pain, and as tolerance increases, more medications are needed, resulting in abuse and possibly addiction. When medications are taken on a schedule whether pain is being experienced or not, better symptom reduction is usually obtained, the reinforcing properties of the drug are undercut, patients are less manipulative, and there is less potential for abuse or addiction. One widely used method to reduce narcotic dependence is to place the patient's initial narcotic dose in an inactive solution (so that the patient does not know how much medication he or she is receiving) and gradually over time reduce the amount of medication in this "pain cocktail" until a moderate or reasonable level is achieved (Fordyce, 1976).

In addition to reducing dependence on prescription medications, pain clinics teach patients to take an active role in the maintenance and improvement of their own health. Toward this end proper body mechanics, diet, and exercises are taught. Patients are often involved in physical and occupational therapy programs. Biofeedback, self-hypnosis, relaxation training, and instruction in the use of transcutaneous nerve stimulators may also be part of the treatment program. Activity is stressed and being inactive because of pain symptomatology is discouraged. Patients also learn their own capabilities and limitations, learning not to overdo activities on "good days" or overly restrict activities on "bad days." Expectations for improvement are also addressed, and patients learn that they can have full and normal lives, and take pride in the fact that they successfully cope with a chronic pain problem.

Because pain symptomatology is manifested in the behavioral sphere, pain clinics give operant or reinforcing factors careful attention. Behavioral management principles followed in pain clinics may include all or some of the following:

1. Pain talk and pain behavior may be ignored by the staff, and it is explained to patients that talking about pain seldom does much to improve it.
2. When patients insist on reporting their complaints they may be instructed to write them down or tape record them for the physician, thereby eliminating or reducing reinforcement from staff.
3. Consistent reinforcement for well behaviors (i.e., active behaviors incompatible with pain debilitation) and the shaping of these behaviors.
4. Pain complaints or behaviors are not accepted as excuses for nonattendance or nonparticipation in clinic activities.
5. Skill building in areas such as relaxation, self-hypnosis, assertiveness, etc.
6. Extinction of verbalizations suggesting, "I am a helpless victim," and reinforcement for verbalizations suggesting, "I am responsible for my condition and competent to deal with my pain."

Aftercare is also important in successful pain management. It is not enough to shape effective pain management behaviors in the clinic, for success requires that these behaviors generalize to the patient's discharge environment. Pain clinics will often run groups for spouses and family members to facilitate this process. While these meetings will vary in their structure and process, a major goal is to teach family members how to reinforce well behaviors and extinguish pain behaviors (Block, 1982).

Although pain clinics are not a perfect solution to the problem of chronic pain, for many they have been effective in reducing dependency, and in facilitating more active and rewarding lives. At the time of this writing there is no operative accreditation mechanism for pain clinics (although CARF and other organizations are exploring them), and the rehabilitationist should therefore carefully investigate a clinic before recommending that a client be referred to it.

LOW BACK INJURIES

After headaches, back pain (especially pain in the lower back) is probably mankind's most frequent and troublesome physical complaint. It has been estimated that 75 million Americans have some sort of back problem, and that there are seven million new back sufferers each year (Tonfexis, 1980). Of these new suffers, five million are partially disabled by their back pain, and two million become unemployed. Moreover, 93 million work days are lost each year because of back problems, and five billion dollars are spent on treatment. Billions more are spent on law suits, out-of-court settlements, and disability claims (Tonfexis, 1980).

In private sector rehabilitation, low back injuries are the most frequently seen disability. Sanchez, Workman, Morris, Miller and Edelstein (1981) reported that for 1979, percentages of workers' compensation injuries served in California were: (a) 46% back injuries; (b) 23% upper extremity injuries, (c) 19% lower extremity injuries, and (d) 12% head and neck injuries. It is not at all uncommon for private sector rehabilitationists to have caseloads where low back injuries represent 75-80% of their clientele.

Structure of the Back

The human spine is a double "S" shaped structure consisting of 33 vertebrae (bones), most of which are separated from each other by discs, which are soft gelatinous areas that give the spine its flexibility and shock absorbing potential. The spine is supported by an array of muscles, tendons, and ligaments; which collectively keep it from collapsing on itself, and provide the structure with its strength for lifting, bending, and related activities. Numerous nerve bundles run up and down the spinal column and nerves exit between facet joints behind the vertebrae to innervate different muscle groups and to relay nerve impulses from different areas of the body to the brain.

Low back pain usually originates from injuries in and around the lower lumbar area of the spine. This area consists of five vertebrae and their adjoining structures. Immediately above the lumbar vertebrae are 12 thoratic vertebrae, and above these seven cervical vertebrae. Below the lumbar spine are five sacral vertebrae within the pelvis and four coccygeal vertebrae. In adults the sacral vertebrae are fused in a bone called the sacrum and the coccygeal vertebrae form a bone called the coccyx which is the vestige of a tail (Myers, 1965).

Types of Injuries

Low back pain can result from a wide variety of medical conditions including visceral, degenerative, and destructive diseases; congenital abnormalities; and traumatic afflictions (Beaudet, 1983). Any reasonably complete discussion of such varied causes is well beyond the scope of this book. Most cases referred to private sector rehabilitationists, however, result from trauma (even though there may be an underlying disease process such as degenerative disc disease). This section therefore briefly overviews back strains and sprains, disorders of the discs, and fractures and dislocations; all of which are often traced by the patient to some specific traumatic experience, and which collectively represent the vast majority of cases referred because of low back pain.

The most common cause of low back pain is simply overexertion of muscles (muscle strain). This can occur for any number of reasons ranging from standing too long in one place to seriously overdoing athletic activities. When muscles are strained beyond their limits they characteristically enter into a sustained contraction, or even go into spasm. The contraction cuts off or reduces the blood supply to the muscle by closing off tiny capillaries, and the result is further tissue damage (even cell death) and sharp excruciating pain. When back pain results from strained muscles, bed rest, which facilitates muscle relaxation, is often sufficient in itself to effect a cure. The patient may also find relief by wearing a corset for back support, by heat and massage therapy for the involved muscles, through more extensive physical therapy, and through prescribed muscle relaxants and analgesics.

A somewhat more serious injury than muscle strain is a sprain, which involves damage to a joint, and possibly also to ligaments surrounding it (Deutsch and Raffa, 1982). Sprains are often seen in injuries that involve sudden acceleration or deceleration, and twisting or pulling. As with muscle strain, the major treatment modalities include bed rest, back support, physical therapy, and mild analgesics. Traction may also be helpful, and in the most severe cases surgical intervention may be needed. Although strains and sprains are similar soft-tissue injuries and it is often impossible to determine which has in fact occured, on average, a patient with back strain can resume work in two to four weeks, and a patient with back sprain in six to twelve weeks (Novak, 1980).

Certainly one of the most frequently discussed disorders of the lower back is what is commonly (but incorrectly) called a "slipped disc." Many back sufferers incorrectly believe they have a disc problem, when in reality their pain results from a strain or sprain. Discs do not "slip," but rather herniate or rupture. In the herniated situation the gelatinous material of the disc starts to bulge out of its normal position between the vertebrae, and presses on surrounding nerve tissue causing pain. The disc may also rupture, forcing expelled materials against the spinal nerves, which can result in very severe pain (Toufexis, 1980).

Some eventual degeneration of discs in the lumbar spine is virtually inevitable because of the excessive weight bearing which this area must endure and the aging process. The herniated situation may develop somewhat insidiously over time, being facilitated by improper or excessive lifting, and first manifest itself through severe pain after one particular incident. While a disc may herniate or rupture at any level, over 90% are localized to the L4 - L5 or L5 - S1 vertebrae spaces (Deutch and Raffa, 1982).

There are a variety of ways physicians treat herniated and ruptured discs, but the most conservative treatment emphasizes bed rest and immobilization; back support; mild anti-inflammatory drugs and analgesics; and instruction in proper exercise, lifting, and sleeping positions. If this does not improve the patient's situation, a laminectomy may be performed where the herniated or ruptured disc is surgically removed. This procedure was first introduced in 1934 (Novak, 1980), and it is estimated that 200,000 are now performed each year (Tonfexis, 1980). This procedure is sometimes followed by another surgical procedure called fusion, where bone chips, usually from the pelvis, are placed as splints across adjoining vertebrae to make that section of the spine rigid and stable (Tonfexis, 1980). Although laminectomies and fusions bring relief to many patients, they result in increased pressure on adjacent discs, which can subsequently facilitate their herniation or rupture. These procedures are therefore most appropriate after more conservative treatment has failed to bring any relief, or when there is clear evidence of a neurological deficit.

Another common cause of low back pain is fracture and/or dislocation of portions of the lumbar spine or pelvis. Such injuries may be relatively trivial or extremely serious, depending on the portion of bone affected, and whether there is evidence of a resulting neurological deficit. Stable fractures are usually treated conservatively with bed rest and bracing, but unstable fractures and dislocations may require surgical interventions. After unstable or displaced fractures are reduced surgically, conservative treatment of residual pain normally follows.

Limitations

Limitations associated with low back injuries center around the problem of chronic or recurrent pain. The pain is debilitating and may affect the client in any (but not necessarily all) of the following ways:

1. By reducing range of motion – making reaching, bending, turning, and related motions extremely painful or impossible.
2. By restricting activities – where the client takes longer or requires assistance to complete basic activities of daily living, and may be forced to terminate certain social, recreational, and vocational pursuits.
3. By introducing a somatic preoccupation – where because of pain, the client becomes overly focused on his or her body, possibly to the extent of developing hypochondriacal personality features.
4. By creating depression – which occurs because of the loss of reinforcing activities, anger over the absence of a medical solution, and because of a decreased sense of self-worth.
5. By creating sleep problems – where because of pain and inactivity, normal sleep patterns are disrupted.
6. By reducing endurance – which occurs in part from pain and in part from the deconditioning effects of inactivity.
7. By creating resentment and hostility – which may be directed toward the employer, insurance company, physicians, and/or family members; all of whom are potential scapegoats for the client's problems.

From a vocational perspective, low back injuries frequently result in work restrictions in the areas of (see Illustration 4-1):

1. Strength – which refers to the lifting, carrying, pushing, and/or pulling requirements of a job.
2. Climbing and/or balancing requirements.
3. Stooping, kneeling, crouching, and/or crawling requirements.

4. Reaching, handling, fingering, and/or feeling requirements.
5. Daily standing tolerance.
6. Daily sitting tolerance.
7. Daily walking tolerance.

There may also be limitations on the work environments clients can safely function in (see Illustration 4-1). For example, the client's pain may be exacerbated by exposure to excessive cold and/or heat, wet and/or humid conditions, or noise and/or vibration. Certain hazards, such as moving machinery, are also potentially dangerous to clients with mobility restrictions.

Medical Management

The basic goal of medical management is to bring the client to MMI at the earliest possible date. Medical management was discussed earlier in Chapter IV, and the process described there applies to low back injuries as well as other disabilities. The discussion here overviews special issues and concerns in the medical management of low back injury referrals.

First, although early referral for medical management is important in all disabilities, it is especially important in those, such as low back injuries, where the development of learned pain behavior is a distinct possibility. All too often the treating physician places the back injured patient on bed rest, and when the back problem has not improved after two or three months, the claims representative authorizes medical management services. Unfortunately, the patient's situation may have actually deteriorated during this "waiting period" because of muscle weakness and atrophy, ligament laxity, joint stiffness, and the like. The patient may also find reinforcers for pain or sick role behavior, become angry (due to neglect), or depressed. For best results, any back injured client who misses a month of work should immediately be referred for medical management services, and earlier referral is probably preferable (Hadwin, 1983; Huneke, 1982).

With low back injuries, there are a number of medical management issues rehabilitationists should be sensitive to. First and foremost is that the client is not neglected or forgotten during the convalescence period. The rehabilitationist should also make sure the client understands and is following instructions from the treating physician, and that there are not long delays in the scheduling of needed diagnostic tests or additional medical evaluations. The rehabilitationist must also be sensitive to the possibility of abuse of analgesics, over and unnecessary restriction of physical activities, and depression or other psychological complications. The rehabilitationist should, with the physician's permission, teach the patient appropriate exercises, body mechanics, relaxation procedures, and sleeping positions. Instructions in proper lifting procedures as the patient approaches MMI should also be given.

Because the low back injured client will often have residual pain even after reaching MMI, in most cases a return to work should not wait for the total elimination of all pain symptomatology. Hadwin (1983) emphasized that physicians should not demand a complete and full elimination of the pain syndrome before allowing their patient to return to work, for to do so can jeopardize the rehabilitation process and the patient's ultimate recovery. Patients should return to work at the earliest possible date, and many can have an early return if needed modifications are identified and subsequently made in their work schedule (Hadwin, 1983).

Vocational Rehabilitation

When a back injured client works at a sedentary or light job, it is usually possible for the client to return to the preinjury position after reaching MMI. However, when the preinjury position requires medium, and especially heavy and very heavy lifting, this is often not the case. Once the back is injured, there is almost always a greater probability of reinjury. This becomes increasingly true as the worker ages. If the injury is relatively minor, the worker has a good recovery, exercises properly, and practices proper lifting procedures; reemployment at medium and even heavy work may be feasible. If the injury was not so minor and pain is at least a periodic problem, reemployment in a sedentary or light position is usually preferable.

Unfortunately, the worker most likely to injure his or her lower back is one who works at a job requiring heavy or very heavy lifting. Such occupations often involve manual labor and minimal skills, and are performed by workers with limited education. Unskilled heavy and very heavy work characteristically pays far more than unskilled sedentary or light work, and herein lies the principal reemployment dilemma. The injured worker needs to return to heavy or very heavy work for financial reasons (and also often for social, life style, and self-concept reasons), but to sedentary or light work for medical reasons. If injured workers could characteristically make this reemployment transition without special assistance, there would be little need for rehabilitationists.

A major part of the solution to this reemployment dilema is a workers' compensation law that reasonably compensates the injured worker for lost wages forced by this transition. A model wage loss law is the one existing at this writing in Florida, which replaces up to 80% of lost wages for a period of up to 10 years. Such laws encourage reemployment in more readily available lower earning positions, and protect income during the early years of the transition when earnings are likely to be at their lowest. The ten year wage loss payments allow older workers time to reach or nearly reach retirement age. Younger workers have ten years to pay off current debts, and time to retrain on their own for better paying employment, or to adjust their financial expectations for the future.

An adequate retraining provision is another component needed to help injured workers make the transition to less strenuous employment. While it is economically unfeasible to write extensive retraining provisions into workers' compensation laws (because such provisions discourage suitable placements on the basis of transferable skills and prolong disability benefits), two years of retraining is not unreasonable when a rehabilitationist certifies that a suitable placement cannot be arranged on the basis of transferable skills alone. For many injured workers, the opportunity for retraining can make the difference between marginal and periodic employment, or a suitable vocational recovery from the injury.

References

Aronoff, G.M. and Wilson, R.R.: How to teach your patients to control chronic pain. *Behavioral Medicine*, 1978, July, 29-35.

Beaudet, J.: A correlational study: The incidence of depression in patients with organic or nonorganic acute low back pain. Unpublished masters thesis. University of South Florida, 1984.

Block, A.R.: Multidisciplinary treatment of chronic low back pain: A review. *Rehabilitation Psychology*, 1982, *27*:51-63.

Block, A.R., Kremer, E.F. and Gaylor, M.: Behavioral treatment of chronic pain: Variables affecting treatment efficacy. *Pain*, 1980, *8*:367-375.

Cairns, D. and Pasino, J.A.: Comparison of verbal reinforcement and feedback in the operant treatment of disability due to chronic low back pain. *Behavior Therapy*, 1977, *8*:621-630.

Cairns, D., Thomas, L., Mooney, V. and Pace, J.: A comprehensive treatment approach to chronic low back pain. *Pain*, 1976, *2*:301-308.

Chronic Pain. *Rehab Brief* (Vol. 5, No. 7). National Institute of Handicapped Research, Washington, D.C., 1982.

Deutch, P.M. and Raffa, F.A.: Damages in tort actions (Volume 9). New York: Matthew Bender, 1982.

Fordyce, W.E.: *Behavioral Methods for Chronic Pain and Illness*. St. Louis: C.V. Mosby, 1976.

Hadwin, K.: Returning the low back injured client to work. *Rehabilitation Forum*, 1983, *10*:21-22.

Hammonds, W., Brena, S.F. and Unikel, I.P.: Compensation for work related injuries and rehabilitation of patients with chronic pain. *Southern Medical Journal*, 1978, *71*, 664-666.

Huneke, B.: Working with chronic low back clients in rehabilitation: The need for early intervention. *Journal of Applied Rehabilitation Counseling,* 1982, *13*, 1517.

Krusen, E.M. and Ford, D.E.: Compensation factors in low back injuries. *Journal of the American Medical Association,* 1958,*166*:1126-1133.

Luce, J.M., Thompson, T.L. and Byyng, R.L.: New concepts of chronic pain and their implications. *Hospital Practice,* 1979, April, 113-123.

Lynch, R.K.: Vocational rehabilitation of worker's compensation clients. *Journal of Applied Rehabilitation Counseling,* 1978, *9*:164-167.

Maltbie, A.A., Cavenar, J.O., Hammett, E.B. and Sullivan, J.L.: A diagnostic approach to pain. *Psychosomatics*, 1978, *19*:359-366.

Melzach, R.: *The Puzzle of Pain.* New York: Basic Books, 1973.

Melzach, R. and Wall, P.D.: Pain mechanisms: A new theory. *Science,* 1965, *150*:971-982.

Merskey, H.: Diagnosis of the patient with chronic pain. *Journal of Human Stress*, 1978, June, 3-7.

Merskey, H. and Boyd, D.: Emotional adjustment and chronic pain. *Pain*, 1978, *5*:173-178.

Myers, J.S.: *An Orientation to Chronic Disease and Disability.* New York: Macmillan, 1965.

Newman, R.I., Painter, J.R. and Seres, J.L.: A therapeutic milieu for chronic pain patients. *Journal of Human Stress,* 1978, June, 8-12.

Novak, J.: The low back loser. *Rehabilitation Forum*, 1980, *7*:3-4.

Pilowsky, I.: Pain as abnormal illness behavior. *Journal of Human Stress*, 1978, June, 22-27.

Report of the Panel on Pain to the National Advisory Neurological and Communicative Disorders and Stroke Counsil (NIA Publication . 79-1912), June, 1979.

Ross, E.: Workmen's compensation rehabilitation: A study of the rehabilitation of injured workers in the United States and member jurisdictions of the International Association of Industrial Accident Boards and Commissions, September, 1976.

Sanchez, I., Workman, E., Morris, G., Miller, J. and Edelstein, M.: *The California Workers' Compensation Rehabilitation System.* New York: Macmillan, 1981.

Singer, D.M.: A study of lump sum settlements and rehabilitation under the Massachusetts workmen's compensation act. Doctoral dissertation (Univ. Micro No. 61-3836) Boston University, 1961.
Sparks, J.A. and Clark, D.W.: Social, psychological, and medical aspects of chronic pain. *Rehabilitation Counseling Bulletin,* 1981, *24*:292-298.

Snyder, S.H.: Opiate receptors and internal opiates. *Science American,* 1977, *236*:44.

Toufexis, A.: The aching back. *Time*, July 4, 1980, 30-38.

CHAPTER VIII

VOCATIONAL EXPERT TESTIMONY

THIS chapter discusses the role of the rehabilitationist as an expert witness on the vocational impact of disability. The chapter is written primarily for rehabilitationists who are involved in the delivery of vocational rehabilitation case management services, and not for consultants who make employability and placeability evaluations, and subsequent testimony, a principal professional activity. Although the methods for developing employability and placeability opinions are the same for the two groups, the rehabilitation case manager is in a somewhat different situation in that he or she will usually have been working with the client toward the development and implementation of a rehabilitation plan, and must therefore testify about the specific plan (or why a plan could not be developed), what services were provided for the client, and the result of services. The professional consultant, on the other hand, is much more likely to be involved only in testimony as to what is vocationally feasible and infeasible, and will have evaluated the client, but usually not delivered services. In other words, the rehabilitation case manager or practitioner testifies not only to what is vocationally feasible and infeasible, but also to what has actually happened.

Another difference between the vocational expert roles of practitioners and consultants is that practitioners will usually be called to testify only on workers' compensation cases where they have worked as limited agents of a carrier. In general, such cases will not be going well from a rehabilitation perspective because the degree of disability and needed benefits are in dispute. While professional consultants may be involved in workers' compensation cases, vocational consultants are also hired for employability and placeability assessments in nonindustrial personal injury cases involving catastrophic and noncatastrophic disability (e.g., medical malpractice, product liability). In such cases, one party is suing another for wrongful injury, and is seeking an out-of-court settlement or court award for damages.

In most states, the legal proceedings in workers' compensation and tort or civil law cases are different. In workers' compensation there will usually be a workers' compensation judge or commissioner who will make a ruling based on evidence presented and statutory provisions of the workers' compensation law. Appeals to civil courts are normally allowed for procedural issues only, and not for disputed facts. In wrongful injury cases a judge will preside, and a jury will hear evidence and determine liability. If the defendant is found liable, the plaintiff will normally receive an award for damages.

Both workers' compensation and wrongful injury cases may involve depositions, where attorneys for both sides examine and cross examine witnesses to discover facts and to evaluate the strengths and weaknesses of their respective cases. Depositions are sworn statements and answers to questions which are taken down by a court recorder. In some cases they may be entered as evidence at a hearing or trial in lieu of an actual appearance by the witness. More often, however, the attorneys again ask their deposition questions in the courtroom, and if testimony is given at the hearing or trial that is inconsistent with the earlier deposition, clarification will be sought by the side adversely affected. If a deposition was taken, the witness should review it before the hearing or trial. A witness can change his or her deposition testimony, but must be prepared to explain any alteration (e.g., did not fully understand the earlier question, misspoke).

In addition to workers' compensation and wrongful injury cases, the Social Security Administration uses vocational experts, through its Vocational Consultants Program, to assist administrative law judges in rulings on disability benefit appeals. The role of the vocational expert is more structured under social security than in workers' compensation hearings or personal injury litigation, and the vocational opinion must conform to the Social Security Administration's definition of disability (see Carter and Saxon, 1977; Field, McCroskey, Sink and Wattenbarger, 1978; Grossman, 1979).

The use of vocational experts in all these areas is relatively new, and reflects the development of social and especially legal recognition of the expertise of rehabilitation professionals. Some attorneys are even starting, for example, to use vocational experts in divorce litigation (Workman, 1983) where the capacity of the wife to support herself is disputed. With the use of vocational experts being so widespread and generally accelerating (except at the time of this writing within the Social Security Administration) it is important for every rehabilitationist to know how to prepare and present an opinion on the vocational impact of disability.

BASIC WORKERS' COMPENSATION TESTIMONY

As indicated earlier, the practitioner will usually be called upon to testify in a case that he or she has worked on. As such, the rehabilitationist must be prepared to present and describe all of his or her activities on the case, the rationale for those activities, and their result. If a rehabilitation plan was developed, the rehabilitationist should be prepared to present and discuss the plan, including all reports, test results, medical evaluations, and other information utilized in its development. The rehabilitationist should be thoroughly familiar with the client's past work history and earnings, and should be prepared to discuss the client's transferable skills and how they relate to the rehabilitation plan and other vocational possibilities.

In preparing to present and discuss past activities with and on behalf of a client, the rehabilitationist should carefully review his or her file notes and billings. In some cases, especially longstanding ones, it may be helpful to transcribe these case service records into a condensed chronological time line so that major activities and their dates can be more easily seen and highlighted. For example, such a time line might indicate major activities as shown in Illustration 8-1.

Illustration 8-1

CASE SERVICE TIMELINE

May 5:	Received referral of Mr. Jones from Mr. Black at Worldwide Insurance.
May 7:	Spoke with Mr. Jones on the telephone and scheduled office interview for 9 a.m. on May 10th.
May 10:	Mr. Jones did not show for scheduled interview.
May 11:	Called Mr. Jones — no answer.
May 12:	Called Mr. Jones — arranged to see him at home on May 15th. Mr. Jones said he forgot his May 10th appointment.
May 14:	Received and reviewed reports of Dr. Smith (dated April 15th) and Dr. Harper (dated April 2nd).
May 15:	Interviewed Mr. Jones in his home. Was informed client is represented by Mr. Wilson (attorney). Called Mr. Wilson from client's home for permission to work with Mr. Jones — granted. Collected work and educational history. Scheduled second appointment for May 22nd at 3:30 p.m.
May 22:	Mr. Jones came one hour late for interview and I had left for the day.
May 23:	Called and rescheduled interview in client's home for May 27th.
May 27:	Went to client's home — no one answered door.
May 28:	Called and rescheduled home visit with Mr. Jones for May 30th.
May 30:	Went to conduct home visit — Mr. Jones said he was not feeling well from flu. Would not make another appointment at that time.
June 4:	Called and Mr. Jones said he was too disabled to work. He would not schedule another meeting.
June 4:	Called Mr. Wilson who said Mr. Jones was going to be seen by Dr. Silver — and rehabilitation efforts should hold pending his report. Contacted Mr. Black to inform him of developments in the case.

Although a case service timeline is sometimes helpful in organizing what has happened in a case, the rehabilitationist should remember that everything he or she writes about a client and places in the case file is subject to review by attorneys representing the client or carrier. This being the case, it is only prudent (and professional) to be as objective and factual as possible. Subjective opinions, interpretations of behavior, and speculations should be kept out of case files. If a client misses several appointments, for example, the client's excuses (if any) should be recorded, but the rehabilitationist should refrain from adding a subjective opinion to the case record such as, "Mr. Jones does not appear to be very motivated for rehabilitation services." If a workers' compensation judge asks your opinion on whether Mr. Jones has been cooperative you can give it, but it is best to leave unsolicited opinions out of written case records.

Another point to be cognizant of in workers' compensation cases where a private insurer is involved is that the rehabilitationist is technically a limited agent of the carrier (i.e., under contract with the carrier to deliver a service). The rehabilitationist or the company he or she works for may have a number of cases from the carrier, and a financial interest in maintaining the carrier's good will. Nevertheless, this relationship with the carrier or its representatives must not be allowed to influence the rehabilitationist's testimony. Testifying to the facts (i.e., what you did and what happened) and leaving subjective opinions and interpretations out of your testimony is the key to providing fair, factually accurate, and unbiased testimony. If you do not know the answer to a question, or are asked for an opinion you have not formulated, do not be afraid to answer, "I don't know."

DEVELOPING VOCATIONAL OPINIONS

According to Lynch (1983), the development of a vocational opinion is a threefold process involving: (a) assessing vocational assets and limitations; (b) identifying occupations that are consistent with the individual's residual capabilities; and (c) establishing the existance, availability, and earnings for these occupations in the general geographic area where the client resides. The first two parts of Lynch's process involve the formation of an employability opinion, which is whether there are occupations the worker is still capable of performing. The third component addresses placeability and future earnings, placeability being whether the worker would likely be hired for an occupation he or she is capable of performing.

Employability Assessment

Employability refers only to the individual's ability to meet the physical and mental demands of an occupation, and has nothing to do with whether there are current openings in the occupation, or whether the worker would be hired for any present or future openings. In developing an employability opinion the rehabilitationist matches the residual capabilities of the client with the demands and requirements of different jobs. If there are no discrepancies between the qualifications and abilities of the worker, and requirements of the job, then the worker is *employable* at that job.

The first step in employability assessment is to determine the residual physical capacities of the client. This requires a careful review of medical records and reports. It is also important to have the primary or attending physician(s) complete a physical capacities form (see Illustration 4-4) since this translates medical findings into the functional realm that is germane to the development of the employability opinion.

Unfortunately, in some cases physicians disagree on functional limitations and residual capacitities. In such cases it is often necessary to present employability opinions based on the different medical assessments or hypothetical situations presented by attorneys. Another occasional problem is that the primary or attending physician(s) may be unable or unwilling to complete all or part of a physical capacities form. In this situation additional diagnostics may be needed, or it may be necessary to have the client examined by another physician. Referral for vocational evaluation can also provide valuable physical capacities information, especially in regard to functional usage of the upper extremities and work tolerance.

Mental variables such as intelligence, aptitudes, achievement levels, interests, temperaments, and the like may be evaluated by referring the client to a vocational evaluation center (which is the most comprehensive approach) or through selective office based testing. However, in workers' compensation cases, the rehabilitationist usually relies primarily on the work history as an indicator of minimum worker capabilities. This is possible because central tendency data exists on the mental and physical demands of different jobs, and if a worker has successfully performed a job, it can be inferred that he or she possesses, unless modified by disability, at least the minimum mental and physical abilities demanded by the job. Work history data is supplemented by the educational history of the client and reported avocational activities (e.g., hobbies, past accomplishments). The occupationally relevant residual capabilities that are identified through this assessment process are called transferable skills.

Some rehabilitationists still use the 1965 edition of the *Dictionary of Occupational Titles* (Volumes I and II) and its supplements to assess transferable skills related to the past work experiences of the client. This is primarily because the 1977 edition of the *DOT* and corollary publications (*Guide for Occupational Exploration, Selected Characteristics of Occupations Defined in the Dictionary of Occupational Titles*) do not report data on minimum job aptitudes, interests, and temperaments; which were previously available in the 1965 edition. The above information, however, is currently available through *The Classification of Jobs According to Worker Trait Factors*, which is published by the VDARE Service Bureau (P.O. Box 1945, Athens, GA 30603) rather than U.S. Department of Labor. This later publication is a more than adequate replacement for the data on aptitudes, interests, and temperaments previously available through the federal government, and is additionally helpful in that it identifies sedentary and light jobs by *GOE* code, and DPT (data/people/things) numbers (Field and Field, 1982). The employability opinion is formulated with this data by comparing the highest levels of previous worker performance (see VDARE discussion in Chapter V), as modified by the disability, to the requirements and demands listed for different jobs.

In formulating an employability opinion the rehabilitationist relates the transferable skills of the client to the demands of jobs. Job demands are not inferred only from

DOT job descriptions and central tendency data available through publications such as *The Classification of Jobs According to Worker Trait Factors,* but are validated by actual job analyses of positions in the community. This is critical because incidental, infrequent, or unreported job demands may totally reverse an employability assessment. In illustrating this point, Mckee (1983) wrote:

> ...I once had a case where an employer offered a man with a low back problem a job as a paper cutting machine operator. We videotaped the job. The man stood at the machine, all paper to be cut was raised by hydraulic lifts, waste paper was automatically removed, cut paper was taken away by conveyor. On cross-examination, the witness was asked if the operator of the machine would have to do anything else at all. "Just change the blades," was the innocent reply. As it developed, changing the blades involved holding the three foot blades at arm's length and pushing them up into the machine – each blade weighed between 50 and 60 pounds (pg. 24).

The employability assessment is complete when the rehabilitationist has related the residual physical and mental capacities of the client (transferable skills) to the demands of jobs that exist in the local community, identifying those which the client could still perform. The next issue which must be addressed is placeability – whether the client would actually be hired, and if so what the compensation would be.

Placeability Assessment

Although placeability and employability are discussed here separately, the two assessments naturally go together. For example, when a job analysis is done to determine if a position is suitable, it will usually be ascertained whether openings exist or are expected, whether the employer would consider hiring a person with a certain disability, what salary would be paid, etc. The rehabilitationist will often collect and evaluate information on employability and placeability simultaneously, but when testifying the issues should be kept separate.

As indicated earlier, employability can be partially assessed by using published data on jobs, but this data is no full substitute for actual on-site job analyses. The same is true for placeability, which can be partially assessed by using published labor market and employment outlook data, but again, such data is not a substitute for first hand information (e.g., that there is a current job opening for a security guard at Ajax Lumber and they would consider someone with a low back injury). A consultant might rely more on published data, but practitioners should be prepared to relate their placeability assessments to the local labor market as they know it, and to their specific placement activities on behalf of the client.

There are a number of resources that may be helpful in formulating or developing placeability opinions. They include:

1. Publications of the Bureau of Labor Statistics, U.S. Department of Labor; such as the *Occupational Outlook Handbook, Occupational Outlook Quarterly, Occupational Projections and Training Data, National Industry-Occupation Employment Matrix,* and *Area* and *National Wage Surveys.*

2. Publications of state Departments of Labor, such as occupational projections and other business/growth data.
3. Publications of the U.S. Chamber of Commerce, such as the *Monthly Labor Review*.
4. Publications of state and local Chamber of Commerces, such as industry directories.
5. Business and trade journals.
6. The local telephone book and newspaper.

From the above list, the practitioner will usually find the local industry directory, telephone book, and newspaper the most valuable placeability resources. The industry directory will usually list all major employers, including number of employees and goods and/or services produced. The telephone book lists all employers who interface with the public, and is especially useful for identifying smaller employers, and the number of separate businesses that produce certain goods or services. Newspapers of course list current job openings, and these listings can be supplemental by calling the local branch of the state employment office. The other listed resources are useful in more general assessments of placement probability.

In placeability assessment, the rehabilitationist must consider how factors such as client appearance, age, sex, race, educational level, interview behaviors, employer hiring practices and attitudes, architectural barriers, and the like affect the probability that the client would be hired for jobs he or she is capable of performing (Deutsch and Raffa, 1982; Lynch, 1983). These factors cannot be as readily assessed as physical capacities and job demands, and this means that placeability opinions are more subjective.

Again, it is important to emphasize that in an actual workers' compensation hearing, the judge or referee will be most interested in what placement activities the rehabilitationist has performed and the results. For example, what were the findings of any labor market surveys? How many employers were contacted? Where are there appropriate job openings? Were any job interviews scheduled? Did the client keep interview appointments? Were any jobs offered? If jobs were not offered, what factors account for this?

When a client is both employable and placeable in certain occupations, the rehabilitationist must be prepared to testify as to what remuneration the client would receive when so employed. Most clients will begin a new occupation at an entry level wage, so the rehabilitationist should be prepared to project how earnings will rise with experience. It is also helpful to know what fringe benefits are available through different employers, what work-related expenses the client will have (e.g., union dues), whether overtime employment is available, and whether occasional layoffs are characteristic of the position? How the above information was learned or established should be well documented (i.e., referenced to sources).

TESTIFYING

In preparing for court testimony, the rehabilitationist should carefully review all assessment procedures, medical reports, and related data; highlighting information pertinent to vocational rehabilitation planning. The rehabilitationist should be prepared to chronologically list his or her major activities with the case, explaining the relevance of each to the development or implementation of the rehabilitation plan. Actual courtroom testimony (including depositions and hearings) may be conveniently divided into four sequential activities: (1) establishment of qualifications, (2) direct examination, (3) cross-examination, and (4) redirect examination. In workers' compensation hearings, these may not be strictly adhered to, and the judge or referee may take considerable latitude in personally questioning witnesses. The witness may also be asked hypothetical questions (Anderson, 1979) since facts may be in dispute.

Qualifications and Direct Examination

Most courts will accept an individual as a vocational expert based upon either work experience or education. No minimum standards exist for either area, and the acceptance of any expert is the perogative of each court. Field and Sink (1981) suggested that a bachelors degree in the behavioral sciences, work experience as a rehabilitationist, and membership in one or more relevant professional associations would generally be sufficient to establish credentials as a vocational expert. Graduate degrees in rehabilitation, certification, and extensive work experience would obviously further enhance the expert's credentials.

Qualifications of the rehabilitationist are normally not a major area of contention in workers' compensation hearings, simply because the rehabilitationist, well qualified or not, has been working with the client and the judge needs to know what has transpired and why. In personal injury litigation the qualifications of the expert may be a major area of contention because one side will be anticipating damaging testimony from witnesses brought forward by the other. That being the case, the side not calling the expert will often want to establish weaknesses in the expert's qualifications, thereby reducing the credibility of the testimony. If one side refuses to accept an individual as an expert (which happens infrequently) the court will rule on whether the individual can so testify.

When called to testify, the rehabilitationist should bring at least one copy of his or her vita. The rehabilitationist should be prepared to explain his or her work experience, educational background, degrees received, and certifications held. Most rehabilitationists familiar with courtroom testimony provide the attorney who called them with a list of questions to ask (and answers that will be received) in the establishment of professional qualifications, which is the first part of direct examination. A logical sequence of qualification questions would be:

1. What is your name?
2. What is your position and who do you work for?
3. What are your job duties?
4. How long have you been employed in that position and similar positions?
5. What is your educational background?
6. Are you a member of any professional associations?
7. Do you hold any certifications?

Direct Examination

After questions dealing with the experts qualifications have been answered, the examining attorney will ask the court to accept the individual as an expert in the area of vocational rehabilitation. If there are no objections, the attorney will then focus direct examination questions on issues pertaining to the case itself. In personal injury litigation there may be a series of questions preceeding case specific questions where the rehabilitationist explains to the jury the vocational relevance of concepts such as physical capacities, job analysis, transferable skills, and the like; because these concepts are pertinent to understanding the expert's testimony. This is normally unnecessary in workers' compensation hearings where only a judge or referee is involved. For example:

Attorney: "Have you evaluated the vocational potential of Mr. Jones?"

Expert: "Yes I have."

Attorney: "What information have you reviewed, collected, or otherwise used in your evaluation?"

Expert: (Presents source data)

Attorney: "Specifically, what must be evaluated in determining vocational potential?"

Expert: (Lists major areas assessed such as physical capacities, transferable skills, job demands, aptitudes, interests, labor market conditions)

Attorney: (Asks follow-up questions where rehabilitationist explains concepts such as physical capacities and transferable skills, and their relevance to work)

After these questions, direct examination will turn to specific issues in the case such as the following:

1. Considering all the data, can the client perform the preinjury job?
2. If not, why not?
3. Could the job be modified so that the client could perform it?
4. If yes, would the employer do this?
5. What other jobs are suitable for the client?
6. Where are they located and how many are there?
7. Are there current job openings?
8. Would the client likely be hired for any of these jobs?
9. If not, why not?
10. Have job interviews been scheduled or completed?
11. What was their result?
12. How much could the client earn if hired?

Direct examination ends when the attorney who called the witness has asked and received answers to all of his or her questions. Attorneys, especially those unfamiliar with vocational issues, often have difficulty asking, during direct examination, appropriate questions which bring to light pertinent vocational issues in a case. For this reason, many experts present attorneys with a list of questions for direct examination, and go over with the attorney what their answers will be (see Field and Sink, 1981; Lynch, 1983). This is more common in personal injury litigation than in workers' compensation hearings.

Cross and Redirect Examination

Cross examination is where the attorney who did not call the witness is allowed to question the witness. According to Kornblum (1974), there are five possible goals in the cross examination of an expert:

1. To question qualifications.
2. To show reason for bias.
3. To show that questionable or improper procedures were employed in the development of the opinion.
4. To discredit facts used in the development of the opinion.
5. To establish favorable facts through admissions by the expert.

Although cross examination can be a trying and difficult experience, sound preparation will considerably lessen anxiety (Lynch, 1983). Questions should be carefully listened to (Brodsky, 1977) and should be answered directly and to the point. A witness should also not be afraid to state in an authoritative manner that he or she does not know the answer to a question (Brodsky and Robey, 1972). Most importantly, regardless of the attorney's questions or demeanor, the expert should remain polite and courteous at all times (Kornblum, 1974).

After cross-examination, the side that called the witness has an opportunity to recover from any cross-examination damage to the testimony through redirect examination. This normally consists of no more than several questions, which are intended to clarify, for benefit of judge or jury, what the expert's actual testimony is.

Fine Points of Testimony

There are some fine points of behavior on the witness stand that generally serve all experts well. Some of these have already been mentioned, such as remaining polite and courteous regardless of provocations, answering questions directly and to the point, and saying "I don't know" with some authority rather than apologetically. Other points to remember when on the witness stand (see Brodsky, 1977, 1981a, 1981b; Kornblum, 1974; Neff, 1983) include:

1. Always be honest. Remember that you are not there to try to "win" a case, but rather to present facts as you know them to the court. Do not overstate your findings or conclusions.
2. Take time to think before you respond to a question, but do not repeat the question. In general, go slow. Do not rush your answers due to anxiety or a desire to get off the witness stand.
3. Be sure you are speaking in a clear and audible voice, and keep your hands away from your face.
4. Don't be flattered by or accept an offer to waive the presentation of your credentials. Your credentials lend credibility to your testimony.
5. If a question requires only a "yes" or "no" response, answer it that way. Don't volunteer information not requested. Remember that many witnesses get into trouble by talking too much.

6. Don't try to interject humor or frivolity into your testimony because this weakens it. Avoid being too casual or going "off the record" too much.
7. If you misspeak, correct your error. If in court you contradict your deposition testimony say, "If I did say that I made a mistake, my testimony is..."
8. Admit to being uncertain if you are uncertain. However, you must also avoid unnecessary equivocation (e.g., "It is *probably* true that he could do that job") and take a definite position based upon your knowledge of the facts.
9. Avoid using unnecessary technical terms. When you must use technical terms explain what they mean.
10. Try to anticipate where the attorney is going with a line of questioning. Never say that a question is irrelevant because it is the court that decides relevancy.
11. Do not speak for other experts. If challenged with incompatible testimony from another expert say, "I cannot speak for that individual, only for myself."
12. Do not ask the judge or hearing officer for advice. Always stop talking when a judge or hearing officer interupts you.
13. Keep materials you bring to the witness stand to a minimum. Attorney's may take these materials away from you and question you on them.
14. If you have been on the witness stand for a substantial period of time you may ask the judge for a five minute break to go to the restroom or get a drink. Remember that you cannot discuss the case on the break.

VOCATIONAL EXPERT CONSULTATION

An area where some rehabilitationists have applied their skills is vocational expert consultation. As indicated earlier, this does not involve the delivery of case management services, but rather the determination of the vocational impact of disability, whether the individual is employable and placeable, what they would earn after placement, and what reemployment-related services are necessary? The two principal areas where consultants work are in personal injury litigation and Social Security disability appeals.

Personal Injury Litigation

When someone is physically injured and another party has some liability for the injury, the injured part is entitled to compensation from the liable party. If the injury results in an employment problem, the court hearing the case is often at a loss to determine the true employment significance of the injury because of a lack of expertise in evaluating a disability/employment interface. This issue is of considerable importance to the court, however, since a vocational impact may affect earnings and any financial loss should be compensated. If there is no vocational impact, the court needs to know this also. Hence the need for a vocational expert.

The services of a vocational expert may be secured by either the attorney(s) for the plaintiff (Treon, 1979) or defense (Cross, 1979; Trimble, 1977). To the author's knowledge no statistics exist on the relative use of vocational experts by either side, but personal experience suggests that vocational expert services are more frequently engaged by the plaintiff's attorney when liability is seriously in doubt, and by the defense when it is not. This is because in cases of substantial loss where liability is questionable, a trial will usually occur, and if the plaintiff wins liability, the award will be based upon the evidence presented for damages. On the other hand, when the defense knows it likely has some liability in the injury, it then has an interest in showing that damages are minimal, thereby reducing the requested settlement or court award. When the defense is convinced it is not liable, it is focused strongly on the liability defense, and is not as concerned with "damage control" in the event liability is lost. The plaintiff's attorney, however, cannot take this position since after winning liability, the award is based on damages.

In personal injury cases the rehabilitationist evaluates employability and placeability essentially the same as in workers' compensation cases, but of course gives no consideration to any disability definitions or medical/rehabilitation benefits specified by the state's workers' compensation law since they do not apply. The economic impact of the injury is the "bottom line," and the vocational expert must be prepared to indicate what jobs the client could be employed at and what would be earned at those jobs now and in the future. Although some vocational experts know how to project pre and post disability earnings for the work life of a client and reduce their difference to a present value (see Deutsch and Raff, 1982a; Field and Sink, 1981) this is usually done by an economist, who is also called to testify as an expert witness. The economist will also compute the present value of projected medical, attendant care, and related expenses as these too are important in the determination of an award or settlement.

Rehabilitationists interested in working as vocational consultants in personal injury litigation normally develop their clientele (i.e. attorneys) either through direct contact in workers' compensation or Social Security cases, or through marketing activities. Credentials and courtroom skills are very important because any case may end up in trial before a jury. The most successful consultants generally have a doctorate in rehabilitation, are certified, have substantial rehabilitation work experience, and have attended workshops on how to prepare and deliver expert testimony.

Social Security

When someone applies for Social Security disability benefits their application is evaluated by a state disability determination unit. If this unit rules that the applicant is not disabled, the applicant can ask for a reconsideration, and if still dissatisfied, may appeal the ruling to the Office of Hearings and Appeals. Here the case is heard (with or without attorneys) by a Social Security administrative law judge, who's basic task is to determine whether the applicant is entitled to benefits under the provisions of the law (Grossman, 1979).

Under the Social Security Act, the definition of disability (except in some cases of blindness) is the "inability to engage in substantial gainful activity by reason of any medically determinable physical or mental impairment which can be expected to result in death or which has lasted or can be expected to last for a continuous period of not less than twelve months" (see section 223). An inability to do the former job does not qualify the applicant for benefits. The applicant must also be unable to engage in any kind of "substantial gainful work which exists in the national economy" (see section 223), taking into consideration the applicant's age, educational level, and work experience. The Social Security definition of disability emphasizes employability rather than placeability. If jobs that the applicant could do exist in substantial numbers in the applicants region or in several other regions of the national economy, then the applicant is not disabled.

Although this definition of disability is relatively straightforward, its application to specific cases can be quite difficult. According to the "Kerner criteria" (established in *Kerner vs. Fleming*) the Social Security Administration must show what jobs an applicant can still do, and must do so on an individual rather than "theoretical" basis to deny benefits (see Field, McCroskey, Sink and Wattenbarger, 1978). When an application is appealed, an administrative law judge may find it very helpful to have the opinion of a vocational expert as to whether any jobs exist that a specific individual could engage in, how many there are, and where they are. The judge may question the expert quite liberally and hypothetically in the process of formulating a decision.

In order to provide a considered and impartial vocational opinion on a case by case basis, the Office of Hearings and Appeals established the Vocational Consultants Program in 1962 (Field, McCroskey, Sink and Wattenbarger, 1978). Professionals interested in developing and presenting vocational opinions are registered through this program, and may be called to render opinions on cases heard in the geographical area where they reside. The development of a vocational opinion is far more structured under Social Security than in workers' compensation or personal injury cases, and vocational experts must follow set guidelines in developing opinions. This helps to insure more uniform and consistent opinions, regardless of which expert is called.

SUMMARY

Regardless of the area where vocational expert testimony is given, the rehabilitationist must remember that he or she is called to help discover the "truth" in a case, and the opinion must be impartial, and the best the rehabilitationist can formulate with the information available. The rehabilitationist's opinion may sometimes be wrong, but the process of developing it must always be beyond reproach.

References

Anderson, R.H.: Vocational expert testimony: The new frontier for the rehabilitation professional. *Journal of Rehabilitation*, 1979, *45*:39-40, 74.

Brodsky, S.: Ten commandments for an expert witness. *Social Action and the Law*, 1981a, *7*:7.

Brodsky, S.L.: *The Expert Witness* (unpublished training booklet), 1981b.

Brodsky, S.L.: The mental health professional on the witness stand: A survival guide. In B.D. Sales (Ed.). *Psychology in the Legal Process.* New York: Spectrum, 1977.

Brodsky, S.L. and Robey, A.: On becoming an expert witness: Issues of orientation and effectiveness. *Professional Psychology*, 1972, Spring, 173-176.

Carter, J.W. and Saxon, J.P.: The role of the vocational expert witness in social security administrative hearings. *Journal of Applied Rehabilitation Counseling,* 1977, *8*:247-250.

Cross, D.L.: A defense attorney looks at private rehabilitation. *Journal of Rehabilitation,* 1979, *45*:37-38, 74.

Deutsch, P.M. and Raffa, F.A.: *Damages in Tort Actions* (Volume 8). New York: Matthew Bender, 1982.

Field, T.F. and Field, J.E.: *The Classification of Jobs According to Worker Trait Factors.* Athens: VDARE Service Bureau, 1982.

Field, T.F., McCroskey, B.J., Sink, J. and Wattenbarger, W.: The role and functions of the vocational expert in judicial hearings. *Psychosocial Rehabilitation Journal*, 1978, *2*:17-27.

Field, T.F. and Sink, J.M.: *The Vocational Expert.* Athens: VDARE Service Bureau, 1981.

Grossman, H.I.: A new concept of disability. *Journal of Rehabilitation*, 1979, *45*:41-49, 71.

Kornblum, G.: The expert as witness and consultant. *The Practical Lawyer,* 1974, March.

Lynch, R.K.: The vocational expert. *Rehabilitation Counseling Bulletin,* 1983, *27*:18-25.

McKee, W.J.: Zen and the art of vocational rehabilitation or: Being prepared to testify. *Rehabilitation Forum*, 1983, *10*:23-25.

Neff, W.J.: Testifying as a competent and credible witness. *The Journal of the College and University Personnel Association,* 1983, *34*:42-45.

Treon, R.T.: Private rehabilitation of injured persons: A plaintiff-lawyers perspective. *Journal of Rehabilitation*, 1979, *45*:34-36.

Trimble, Mr.: The defendant's vocational rehabilitation expert witness. *The Chronicle,* 1977, *23*:886-891.

Workman, E.L.: Vocational rehabilitation in the private, profit making sector. In E.L. Pan, T.A. Backer and C.L. Vash (Eds.) *Annual Review of Rehabilitation* (Volume 3). New York: Springer, 1983.

CHAPTER IX

BUSINESS ASPECTS

PRIVATE sector rehabilitation was defined in Chapter I as the delivery of medical and/or vocational rehabilitation case management services to clients having third party coverage. Indeed, what principally distinguishes the public and private sectors is that rehabilitation services are supported by tax dollars in the public sector, and by insurance premiums or assessments on insurers in the private sector. With the exception of in-house corporate and insurance company programs, private sector rehabilitation is a service which insurance companies, self-insuring employers, and workers' compensation agencies contract for on an as-needed basis. The self-employed professionals and corporations which provide these services constitute the actual "business" of private sector rehabilitation.

There are many important business aspects of private sector rehabilitation. This chapter overviews some of the more important ones. Areas addressed include the scope of the business, business models, staffing models, marketing, billing systems, accountability, and future trends.

Scope of the Business

As indicated in Chapter I, private sector rehabilitation began growing rapidly in the mid 1970's. It started first in California, and spread to other states as they too modified their workers' compensation laws to encourage or mandate rehabilitation services. Although private sector referrals are generated from all the personal injury lines of insurance (workers' compensation, auto no-fault, auto liability, general liability, and long term disability), the vast majority of referrals stem from industrial injuries. With the exception of federal employees, harbor workers, and railroad workers; rehbilitation benefits in industrial injury cases are defined by each state workers' compensation law. The workers mentioned above are covered by federally administered laws (i.e., Federal Employees Compensation Act, Longshoremen and Harbor Workers' Act, Railroad Retirement Act/Employer's Liability Act, respectively).

Because workers' compensation is a state responsibility, the scope of the business varies on a state by state basis. In some states (e.g., California, Michigan, Florida) the private sector is very large, and in others it does not even exist as a distinct business entity. Since workers' compensation laws can be modified every time a state legislature convenes, the private sector can be rapidly expanding in one state while it is contracting in another. To date, the sector has only experienced growth and expansion, but as there are a limited number of state laws to modify favorably toward rehabilitation, and a finite number of industrial injuries, the rapid growth of the late 1970's and early 1980's cannot be maintained forever. Moreover, in many states the public rehabilitation agency is repositioning itself to more effectively seek and serve workers' compensation referrals (see Smith and Sawisch, 1983), and if this trend continues it could slow the growth of the private sector.

There are a number of ways to measure the scope or size of businesses that exist in the national economy. Unfortunately, private sector rehabilitation is so new and so decentralized that no truly reliable data exists for any of the customary measures. The Tenth Institute on Rehabilitation Issues (1983), however, reported the following estimates by Richard LaFon (a former NARPPS president): (a) $450 million in billings during 1982, (b) 6,000 private proprietary professionals employed in the United States in 1983, and (c) more than 1,000 private proprietary organizations in 1983. Gutowski, Harder and Koshel (1980) estimated that 150,000 to 200,000 clients were served annually.

Business Models

Rehabilitation services are sometimes provided by in-house corporate or insurance company rehabilitation units, and the workers' compensation agency itself may have a rehabilitation staff. There are also, however, "private vendors" who constitute most of the private rehabilitation sector. These vendors hope to make a profit by delivering rehabilitation services in cases referred to them by employers, insurance companies, or workers' compensation agencies. Their businesses may be organized as sole proprietorships, partnerships, or corporations.

A sole proprietorship is the oldest, simplest, and most common form of business organization. It is most commonly utilized in the United States in small retail stores, service businesses, and in professions such as private sector rehabilitation. In a small proprietorship one person owns the business. He or she is the president, general manager, board of directors, and stockholder all rolled into one (Newcomer, 1974).

There are a number of business advantages in being organized as a sole proprietorship. First, the business is easy to start and close. There is no legal distinction between the owner and the business itself, and for this reason sole proprietorships escape most government regulation. Often the only legal requirement is an occupational or business license. In the case of a private rehabilitation enterprise, registration with and approval from the workers' compensation agency may be necessary. If the owner wishes to operate the business under some title other than his or her own name (e.g., Center City Rehabilitation Services) the business name must be registered, but that does not change the legal status of the business. The sole proprietor owns all the assets and profits of the business, and he or she is liable for all its debts and obligations. Sole proprietorships pay no separate taxes, earnings and expenses being reported on the owner's personal tax return.

Many individuals find sole proprietorships attractive because they offer the opportunity to "be your own boss," and to earn more than would likely be earned as an employee of someone else. They can be started on a part-time basis with limited capital, and can conceivably grow into major corporations. Examples of sole proprietorships that became a major success include Sears and Roebuck, J.C. Penney, Ford Motors, the Bank of America, and Kentucky Fried Chicken (Preston and Zimmerer, 1976). In private sector rehabilitation, the third largest company (largest unaffiliated with an insurance company), Vocational Placement Services, began in the Richmond, Virginia home of Mary Gambosh ("Who's Who in Rehabilitation, 1982).

Although sole proprietorships can grow into major corporations, the majority fail, sometimes bringing financial disaster to their owner. Sole proprietorships fail for a number of reasons. One is that the proprietor may lack adequate managerial skills. Another is that there may be insufficient capital. It is very difficult for sole proprietorships to obtain substantial bank loans and other outside financing because there is often insufficient collateral to secure a major loan. It is also hard to maintain good employees because sole proprietorships offer less security and fewer opportunities for advancement than large corporations. When all things are considered, starting a sole proprietorship involves assuming many risks.

The report of the Tenth Institute on Rehabilitation Issues (1983) noted that many private sector rehabilitation services are delivered by sole proprietors. Some begin on a part-time basis while maintaining full-time employment in an agency setting. If they can generate enough business, they eventually enter the field full-time, and may expand by hiring other professional employees. Typical business expenses include: (a) office rent, furnishings, and utilities; (b) printing and office supplies; (c) typing, telephone answering, legal and accounting services; (d) transportation; and (e) liability insurance. To be successful, a sole proprietor should generate a pre-tax income of at least $20,000; and $80,000 is about as much as one professional could hope to earn. In addition to having referral sources and experience working in private sector rehabilitation, the successful sole proprietor must be well-organized and a self-starter (Tenth Institute on Rehabilitation Issues, 1983).

Another business model which is legally similar to the sole proprietorship is the partnership. The advantages of partnerships include: (a) larger capital resources, (b) better credit standing than a single individual, (c) risk sharing, and (d) more managerial and service talent (Hastings, 1968). Like the sole proprietorship, partnerships do not pay separate taxes and in *general* partnerships (which are the most common) the partners have unlimited liability for business debts and obligations. In a *limited* partnership a partner may invest *X* dollars in the business and have liability limited to its loss, but the limited partner cannot become involved in business affairs or management. If the limited partner acts as more than an investor, he or she may be treated by the courts as a general partner.

Disadvantages of partnerships include: (a) the possibility of serious business disagreements, (b) being bound to contracts made by other partners, (c) the uncertain life of the business enterprise, and (d) possible difficulty in withdrawing from the business (Shilt, Carmichael and Wilson, 1967). It is fair to say that honesty and responsibility are indispensable qualities of "good" partners. A person should never go into business with someone they do not trust or cannot rely on.

Although partnerships can be formed orally, in almost all cases a legal agreement is signed which specifies the business responsibilities of each partner and how proceeds will be divided. In the United States, partnerships are usually regulated by the Uniform Partnership Act, a model code which most states have adopted, thereby standardizing partnership law to a large extent throughout the nation (Keith and Gubellini, 1967; Newcomer, 1974).

For readers interested in beginning a private rehabilitation enterprise, the partnership business model should be given serious consideration. For one thing, the cost of two people being in business together is not much more than one in business alone. Also, one of the major problems rehabilitationists have when they start on their own is that after their marketing efforts produce cases, they must stop marketing to deliver services, and cannot again engage in substantial marketing until their caseload goes down. Since they are not able to market themselves, that usually happens. The result is that there is either too much work (which undercuts the quality of their services and reputation with referral sources) or not enough, and highly variable monthly income. Partners can avoid this in that one can keep a substantial percentage of his or her time committed to marketing. When this time starts to be encroached upon, it is probably time to expand the business by hiring an employee. If business keeps expanding, the partners may eventually chose to form a corporation.

Corporations differ from sole proprietorships and partnerships in that corporations exist as separate legal entities. A corporation pays taxes, can sue or be sued, and those who own it have no personal liability for its debts and obligations. Corporations are chartered on a state-by-state basis, and have articles of incorporation which state the name of the business, business objectives, and responsibilities of officers and directors. Unlike a sole proprietorship or partnership, which end with the death or retirement of the owner(s), corporations continue indefinitely, so long as they remain financially solvent.

Most large businesses (i.e., gross earnings of $1,000,000 per year or more) and even many smaller ones are organized as corporations. Advantages of the corporate model include: (a) limited liability in that the owners can lose only their investment in the company, (b) capital is raised more easily through bank loans, bonds, or sale of additional stock, (c) permanency of existence, and (d) ease of transferring shares of ownership. Disadvantages include: (a) higher starting costs due to legal fees associated with incorporation, (b) greater government regulation, (c) business restrictions imposed by the charter, and (d) taxes on both corporate earnings and profit distributions (dividends) paid to owners (Preston and Zimmerer, 1976; Shilt, Carmichael and Wilson, 1967).

Although corporations must pay taxes on their earnings and shareholders taxes on their dividends, even for small businesses with one or two owners, incorporation can sometimes produce a net tax savings, and a successful sole proprietorship or partnership should therefore investigate the tax ramifications of incorporation. When all things are considered, large businesses with substantial capital and multiple owners can seldom be satisfactorily run as partnerships, so the corporate model is needed. This is true for rehabilitation where local and sometimes statewide firms are run as proprietorships or partnerships, but where regional and nationwide firms are incorporated.

Staffing Models

Even a sole proprietor, starting into the rehabilitation business on a part-time basis and working out of his or her home, must consider certain staffing issues. For example, who will take business telephone messages while the rehabilitationist is in the field — a telephone answering machine, professional answering service, or spouse? Who will type reports, letters, and the like? Who will prepare the billings for professional services and monitor whether they are paid? Who will keep track of business operating expenses, order supplies, and balance the books? Does the rehabilitationist need a secretary/bookkeeper on a full- or part-time basis, should the rehabilitationist contract for these services with an outside firm, or can he or she handle these tasks in addition to marketing and case management services?

There are no easy answers to any of the above questions, but obviously how well these "nonprofessional" job tasks are handled can mean the difference between whether a business is a success or failure. This is true whether the business is new or established. The owner or manager must accurately assess what support services are needed, hire suitable personnel, and when necessary dismiss them. Moreover, as the business grows, staffing and management issues require more time and become increasingly complex.

There are entire books written on personnel and business management, and this discussion therefore only addresses some specific issues related to the hiring and management of professional rehabilitation staff. These include: (a) duties and qualifications of professional staff, (b) compensation methods, and (c) noncompetition agreements.

As indicated in Chapters V and VI, matching the right worker with the right job involves understanding both the qualifications of the worker and duties of the job. In relation to professional staff, qualifications take the form of degrees and work experiences. Job duties take the form of either specific case service responsibilities (total or compartmentalized) or type of caseload (general or specific) which the professional will carry.

In most private rehabilitation companies, professional staff deliver total case management services (from the initial interview to placement follow-up) for all clients assigned to them. This is especially true with smaller companies, where because of their size, the staff must be versatile. As a company grows, however, one natural division of labor is to assign cases with more outstanding medical issues to staff with strong medical backgrounds, and cases which are ready for vocational services to staff with strong vocational backgrounds. For some companies, this has translated into having rehabilitation nurses and rehabilitation counselors as case managers, respectively. Because most companies are primarily focused on the delivery of vocational services, some also hire specialists such as vocational evaluators and job developers to respectively assist their rehabilitation case managers in assessment and placement functions.

While degrees and work experiences are important in determining how assignments (specific job duties or cases) should be divided among professional staff, staff qualifications are critical in establishing the credibility of the company as a legitimate rehabilitation service provider. Without appropriately credentialed staff, a so-called rehabilitation company may be little more than an employment agency. Employment agencies make their profit through a volume business serving the most marketable of job seekers, and their employment counselors are not characteristically qualified to address the multifaceted medical and vocational issues which impact handicapped clients. Increasingly, workers' compensation agencies, insurance companies, and attorneys are insisting on service delivery by "qualified" professionals. Although a bachelors degree in health support services or an R.N. license are minimum qualifications today, in the future, professional credibility will most likely require certification through the Bureau for Rehabilitation Certification as either a rehabilitation counselor or insurance rehabilitation specialist.

As part of the process of hiring professional staff, a rehabilitation company must determine at what level and through what method to compensate them. In relation to level of compensation, starting salaries for experienced and unexperienced rehabilitationists vary on a state and company basis. Deneen and Hessellund (1981) estimated starting salaries for master's level unexperienced rehabilitationists at between $1,100 and $1,400 per month. In Florida, the author personally knows a number of experienced caseload carrying rehabilitationists earning salaries above $20,000 per year. Salaries above $25,000 per year (in Florida and at the time of this writing) are more commonly paid to supervisors and administrators. Again, salaries vary widely on a state and company basis.

Most private sector rehabilitationists are hired on either a full- or part-time basis, and are subsequently paid at a flat hourly rate for a set number of hours, regardless of how many hours (more or less) they actually put in. Staff are normally hired on a full-time basis. Part-time employment is utilized when a caseload is small, and this occurs most frequently in companies that have recently opened or are expanding into some new geographic area. Part-time positions usually become full-time when and if the caseload grows.

Although most companies pay a flat hourly rate for full- or part-time employment, some companies reimburse professional staff on a fee-splitting basis. In this model, the rehabilitationist's compensation is a percentage of each billed hour. For example, if the company bills at a rate of $45 per hour, and the rehabilitationist's contract calls for payment at a rate of one-third for each billed hour, then if the rehabilitationist bills 35 hours in a given week, gross earnings for that week would be $525 ($15 times 35 hours). The other two-thirds of each billed hour cover the business operating expenses and provide a profit for the company.

Deneen and Hessellund (1981) pointed out that when professional staff are reimbursed on a fee-splitting basis they can work longer hours if they want higher earnings, and are more likely to be available to their clients at odd hours of the day or night. They also noted that entry level percentages generally range from 25% to 33⅔% of billable hours, and that 40% is about the maximum that a company with three to ten employees can afford to pay. When all things are considered, for the fee-splitting model to work well for a rehabilitationist, he or she must have excellent time management skills and an adequate number of active cases. It is very easy to lose billable hours through casual socializing with co-workers, excessive time on reports, sessions with supervisors, and the like (Deneen and Hessellund, 1981). Other problems with the fee-splitting model are that income is variable and therefore less predictable, and some professionals may develop workaholic behaviors that undermine mental and/or physical health, and ultimately the quality of their services.

Another staffing issue which deserves mention is the noncompetition agreement which many companies require professional staff to sign. A noncompetition agreement specifies a length of time (usually at least a year) and/or geographical area (usually at least 100 miles) where the rehabilitationist will not compete with their immediate past employer (Tenth Institute on Rehabilitation Issues, 1983). The rationale for such an agreement is to prevent a rehabilitationist from learning all about the employer's private sector rehabilitation business while an employee, developing referral contacts (i.e., claims representatives), and then using that knowledge and those business contacts to set-up a business that would directly compete with the employer's. Although noncompetition agreements are hard to subsequently enforce, they are very common. Today they protect not so much the employer's private sector knowledge and business practices (because the private sector is not the "secrete" it was five years ago), but rather encroachment upon referral sources which the employer has developed.

Marketing

Marketing has been defined by the American Marketing Association (1960) as "the set of activities by which the demand structre for goods, ideas, and services is managed in order to facilitate the exchange process satisfactorily" (p. 15). Activities that fall within this domain include: (a) market research, (b) product or service development and modification, (c) pricing, (d) arranging and managing the distribution of products and services, (e) advertising and promotion, and (f) personal selling and following-up on customer satisfaction (Cunningham and Cunningham, 1981; Kinnear and Bernhardt, 1983). In private sector rehabilitation, marketing activities primarily center around research and personal selling.

In relation to market research, a rehabilitation company must determine the demand for rehabilitation services within the geographical area(s) it is considering entering. Demand is largely a function of the state workers' compensation law. If, for example, the state law mandates vocational rehabilitation services, there will be considerable demand. If the state law is supportive of those services, there will be some demand, but less than under mandatory laws. Even in states where the workers' compensation law does not create a significant demand for rehabilitation services, there may be some demand created by federally administered workers' compensation programs and other personal injury lines of insurance. Because most private sector cases stem from industrial injuries, a careful review of the state's workers' compensation law, and any new statutory modifications or court interpretations, is an indispensible aspect of market research.

When studying workers' compensation laws and other insurance contracts, it is important to determine the specific liability of carriers. To be successful, a service must address the needs of those who will purchase it, and this cannot be done unless those needs are fully understood. In explaining the early success of Vocation Placement Services where so many other companies had failed, Manny Gambosh stated:

> The key was that I knew I had to have more knowledge of the insurance benefit system. And so I made it my business to learn what the insurance companies' responsibilities are to the injured person so I could tailor what I did to meet the needs of the claimant and the insurance company (Who's Who in Rehabilitation, 1982, p. 5).

This is only possible through effective market research. A rehabilitation company must understand the needs of its potential customers if it is to develop and offer services they will buy.

Identifying potential referral sources and competitors is also part of the process of assessing demand. Market research must identify potential referral sources as fully as possible since these will later be targeted for advertising and personal selling efforts. The services offered by competitors should be studied to whatever extent is ethically possible, and the prices of their different services should be identified. A market can be large, but saturated with service providers, and if a new company is going to enter such an area and compete effectively, its services must be as good or better than those of its competitors and reasonably priced. Surveying potential referral sources by mail, telephone, or through personal contact is how most market research is conducted.

Most private sector rehabilitation companies advertise their services in one way or another. Although some have used television and radio commercials (Tenth Institute on Rehabilitation Issues, 1983) for most advertising takes the form of bulk rate mailings of information packets, referral forms, brochures, letters with attached business cards, and the like. Advertising is a good way of getting the firm's name, address, and telephone number into the hands of potential referral sources, but in and of itself it generates few referrals. This is because private sector rehabilitation is a very "person centered" business, and claims representatives and managers usually want to know who they are dealing with. This can only be ascertained through personal contacts.

Initial referrals from carriers and employers are usually obtained from personal selling (i.e., sales oriented contacts on a one to one or small group basis). Large private sector rehabilitation companies have full-time personnel who promote the company and solicit referrals on a local, state, regional, and even national basis. In other companies, generating new business and keeping all companies satisfied is usually the responsibility of district or office managers, and in some an adjunct role for caseload carrying rehabilitationists as well.

Soliciting new business is a "sales" activity. It involves contacting potential referral sources, arranging appointments, and making presentations on how the company's services can address needs experienced by the buyer. Presentations may be formal (e.g., given to groups) or informal (e.g., over lunch). They may be very sales oriented or more social and informational. Formal presentations may include the use of professionally prepared media aids such as charts, graphs, films, audio-visual tapes, and the like.

According to Wilmshurst (1978), there are two qualities that are essential in a good salesperson. The first is empathy – or an ability to feel and see the world as the customer does, and the second is ego drive – or a strong personal need (not simply a monetary incentive) to make a sale. In addition to these personal qualities, an effective salesperson must have a sound knowledge of the company and its products or services, technical knowledge to converse in the buyer's field, procedural knowledge as to how orders (referrals) are taken and processed, and professional knowledge about the job of selling (Wilmshurst, 1978). Because of the "technical"nature of the rehabilitation and insurance industries, most companies utilize an experienced rehabilitationist for personal selling rather than outside persons with extensive sales experience. Although knowing how to prepare for, approach, and close a sale is critical, knowledge and experience in rehabilitation is also important.

Although initial referrals from carriers and employers are usually generated through personal selling, subsequent referrals are generated by satisfaction with the company's earlier casework. Deneen and Hessellund (1981) noted that positive "street-talk" (i.e., informal communications between claims personnel and attorneys) is the best marketing a company can have. If a claims representative refers a case and is satisfied with the quality and effectiveness of the rehabilitation casework, he or she will be naturally inclined to refer again. In the final analysis, good casework is the cornerstone of private sector marketing.

Billing Systems

Private sector service providers receive no funding from any source other than their own work. For this reason, it is of critical importance that they keep track of all the work they perform, and bill for their services in an accurate and timely manner. Private providers must also monitor their accounts receivable to insure that payments are in fact received for services rendered. Delinquent accounts must be identified and subsequently contacted for payment.

In some states, private sector bills for workers' compensation rehabilitation services are paid directly by the employer or carrier. In other states they are paid by the workers' compensation agency from a rehabilitation fund. In nonindustrial injury cases, the bill is always sent to the insurance company which contracted for the rehabilitation services. Rarely does a client or family directly pay for rehabilitation services.

Most private sector rehabilitation companies use distinct service codes to communicate to the carrier or agency what rehabilitation services were actually provided. They also bill for these separate services in fractions of working hours. It is not enough, for example, to submit a bill which states, "Five and one-half hours from May 1st through May 7th for rehabilitation case management services with Mr. John Doe." The payee will normally want to know what services were provided each day and how much time each service required.

In most states, there are no mandatory codes for reporting workers' compensation rehabilitation services, this being left to the discretion of each company (Deneen and Hesselund, 1981). Accordingly, service codes vary between different rehabilitation companies. Illustration 9-1 shows service codes which could be used by a rehabilitation company. For each case, these different services would be billed in hourly fractions at some set hourly rate. For example, if the hourly rate for professional time was $50 per hour and for Mr. John Doe the rehabilitationist conducted a one hour initial evaluation interview, two hour job analysis, and spent two and one-half hours on labor market surveying in his behalf; the total charge would be $275 (5.5 hours at $50/hour). Some companies bill for what they consider to be "nonprofessional time" (e.g., time spent driving, waiting in a doctor's office) at a lower hourly rate. Billable hours are normally broken into one-tenth (.1) hour units, meaning that evey six minutes of service are accounted for.

Illustration 9-1

EXAMPLE OF BILLING CODES

01	Case file review
02	Medical record review
03	Vocational evaluation report review
04	Correspondence review
05	Client evaluation interview
06	Client contact
07	Carrier contact
08	Workers' compensation agency contact
09	Attorney contact
10	Physician contact
11	Employer contact
12	Other case related contact
13	Rehabilitation plan development
14	Rehabilitation report
15	Progress note
16	Conference preparation
17	Rehabilitation conference
18	Job seeking skills training
19	Resume preparation
20	Vocational testing
21	Test interpretation
22	Vocational guidance and counseling
23	Job readiness counseling
24	Medical research
25	Travel and waiting time
26	Correspondence
27	Job analysis

28	Job modification
29	Job development
30	Labor market survey
31	Placement consultation
32	Placement follow-up
33	Preparation for testimony
34	Testimony

In order for any billing system to work, the rehabilitationist must record, on a daily basis, exactly what services were provided for each case, and how much time each service required. These daily records are then compiled at the end of the week and turned into the company, which subsequently bills for the recorded services. Although precise record keeping is difficult, it is nevertheless the foundation of the private sector billing system. Effective time management is the key to accurate record keeping, staying on task, and avoiding substantial periods of nonbillable time.

Accountability

All government run human service programs have a legislated mandate to accomplish some mission(s), and a budget allocation to do so. Because the mission is in the public good, government supports it with tax dollars. Those charged with accomplishing the mission and given stewardship of tax monies are required to account for their actions, showing that funds were appropriately and legally spent, and that the mission has or is being accomplished. In almost all cases, governments require that the effectiveness and efficiency of their human service programs be studied and improved through program evaluation.

Matkin (1981) noted that legislative statues have mandated that program evaluation is to be the principal mechanism by which the state – federal rehabilitation program and nonprofit rehabilitation sector account for the efficacy of their services. Because of this, in the public sector, accountability and program evaluation are virtually synonymous. This is not true in the private sector, because workers' compensation statues and administrative rules do not require rehabilitation companies to study and report on the effectiveness of their services. The workers' compensation agency (usually through its rehabilitation bureau) studies the overall economic and reemployment impact of rehabilitation services, and although this data may be used to modify the program as a whole, it does not address the adequacies, or inadequacies, of specific service providers.

Because there is no legislated mandate requiring company specific program evaluation studies, companies can choose to ignore program evaluation issues. Many do so because they see themselves as primarily accountable to their referral sources. Employers and carriers do not characteristically ask private rehabilitation companies to present program evaluation data as a prerequisite to case referral, but instead refer to those they perceive as effective in resolving vocational issues and ignore those they perceive as ineffective. Hence, there has been no economic rationale for private rehabilitation companies to undertake program evaluation studies.

If the private sector is not required to engage in program evaluation, then how is accountability addressed? First and foremost, there is the profit incentive and competition of the free enterprise system. Employers and insurance companies expect the resolution of outstanding vocational issues, and they will not continue to refer cases to companies that consistently fail to return clients to work (Scher, 1979). Poor and marginally effective service providers go out of business, and effective service providers expand because of an increasing demand for their services. This type of "marketplace" accountability is not experienced at all by government supported human service programs, but it is the essence of accountability for "business" activities.

The presence of so many outside observers also contributes to accountability in private sector rehabilitation. For example, in industrial injury cases, the carrier and workers' compensation agency normally both oversee rehabilitation services, reviewing and approving individual plans. Moreover, if the claimant has an attorney, this individual specifically seeks to protect his or her rights. In government run human services, there are usually no outside observers, only agency personnel and clients.

The adoption and enforcement of minimum practitioner standards by workers' compensation agencies also contributes to accountability in private sector rehabilitation services (see Couch, 1979; Matkin, 1984; Nadolsky, 1979). In the future, the CIRS and CRC certification processes may come to be the only recognized credentials for private sector rehabilitationists. Enforced professional codes of ethics, such as the code adopted by NARPPS, also contribute to private sector accountability.

Future Trends

The private rehabilitation sector should continue to expand, at a more moderate pace, for at least the next several years. The field will be more closely regulated by state workers' compensation agencies, and accountability (in one form or another) will become increasingly important. Because workers' compensation is very much a state political arena where powerful economic forces vie for influence (e.g., large employers, business associations, unions, trial attorneys, insurance companies) the stability of rehabilitation provisions in any state law can never be taken for granted. The "business" of rehabilitation will need to demonstrate, on a continuing basis, that it successfully returns industrially injured workers to the work force, and in so doing helps hold down the cost of workers' compensation within the state.

Although workers' compensation is a state affair, to no small extent, the future of the state managed system will be influenced by the overall performance of vocational rehabilitation services. If greater numbers of industrially disabled workers can be successfully returned to work, then it will be economically feasible to provide increased benefits for those who cannot. As a whole, the states are still far from actualizing the 19 "essential" and other recommendations of the National Commission. Although the threat of federalization has diminished because of the state rush toward reform, it could again return. The federal government already administers workers' compensation and other disability programs, and given the right political climate, Congress could some day federalize the system.

Although state workers' compensation programs will probably always account for the majority of private sector referrals, in the future, other major referral sources could develop. For example, the Social Security Administration may some day primarily utilize the private sector for rehabilitation services. They already rely on private practitioners for vocational expert opinions. It is also possible that the public sector may some day purchase job placement and even case management services from the private sector, focusing its efforts on case finding, eligibility determination, and quality assurance.

From an organizational perspective, the future trend should be toward larger insurance affiliated, nonaffiliated, and in-house corporate rehabilitation programs (Ashton, 1979); and away from small proprietorships and partnerships. This does not mean, however, that entrepreneurs will not establish new and successful private sector practices. The rehabilitation business is a very "person centered" activity, and many claims representatives prefer to deal with smaller firms where they know the rehabilitationist and receive more personalized service. The successful future entrepreneur, however, will probably need to obtain work experience with an established company before working independently. The time when rehabilitationists could learn the insurance rehabilitation system as they worked cases is definitely over.

Larger rehabilitation companies will also provide a foundation for expansion into other human service areas. In the future, it is likely that the larger rehabilitation companies will offer multiple services, some of which may be quite different from rehabilitation case management. For example, Reagles (1983) described Pelion, Inc. (pronounced "Pee-lee-on") a multiprogram private sector company which offers a prescription drug misuse program, chronic pain rehabilitation program, evaluation and assessment program, community health education program, employee assistance and wellness services, and readjustment counseling for Vietnam-era veterans. Other service areas that rehabilitation companies may expand into include affirmative action consultation, outplacement counseling for displaced workers, preemployment testing, consultation to rehabilitation facilities, and general employment agency services (see Garvin, 1983; McMahon, Matkin, Growick, Mahaffey and Gianforte, 1983). Of all the areas mentioned, it appears that employee assistance and wellness programming will offer the greatest potential for private sector expansion (see Dickman and Emener, 1982; Dickman, Emener and Hutchison, 1984).

All indicators suggest that private sector rehabilitation will be around for quite some time to come. The field of rehabilitation will be characterized, like never before, by the existance of two parallel rehabilitation systems — one for individuals who have some sort of insurance coverage and another for those who do not. The different nature of the clientele and service issues differentiating the two sectors will need to be increasingly addressed in preservice rehabilitation education programs. What the future holds in terms of cooperation, competition, or eventual ascendance of one sector over the other cannot be predicted. We will just have to wait and see.

References

American Marketing Association, Committee on Definitions, *Marketing Definitions: A Glossary of Marketing Terms.* Chicago, 1960.

Ashton, P.C.: Rehabilitation in a major corporate setting. *Journal of Rehabilitation*, 1979, *45*:26-29.

Couch, R.H.: Keeping score and looking good: The dilemma of certification in the private rehabilitation sector. *Journal of Rehabilitation,* 1979, *45*:62-64.

Cunningham, W.H. and Cunningham, I.: *Marketing: A Managerial Approach.* Cincinnati: South-Wester Publishing Co., 1981.

Deneen, L.J. and Hessellund, T.A.: *Vocational Rehabilitation of the Injured Worker,* San Francisco: Rehab Publications, 1981.

Dickman, J.F. and Emener, W.G.: Employee assistance programs: An emerging vista for rehabilitation counselors. *Journal of Applied Rehabilitation Counseling,* 1982, *13*:18-20, 24.

Dickman, J.F., Emener, W.G. and Hutchison, W.S. (Eds.): *Counseling the Troubled Person in Industry.* Springfield, Il.: Charles C Thomas, 1984.

Garvin, R.E.: Industrial relations: A service-oriented approach to job development. *Journal of Applied Rehabilitation Counseling,* 1983, *14*:44-46, 50.

Gutowski, M., Harder, P. and Koshel, O.: *Forecasting Manpower Needs in the Rehabilitation Industry.* The Urban Institute, Washington, D.C., December, 1980.

Hastings, P.G.: *Introduction to Business.* New York: McGraw-Hill Book Company, 1968.

Keith, L.A. and Gubellini, C.E.: *Introduction to Business Enterprise.* New York: McGraw-Hill Book Company, 1967.

Kinnear, T.C. and Bernhardt, K.L.: *Principles of Marketing.* Glenview, Il.: Scott, Foresman and Company, 1983.

Matkin, R.E.: Credentialing insurance rehabilitation specialists. *Rehabilitation Forum,* 1984, *11(1)*:12-17.

Matkin, R.E.: Program evaluation: Searching for accountability in private rehabilitation. *Journal of Rehabilitation,* 1981, *47*:65-68.

McMahon, B.T., Matkin, R.E., Growick, B., Maheffey, D. and Gianforte, G.: Recent trends in private sector rehabilitation. *Rehabilitation Counseling Bulletin,* 1983, *27*:32-47.

Nadolsky, J.M.: Profit and certification in vocational rehabilitation programs. *Journal of Rehabilitation,* 1979, *45*:65-70.

Newcomer, H.A.: *Private Business Enterprise.* Columbus: Charles E. Merrill Publishing Company, 1974.

Preston, P. and Zimmerer, T.: *Business: An Introduction to American Enterprise.* Englewood Cliffs: Prentice-Hall, 1976.

Reagles, K.W.: Rehabilitation in a multiprogram private sector company. *Rehabilitation Counseling Bulletin,* 1983, *27*:48-53.

Scher, P.L.: NARPPS – Key to the survival of rehabilitation in the 1980's *Journal of Rehabilitation,* 1979, *45*:50-51, 74.

Shilt, B.A., Carmichael, D.L. and Wilson, W.H.: *Business Principles and Management.* Cincinnati: South-Western Publishing Company, 1967.

Smith, H.R. and Sawisch, L.P.: Injured worker rehabilitation in Michigan: Two decades of maturation. *Rehabilitation Counseling Bulletin,* 1983, *27*:5-11.

Tenth Institute on Rehabilitation Issues. *Proprietary Rehabilitation: A Better Understanding.* Research and Training Center, University of Wisconsin-Stont, Menomonie, Wisconsin, June, 1983.

Who's Who in Rehabilitation. *Rehabilitation Reports,* Vol. 2, No. 1, Adelphi, Maryland, 1982.

Wilmshurst, J.: *The Fundamentals and Practice of Marketing.* Bath: Pitman Press, 1978.

Workman, E.L.: Vocational rehabilitation in the private, profit-making sector. In E.L. Pan, T.E. Backer and C.L. Vash (Eds.) *Annual Review of Rehabilitation* (Volume 3). New York: Springer Publishing Company, 1983.

APPENDICES

Appendix I

WORKERS' COMPENSATION AGENCIES

APPENDIX I

WORKERS' COMPENSATION AGENCIES

STATE AGENCIES

Alabama
Workmen's Compensation Division
Department of Industrial Relations
Industrial Relations Building
Montgomery, Alabama 36130

Alaska
Workmen's Compensation Division
Department of Labor
P.O. Box 1149
Juneau, Alaska 99811

Arizona
Industrial Commission
1601 West Jefferson
P.O. Box 19070
Phoenix, Arizona 85005

Arkansas
Workers' Compensation Commission
Justice Building
State Capital Grounds
Little Rock, Arkansas 72201

California
Division of Industrial Accidents
P.O. Box 603, Room 617
San Francisco, California 94101

Colorado
Division of Labor
1313 Sherman Street, Room 314
Denver, Colorado 80203

Connecticut
Workers' Compensation Commission
295 Treadwell Street
Hamden, Connecticut 06514

Delaware
Industrial Accident Board
State Office Building, 6th Floor
820 North French Street
Wilmington, Deleware 19801

Florida
Division of Workers' Compensation
Department of Labor and Employment Security
1321 Executive Center Drive-East
Tallahassee, Florida 32301

Georgia
Board of Workers' Compensation
1800 Peachtree Street, N.W.
Suite 400
Atlanta, Georgia 30309

Hawaii
Disability Compensation Division
Department of Labor and Industrial Relations
825 Mililani Street
Honolulu, Hawaii 96813

Idaho
Industrial Commission
317 Main Street
Boise, Idaho 83720

Illinois
Industrial Commission
160 North LaSalle Street
Chicago, Illinois 60601

Indiana
Industrial Board
601 State Office Building
100 North Senate Avenue
Indianapolis, Indiana 46204

Iowa
Industrial Commissioner's Office
507 10th Street
Des Moines, Iowa 50319

Kansas
Division of Workers' Compensation
Department of Human Resources
6th Floor
535 Kansas Avenue
Topeka, Kansas 66603

Kentucky
Workers' Compensation Board
127 Building
U.S. 127 South
Frankfort, Kentucky 40601

Louisiana
Department of Labor
1045 State Land and Natural
Resources Building
Box 44094
Baton Rouge, Louisiana 70804

Maine
Workers' Compensation Commission
State Office Building
Augusta, Maine 04333

Maryland
Workmen's Compensation Commission
108 East Lexington Street
Baltimore, Maryland 21202

Massachusetts
Industrial Accidents Board
Leverett Saltonstall Office Building
100 Cambridge Street
Boston, Massachusetts 02202

Michigan
Bureau of Workers' Disability Compensation
Department of Labor
309 North Washington Square
Lansing, Michigan 48909

Minnesota
Workers' Compensation Division
Department of Labor and Industry
444 Lafayette Road
St. Paul, Minnesota 55101

Mississippi
Workmen's Compensation Commission
1404 Walter Sillers State Office Building
P.O. Box 987
Jackson, Mississippi 39205

Montana
Division of Workers' Compensation
815 Front Street
Helena, Montana 59601

Nebraska
Workmen's Compensation Court
State House, 12th Floor
Lincoln, Nebraska 68509

Nevada
Industrial Commission
515 East Musser Street
Carson City, Nevada 89714

New Hampshire
Department of Labor
19 Pillsbury Street
Concord, New Hampshire 03301

New Jersey
Division of Workers' Compensation
Department of Labor and Industry
P.O. Box CN 381
John Fitch Plaza
Trenton, New Jersey 08625

New Mexico
Labor and Industrial Commission
509 Camino De Los Marquez
Suite 2
Santa Fe, New Mexico 87501

New York
Workers' Compensation Board
Two World Trade Center
New York, New York 10047

North Carolina
Industrial Commission
Dobbs Building
430 North Salisbury Street
Raleigh, North Carolina 27611

North Dakota
Workmen's Compensation Bureau
Russell Building
Highway 83 North
Bismarck, North Dakota 58505

Ohio
Bureau of Workers' Compensation
246 North High Street
Columbus, Ohio 43215

Oklahoma
Oklahoma Workers' Compensation Court
Jim Thorpe Building
2101 North Lincoln
Oklahoma City, Oklahoma 73105

Oregon
Workers' Compensation Department
Labor and Industries Building
Salem, Oregon 97310

Pennsylvania
Bureau of Workers' Compensation
Department of Labor and Industry
3607 Derry Street
Harrisburg, Pennsylvania 17111

Rhode Island
Workers' Compensation Commission
25 Canal Street
Providence, Rhode Island 02903

South Carolina
Industrial Commission
Middleburg Office Park
1800 St. Julian Place
Columbia, South Carolina 29202

South Dakota
Division of Labor and Management
Department of Labor
Kneip Building, Second Floor
Pierre, South Dakota 57501

Tennessee
Workers' Compensation Division
Department of Labor
501 Union Building
Nashville, Tennessee 37219

Texas
  Industrial Accident Board
  200 East Riverside, First Floor
  Austin, Texas 78704

Utah
  Industrial Commission
  350 East 500 South
  Salt Lake City, Utah 84111

Vermont
  Department of Labor and Industry
  Montpelier, Vermont 05602

Virginia
  Industrial Commission
  Blanton Building
  P.O. Box 1794
  Richmond, Virginia

Washington
  Department of Labor and Industries
  General Administration Building
  AX-31
  Olympia, Washington 98504

West Virginia
  Workmen's Compensation Commissioner's Office
  P.O. Box 3151
  Charleston, West Virginia 25332

Wisconsin
  Workers' Compensation Division
  Department of Industry, Labor, and Human Relations
  P.O. Box 7901
  201 East Washington Avenue
  Madison, Wisconsin 53707

Wyoming
  Workers' Compensation Division
  State Treasurer's Office
  2305 Carey Avenue
  Cheyenne, Wyoming 82002

District of Columbia
  Government of the District of Columbia
  Office of Workers' Compensation
  950 Upshur Street, N.W.
  Washington, D.C. 20011

Puerto Rico
Industrial Commissioner's Office
G.P.O. Box 4466
San Juan, Puerto Rico 00936

FEDERAL PROGRAMS

For federal workers' compensation programs (i.e., Coal Mine Workers' Compensation, Federal Employees Compensation, and Longshore and Harbor Workers' Compensation) write:

Office of Workers' Compensation Programs
Department of Labor
Employment Standards Administration
Washington, D.C. 20210

CANADIAN PROVINCES AND TERRITORIES

Alberta
Workers' Compensation Board
P.O. Box 2415
9912 107th Street
Edmonton, Alberta T5J 2S5

British Columbia
Workers' Compensation Board
5255 Heather Street
Vancouver, British Columbia V5Z 3L8

Manitoba
Workers' Compensation Board
333 Maryland Street
Winnipeg, Manitoba R3G 1M2

New Brunswick
Workers' Compensation Board
P.O. Box 160
Saint John, New Brunswick E2L 3X9

Newfoundland
Workers' Compensation Board
P.O. Box 9000
Station B
St. John's, Newfoundland A1A 3B8

Northwest Territories
Workers' Compensation Board
P.O. Box 8888
Yellowknife, Northwest Territories X1A 2R3

Nova Scotia
Workers' Compensation Board
5668 South Street
P.O. Box 1150
Halifax, Nova Scotia B3J 2Y2

Ontario
Workmen's Compensation Board
2 Bloor Street East
Toronto, Ontario M4W 3C3

Prince Edward Island
Workers' Compensation Board
60 Belvedere Avenue
P.O. Box 757
Charlottetown, Prince Edward Island C1A 7L7

Quebec
Commission de la Sante et de la
Securite du Travail
524 Bourdages Street
Quebec, Quebec G1K 7E2

Saskatchewan
Workers' Compensation Board
1840 Lorne Street
Regina, Saskatchewan S4P 2L8

Yukon
Workers' Compensation Board
4110 4th Avenue
Suite 300
Whitehorse, Yukon Y1A 4N7

FEDERAL PROGRAMS OF CANADA

Labour Canada
Occupational Safety and Health Branch
Injury Compensation Division
Ottawa, Ontario K1A 0J3

Merchant Seamen Compensation Board
Labour Canada
Ottawa, Ontario K1A OJ2

Appendix II

NARPPS STANDARDS AND ETHICS

Reprinted by permission of the National Association of Rehabilitation Professionals in the Private Sector (NARPPS), 1133 Fifteenth Street, N.W., Washington, D.C. 20005

STANDARDS AND ETHICS

Preamble

NARPPS members recognize the uniqueness of the private rehabilitation field. The conduct of members of a professional organization must be ethical at all times. NARPPS recognizes the free enterprise system and believes that fair competition encourages the development of quality services to both the client and the referral source.

Professional Conduct by Discipline

The member is obligated to maintain technical competency at such a level that the recipient receives the highest quality of services that the member's discipline is capable of offering. The implementation of a rehabilitation plan for a client is a multidisciplinary effort. NARPPS members will conduct themselves in interdisciplinary relationship in such a way as to facilitate the contribution of all specialists involved for maximum benefit of the recipient of services and to bring credit to each discipline.

Minimal Standards for Service Delivery

Standards shall apply to those persons who are providing the services.

The services and submission of reports shall be provided in a timely fashion and shall respond to the purpose of the referral and include recommendations, if appropriate. All reports shall reflect an objective, independent opinion based on factual determinations within the provider's area of expertise and discipline. The reports of services and findings shall be distributed to appropriate parties and in compliance with all applicable legal regulations.

The member shall render only those services that the member is competent and qualified to perform.

The member has an obligation to withdraw from a professional relationship if it is believed that the participation will result in violation of the ethical standards of his/her professional discipline.

There shall be a stated rationale for the provision of services to be rendered to the client in the form of an identified objective or purpose.

The member shall refuse to participate in practices which are inconsistent with the standards established by regulatory bodies regarding the delivery of services to clients.

Members will adhere to all tenets of confidentiality.

At the time of initial referral, the member has the responsibility for identifying to the referral source and to the client what services are to be provided and practices to be conducted. This shall include the identification, as well as the clarification, of services that are available by that member.

Professional Education, Training and Experience

NARPPS supports the principle of accreditation of member rehabilitation companies on a voluntary basis.

NARPPS considers the following standards to be the minimum requirements for a Rehabilitation Practitioner:

A. Professional Rehabilitation Practitioner

1. Holder of a Masters or Doctorate degree in health-support services from an accrdited institution, plus one year of experience in vocational rehabilitation or physical rehabilitation. At least one year shall have been spent in the rehabilitation of disabling conditions and/or diseases; or
2. Holder of a Baccalaureate degree in health-support services from an accredited institution, plus two years of experience in vocational rehabilitation or physical rehabilitation. At least one year shall have been spent in the rehabilitation of disabling conditions and/or diseases; or
3. Diploma in Nursing from an accredited institution, plus a current R.N. license, plus three years of experience in physical rehabilitation or vocational rehabilitation. At least one year shall have been spent in the rehabilitation of disabling conditions and/or diseases; or
4. Holder of any Baccalaureate degree other than listed in No. 2 above from an accredited institution, plus three years of experience in vocational rehabilitation. At least two years shall have been spent in the rehabilitation of disabling conditions and/or diseases.

B. Associate Rehabilitation Practitioner

Holder of an Associate degree or high school diploma, plus continuing education and five years experience in vocational rehabilitation, including counseling, evaluation and direct case services. Three of the five years shall have been spent in the rehabilitation of disabling conditions and/or diseases.

C. Rehabilitation Intern

An individual who meets the minimum education requirements but does not meet the experiential requirements must be supervised by a professional rehabilitation practitioner. The intern shall provide the name of the professional rehabilitation practitioner under whose direct supervision he/she will work. The supervisor will function as the primary case manager.

Advocacy

Advocacy is a term used when referring to the act of pleading the cause or coming to the aid of another. NARPPS members respect the integrity and interest of the people and groups with whom they work. With regard to disabled persons, advocacy takes into account such issues as the legal rights of handicapped people to achieve integration into the social, cultural and economic life of the general community. The role of the NARPPS member as an advocate is to protect and promote the welfare of disabled persons to maximize control over circumstances that interfere with their obtaining vocational independence. When there is a conflict of interest between the disabled client and the NARPPS member's employing party, the member must clarify the nature and direction of his/her loyalty and responsibilities and keep all parties informed of that commitment. NARPPS supports legislation that provides for services and care to the disabled.

Testimony

NARPPS recognizes that a rehabilitation practitioner has a responsibility, when requested, to provide objective testimony.

Rehabilitation Practitioners provide services within the legal system and, in addition to providing primary care rehabilitation services, are called upon to testify as to facts of which they have knowledge or to render a professional opinion on rehabilitation questions or disability factors affecting an individual.

The testimony of a rehabilitation practitioner should be limited to the specific fields of expertise of that individual as demonstrated by training, education and experience. The extent of the practitioner's training, education and experience needed to testify is determined by the legal jurisdiction in which the practitioner is testifying.

It is also permissible for a rehabilitation practitioner to render an expert opinion and answer questions about a disabled or handicapped individual that has been evaluated either in person or hypothetically.

Confidentiality

The purpose of confidentiality is to safeguard information that is obtained in the course of practice. Disclosures of information are restricted to what is necessary, relevant and verifiable with respect to the client's right to privacy. When a third party is involved, the key to confidentiality, when considering personal or confidential information, is to make certain that the client is aware, from the outset, that the delivery of services is being observed by the third party. Professional files, reports and records shall be maintained under conditions of security and provision will be made for their destruction when appropriate.

Business Practices

Individuals and/or organizations in private sector rehabilitation should adhere to all applicable standards and practices common to the general business community. In addition, they should give special attention to and adhere to the following specific points:

1. Members will adhere to all applicable federal, state and local laws establishing and regulating business practices.
2. Members will not misrepresent themselves, their duties or credentials.
3. Members should carry professional liability insurance for the protection of themselves and affected third parties.
4. Rehabilitation Practitioners shall not engage in claims practices as such are defined under the statues and legal precedents in their respective jurisdictions.
5. It is to be encouraged that any discussion and comments or criticism directed toward a fellow Rehabilitation Practitioner or organization shall be positive and/or constructive.
6. Competitive advertising should be factually accurate and shall avoid exaggerated claims as to costs and results.
7. When asked to comment on cases being actively managed by another Rehabilitation Practitioner and/or organization, the reviewer shall make every reasonable effort to conduct an in-person evaluation before rendering his conclusion.
8. A Rehabilitation Practitioner member will not promise or offer services or results he cannot deliver or has reason to believe he cannot provide.
9. A member is not to solicit referrals either directly or indirectly by offering money or gifts other than *de minimis* gifts to a referral source.
10. When recruiting an employee, members should not falsely promise benefits, employment advancement or salaries which they know or have reason to know that they cannot meet.
11. No Rehabilitation Practitioner or organization shall effectuate or participate in the wrongful removal of professional rehabilitation files or other materials upon the initiation of new employment.
12. Rehabilitation Practioners shall not enter into fee arrangements that would be likely to create conflicts of interest or influence their testimony in claims cases. Rehabilitation Practitioners shall advise the referral source/payor of its fee structure in advance of the rendering of any services and shall also furnish, upon request, detailed accurate time records.
13. Member referral sources working for member organizations or individuals shall pay invoices in accordance with normal payment practices.

Standards Compliance Review Board

The function of the Standards Compliance Review Board will be to investigate and rule on alleged infraction of the approved standards and ethics of NARPPS members. The Standards Compliance Review Board will consist of the following:

a. Rehabilitation Counselor
b. Rehabilitation Nurse
c. Vocational Evaluator
d. Placement Specialist
e. Insurance Claimsperson or buyer
f. Private Practitioner (general)
g. Company Administrator

Adopted November 1981.

Appendix III

WORKERS' COMPENSATION PROVISIONS

CHART VI INCOME BENEFITS FOR TOTAL DISABILITY January 1, 1984

JURISDICTION	PERCENT OF WAGES	MAXIMUM WEEKLY PAYMENT		MINIMUM WEEKLY PAYMENT		TIME LIMIT	AMOUNT LIMIT[2]	AUTOMATIC COST OF LIVING INCREASE	OFFSETS[3]	NOTATIONS
		AMOUNT	RATE	AMOUNT	RATE					
ALABAMA	66-2/3	$ 184.00	66-2/3% SAWW	$69.00[1]	25% SAWW[1]	TT—300 weeks PT—Disability	TT—*$55,200*			Annual increase in maximum effective July 1.*
ALASKA	80% of spendable earnings	1,080.00	200% SAWW	110.00*		Disability			Social Security, unemployment compensation	Annual increase in maximum effective January 1.
AMERICAN SAMOA	66-2/3					Disability				Compensation increased 10% if installment without award unpaid after 14 days, 20% if installment following award unpaid after 10 days.
ARIZONA	66-2/3	203.86				TT—Disability PT—Life				Benefits payable monthly. Additional $10 monthly if 1 or more total dependents, not subject to maximum.
ARKANSAS	66-2/3	154.00*		15.00		TT—450 weeks PT—Disability	TT—69,300*		Unemployment compensation	15% penalty for employer's violation of safety laws, payable to Second Injury Fund.**
CALIFORNIA	66-2/3	224.00*		112.00		TT—Disability PT—Life		TT—after 2 years		50% increased compensation if injury due to employer's serious, willful misconduct.
COLORADO	66-2/3	296.80	80% SAWW			TT—Disability PT—Life			Social Security	Annual increase in maximum effective July 1. Compensation increased 50% if employer failed to comply with insurance provisions. Compensation decreased 50% if injury results from worker's failure to obey safety regulations or from intoxication.
CONNECTICUT	66-2/3	345.00 to 517.50	100% SAWW	69.00*	20% SAWW	Disability		October 1		Annual increase in maximum effective October 1. Additional $10 weekly per dependent child under 18, maximum 50% of basic benefit or 75% of wage (whichever is less). Compensation increased to 75% of wages if employer violated OSHA regulation.**
DELAWARE	66-2/3	223.78	66-2/3% SAWW	74.59[1]	22-2/9% SAWW[1]	Disability				Annual increase in maximum effective June 7.
DISTRICT OF COLUMBIA	66-2/3 up to 80% of spendable earnings*	396.78*	100% SAWW*	99.20[1,*]	25% SAWW[1,*]	Disability		PT—October 1, maximum 5%*	Social Security, employer-funded pension	Annual increase in maximum effective October 1*.
FLORIDA	66-2/3	288.00	100% SAWW	20.00		TT-350 weeks PT-Disability	TT—*$100,800*		Unemployment compensation, Social Security	Annual increase in maximum effective January 1. Compensation increased 10% if installment unpaid after 14 days.*
GEORGIA	66-2/3	135.00		25.00[1]		Disability				Board may assess $500 penalty for refusal, unreasonable delay, or willful neglect to make payment.*
GUAM	66-2/3	140.00	66-2/3% SAWW	50.00[1]		Disability	40,000			Compensation increased 10% for late payment without award; 20% if award.
HAWAII	66-2/3	281.00	100% SAWW	TT—70.25* PT—70.25	TT—25% SAWW* PT—25% SAWW	Disability		PT—injuries prior to June 18, 1980		Annual increase in maximum effective January 1. Compensation may be increased 10% for failure to pay within 31 days after decision or award, or within 10 business days for uncontroverted temporary total disability case.
IDAHO	60	249.30 to 346.25	90% SAWW	124.65	45% SAWW	Disability		After 52 weeks		Annual increase in maximum effective January 1. For first 52 weeks benefit is 60% of worker's wages if there are no dependent children under 18; after 52 weeks benefit is 60% of SAWW. Benefit is increased 7% of SAWW per dependent child (up to 5), but may not exceed 90% of wages. 8% interest on late payments.
ILLINOIS	66-2/3	463.44	133-1/3% SAWW	TT—100.90* PT—173.79	PT—50% SAWW	TT—Disability PT—Life		PT—July 15 of 2nd year		Semiannual increases in maximum effective January 15 and July 15.**
INDIANA	66-2/3	156.00*		50.00[1]		500 weeks	78,000*			After 500 weeks, additional benefits are payable from second injury fund in 150-week increments.**
IOWA	80% of spendable earnings	563.00	200% SAWW	(*)		Disability				Annual increase in maximum effective July 1. Benefits increased 50% if late or stopped without good cause.
KANSAS	66-2/3	218.00	75% SAWW	25.00		Disability	TT— 75,000 PT—100,000 (includes TT)			Annual increase in maximum effective July 1. Compensation may be increased up to $100 per week past due (plus up to $25 per week past due for failure to pay medical bill).
KENTUCKY	66-2/3*	294.87	100% SAWW	58.97[1]	20% SAWW[1]	Disability				Annual increase in maximum effective January 1. Compensation increased or decreased 15% if injury caused by safety violation. 12% interest on late payments.
LOUISIANA	66-2/3	245.00*	75% SAWW*	65.00[1]	20% SAWW[1]	Disability			Social Security, unemployment compensation, employer-funded disability, federal workers' compensation	Annual increase in maximum effective September 1. 12% interest on late payments.

[1]Actual weekly wage if less.

[2]Amounts shown in italics have been calculated.

[3]Social Security offsets generally apply by formula up to 50% of basic benefit.

Alab. *Compensation may be increased up to 10% for failure to pay within 30 days after due.

Alaska *Spendable weekly earnings if less.

Ark. *Amounts over $75,000 are payable from Death and Permanent Total Disability Bank Fund.
**10% interest on late installments.

Conn. *80% of average weekly wages, if less.
**12% interest benefits added if undue delay in payment; 6% interest added if undue delay in adjustment (4 weeks presumed undue delay).

D.C. *Maximum is no less than $396.78; minimum is no less than $99.20. Benefits for D.C. government employees are similar to F.E.C.A. (effective 10/1/83, maximum—$654.58 to $736.41, minimum—$67.64 to $76.09).

Fla. *Compensation increased 20% if unpaid 30 days after award.

Ga. *Income payable without award increased 15% if not paid within 14 days unless claim is controverted or Board excuses. Awarded benefits increased 20% if not paid within 20 days unless Board grants review.

Hawaii *Actual wages if less, but no less than $38.

Ill. *Minimum TT benefit is $100.90 if unmarried and ranges up to $124.30 if 4 or more dependents. In all cases claimant receives actual weekly wage if less.
**TT benefits may be increased $10 per day, up to $2,500, for unreasonable delay in payment; 14 days is presumed unreasonable. Compensation may be increased 50% for unreasonable or vexatious delay in payment. Compensation may be increased 25% for employer's willful violation of safety standard.

Ind. *Effective 7/1/83. Effective 7/1/84, maximum is increased to $166.00 and amount limit to $83,000.
**Award is increased 5% if employer loses on court appeal; court may increase to 10%.

Iowa *Minimum earnings presumed to be 35% of SAWW (= $98.00); benefits may not exceed worker's spendable earnings.

Ky. *80% of AWW during rehabilitation.

La. *Effective 7/1/83.

CHART VI □ INCOME BENEFITS FOR TOTAL DISABILITY □ January 1, 1984 (continued)

JURISDICTION	PERCENT OF WAGES	MAXIMUM WEEKLY PAYMENT		MINIMUM WEEKLY PAYMENT		TIME LIMIT	AMOUNT LIMIT[2]	AUTOMATIC COST OF LIVING INCREASE	OFFSETS[3]	NOTATIONS
		AMOUNT	RATE	AMOUNT	RATE					
TEXAS	66-2/3	$ 189.00	(**)	$33.00	(**)	401 weeks*	*$75,789*			Annual increase in maximum effective September 1.**
UTAH	66-2/3	TT—300.00 PT—255.00	TT—100% SAWW PT— 85% SAWW	45.00[1]		Disability*				Annual increase in maximum effective July 1. Additional $5 if spouse, plus $5 per dependent child under 18 (up to 4); total benefit may not exceed maximum.*
VERMONT	66-2/3	262.00 plus dependents	100% SAWW	122.00[1]	50% SAWW[1]	Disability*		July 1		Annual increase in maximum effective July 1. Additional $10 per dependent child under 21; total benefits may not exceed pre-injury wages.**
VIRGIN ISLANDS	TT—66-2/3* PT—75	173.00*	66-2/3% SAWW*	60.00[1],*		Disability		After 2 years on January 1		Annual increase in maximum effective January 1. Total disability benefits begin after medical and vocational rehabilitation end. Compensation increased 15% for injury caused by employer's failure to obey safety order.*
VIRGINIA	66-2/3	277.00	100% SAWW	63.25[1]	25% SAWW[1]	TT—138 weeks PT—Disability*	TT—*138,500*	October 1**		Annual increase in maximum effective July 1. Compensation increased 20% for failure to pay within 2 weeks after due.
WASHINGTON	60	253.17	75% SAWW	42.69*		Disability		July 1	Social Security under age 65	Benefits payable monthly. Annual increase in maximum effective July 1. Additional 5% of wages for spouse, plus 2% of wages per dependent child (up to 5), up to maximum.**
WEST VIRGINIA	70	318.85	100% SAWW	100.21	33-1/3% SAWW	TT—208 weeks PT—Life	TT—*66,321*			Benefits payable monthly. Annual increase in maximum effective July 1.
WISCONSIN	66-2/3	305.00	100% SAWW	30.00		TT—Disability PT—Life			Social Security	Annual increase in maximum effective January 1.*
WYOMING	TT—66-2/3	TT—313.58 PT—209.06 plus dependents	TT—100% SAWW PT—66-2/3% SAWW	TT— 43.38 PT—209.06	PT—66-2/3% SAWW	TT—Disability PT—Life	(*)			Benefits payable monthly. Quarterly increases in maximum effective January 1, April 1, July 1, and October 1. PT benefit fixed at 66-2/3% of SAMW plus $100 per child monthly.
F.E.C.A.	66-2/3 or 75	942.22	66-2/3% or 75% of highest rate for GS-15	145.63[1]	66-2/3% or 75% of lowest rate for GS-2[1]	TT—Disability PT—Life		October 1		Benefits payable monthly. Increase effective 1/9/84. Higher percentage payable if 1 or more dependent.
LONGSHORE ACT	66-2/3	548.34*	200% NAWW*	137.09[1],*	50% NAWW[1],*	Disability		PT—October 1		Annual increase in maximum effective October 1.
ALBERTA	90% of weighted net income	510.31		155.34[1]		TT—Disability PT—Life				PT payable monthly. Maximum annual earnings is $40,000.
BRITISH COLUMBIA	75	434.38	(*)	174.52[1]		TT—Disability PT—Life		January 1 and July 1		PT payable monthly. Maximum annual earnings $30,200. Annual increase in maximum effective January 1.**
MANITOBA	75	403.85	(*)	TT—136.16[1] PT—136.16		TT—Disability PT—Life				PT payable monthly. Maximum annual earnings $28,000. Annual increase in maximum effective January 1.*
NEW BRUNSWICK	90% of weighted net income	350.86 to 381.51*	150% of provincial average wage			TT—Disability PT—Life				PT payable monthly. Maximum annual earnings is $27,500. Annual increase in maximum effective January 1.
NEWFOUNDLAND	90% of weighted net income	587.82	250% of provincial average wage	200.00*		TT—Disability PT—Life				PT payable monthly. Maximum annual earnings $45,500, effective 1/1/83. Board may raise compensation as it deems equitable.
NORTHWEST TERRITORIES	75	380.77		167.54[1]		TT—Disability PT—Life				Benefits payable monthly. Maximum annual earnings $26,400.
NOVA SCOTIA	75	274.04 plus dependents		112.50*		TT—Disability PT—Life		January 1		PT payable monthly. Maximum annual earnings $19,000, effective 1/11/82. Additional $32.31 weekly per child; total benefit may exceed maximum.
ONTARIO	75	367.79		179.00[1]		TT—Disability PT—Life		TT—after 12 months		PT payable monthly. Maximum annual earnings $25.500, effective July 1, 1983.
PRINCE EDWARD ISLAND	75	245.19		60.00*		TT—Disability PT—Life				Maximum annual earnings $17,000, effective January 1, 1983.
QUEBEC	90% of weighted net income	364.85 to 403.41	150% of provincial average wage	35.00[1]		TT—Disability PT—Life		January 1		Maximum annual earnings $31,500. Annual increase in maximum effective January 1.
SASKATCHEWAN	75	475.96	(**)	187.76*		TT—Disability PT—Life			Canada Pension after 1 year	PT payable monthly. Maximum annual earnings $33,000, effective 1/1/84. After 2 years' disability, an amount equal to 10% of compensation is set aside to purchase annuity for benefits after age 65.**
YUKON TERRITORY	75	389.42	(*)	115.23[1],*		TT—Disability PT—Life		January 1		Maximum annual earnings $27,000. Annual increase in maximum effective January 1.*
CANADIAN MERCHANT SEAMEN'S ACT	75	288.46		90.00		TT—Disability PT—Life				Benefits payable monthly. Maximum annual earnings $20,000. Gov.-in-Council may raise benefits to level paid in maritime provinces.

Texas *For life in case of amputation or paralysis of two limbs, loss of vision in both eyes, or permanent insanity.
**Maximum increased $7 and minimum increased $1 per $10 increase in SAWW.

Utah *Disability beyond 312 weeks is payable from Second Injury Fund, minimum $110 weekly.

Vt. *PT benefits payable at least 330 weeks, after temporary disability benefits cease. After 330 weeks, PT benefits continue while there is lost earning capacity.
**Benefits may be disallowed if injury results from worker's failure to use safety device.

V.I. *During vocational rehabilitation, income benefits are 75% of AWW, maximum SAWW, minimum $75 or actual wages if less.

Va. *500-week limit for certain PT cases.
**Recipient of Social Security ineligible for cost of living increases.

Wash. *Plus $8.53 for first child, $7.15 for second child, $5.30 each for third through fifth children, and $6.92 for spouse.
**50% penalty payable to Accident Fund for dependent children, minimum is amount of death benefit payable to spouse fire rescue.

Wisc. *Compensation may be adjusted up or down by 15% (up to $15,000) for failure to use safety device or obey code or order. 10% interest payable on late payments. Employer, insurer, or both may be assessed penalty up to double the amount of compensation (not to exceed $15,000) for bad faith failure to make payments.

Wyo. *Court must approve PT payments after $53,728 (257 times 66-2/3% SAWW).

Longshore *For Nonappropriated Fund Instrumentalities Act, maximum is $506.65 (66-2/3% of GS-12, step 10), and minimum is $129.45 (66-2/3% of GS-2, step 1), effective 1/8/84.

Alta. *Employer must pay half of "costs of the claim" to Accident Fund if injury caused by safety violation.

B.C. *Maximum increased in proportion to increase in provincial average weekly wage (maximum 6% for 1983).
**On application for review, Board may award benefits based on current levels.

Man. *Maximum earning ceiling increased by $1,000 if 10% of workers injured in preceding year earn in excess of maximum.

N.B. *Board must review maximum at least biennially. Higher figure is for married claimant with 2 children.

Nfld. *100% of weighted net earnings if less.

N.S. *Minimum for temporary total disability is 75% of minimum wage.

Ont. *No less than award if worker had been fatally injured.

P.E.I. *Actual wages if less, but Board may set minimum at $15.

Sask. *Actual wages if less for first 2 years' disability.
**Maximum earning ceiling increased by $1,000 if 10% of workers injured in preceding year earn in excess of maximum.

Yukon *Benefits increased annually based on Consumer Price Index, and based on 90% of territory's average wage, effective January 1. Minimum for 1984 unavailable at time of publication.

CHART VI □ INCOME BENEFITS FOR TOTAL DISABILITY □ January 1, 1984 (continued)

JURISDICTION	PERCENT OF WAGES	MAXIMUM WEEKLY PAYMENT AMOUNT	MAXIMUM WEEKLY PAYMENT RATE	MINIMUM WEEKLY PAYMENT AMOUNT	MINIMUM WEEKLY PAYMENT RATE	TIME LIMIT	AMOUNT LIMIT[2]	AUTOMATIC COST OF LIVING INCREASE	OFFSETS[3]	NOTATIONS
MAINE	66-2/3	$ 426.43	166-2/3% SAWW	$25.00		Disability		Anniversary (July 1 if maximum benefit)	Unemployment compensation	Annual increase in maximum effective July 1. Compensation may be increased 10% for failure to pay uncontroverted claim within 10 days.*
MARYLAND	66-2/3	311.00	100% SAWW	TT—50.00[1] PT—25.00[1]		Disability		(*)		Annual increase in maximum effective January 1. If permanent disability exceeds 50% of whole body, worker receives additional compensation from Subsequent Injury Fund after completion of payments by employer.
MASSACHUSETTS	66-2/3	320.29	100% SAWW	40.00*		Disability	TT—*$80,073***			Annual increase in maximum effective October 1. Additional $6 weekly per dependent if total benefit does not exceed $150 or 100% of wages.***
MICHIGAN	80% of spendable earnings	334.00***	90% SAWW	PT—93.00	PT—25% SAWW	Disability*		PT (injury prior to 1/1/82)	Disability, pension, Social Security retirement**	Annual increase in maximum effective January 1. Additional $50 per day for award unpaid after 30 days, maximum $1,500.
MINNESOTA	66-2/3	313.00	100% SAWW	156.50*	50% SAWW*	Disability		Anniversary of injury	Social Security after $25,000 paid**	Annual increase in maximum effective October 1. Late payment may be increased 10% if inexcusably delayed, plus interest.
MISSISSIPPI	66-2/3	112.00*		25.00		450 weeks	50,400*			Additional rehabilitation allowance up to $10 weekly for 52 weeks.
MISSOURI	66-2/3	212.19	70% SAWW	40.00		TT—400 weeks PT—Life	TT—*84,876*			Annual increase in maximum effective July 1. 8% interest for late payments.**
MONTANA	66-2/3	277.00	100% SAWW			Disability*			Social Security	Annual increase in maximum effective July 1. Compensation may be increased 20% if payment unreasonably delayed or refused.
NEBRASKA	66-2/3	200.00		49.00[1]		Disability				
NEVADA	66-2/3	312.83	100% SAWW			TT—Disability PT—Life			Social Security	Benefits payable monthly.* Annual increase in maximum effective July 1.
NEW HAMPSHIRE	66-2/3*	418.00	150% SAWW*	112.00[1]	40% SAWW[1]	Disability		July 1—after 3 years		Annual increase in maximum effective July 1. Double compensation if employer violated prior recorded safety standard.
NEW JERSEY	70	255.00	75% SAWW	68.00	20% SAWW	TT—400 weeks PT—Life	TT—*102,200*		Social Security	Annual increase in maximum effective January 1. After 450 weeks at reduced rate if employed; at full rate if not able to be rehabilitated.
NEW MEXICO	66-2/3	289.20	100% SAWW	36.00[1]		600 weeks	*173,520*			Annual increase in maximum effective January 1. 10% additional compensation payable by employer for failure to provide safety devices.
NEW YORK	66-2/3	255.00*		TT—20.00[1] PT—30.00[1]		Disability				Persons receiving PT benefits may collect full compensation and wages if working, but not in excess of pre-injury wage.
NORTH CAROLINA	66-2/3	262.00	100% SAWW	30.00		TT—Disability PT—Life				Annual increase in maximum effective January 1.
NORTH DAKOTA	66-2/3	278.00 plus dependents	100% SAWW	167.00[1]	60% SAWW[1]	Disability			Social Security	Annual increase in maximum effective July 1. Additional $5 weekly per dependent child under 18; total benefits may not exceed claimant's net take-home pay.
OHIO	72—first 12 weeks 66-2/3—after 12 weeks	335.00	100% SAWW	TT—111.67[1] PT—167.50[1]	TT—33-1/3% SAWW[1] PT—50% SAWW[1]	TT—Disability* PT—Life				Annual increase in maximum effective January 1. If PT benefit plus Social Security are less than $155.63 weekly, Disabled Workers' Relief Fund pays difference; amount increased annually by increase in Consumer Price Index.
OKLAHOMA	66-2/3	212.00	66-2/3% SAWW	30.00[1]		TT—300 weeks PT—Disability	TT—*63,600*			Annual increase in maximum effective November 1. TT may be extended to 500 weeks.
OREGON	66-2/3	316.23 to 341.23	100% SAWW	50.00*		Disability			PT—Social Security	Annual increase in maximum effective July 1. Additional $5 weekly per dependent (up to 5).**
PENNSYLVANIA	66-2/3	320.00	100% SAWW	153.00*	50% SAWW*	Disability				Annual increase in maximum effective January 1.
PUERTO RICO	66-2/3	TT—45.00 PT—28.86		TT—10.00 PT—11.54		TT—312 weeks PT—Life	TT—*14,040* PT—$18,900*			Compensation doubled if due to employer's violation of safety or health law or regulation.
RHODE ISLAND	66-2/3	275.00 plus dependents	100% SAWW	30.00		Disability				Annual increase in maximum effective September 1. Additional $9 per dependent child under 18; total benefit may not exceed 80% of pre-injury wages.*
SOUTH CAROLINA	66-2/3	268.99	100% SAWW	25.00		500 weeks	*134,495*			Annual increase in maximum effective January 1.
SOUTH DAKOTA	66-2/3	238.00	100% SAWW	114.00[1]	50% SAWW[1]	TT—Disability PT—Life				Annual increase in maximum effective July 1.
TENNESSEE	66-2/3	136.00		15.00		TT—Disability PT—550 weeks*	54,400			After 400 weeks PT benefit is reduced to $15.

Maine *Carrier may be assessed up to $25 per day for failure to pay award within 10 days. Added benefits during rehabilitation—$35 weekly.

Md. *Benefits increased October 1 for persons injured any time during July 1, 1965, through June 30, 1978, and receiving PT benefits in July, 1973.

Mass. *Actual wages if less, but no less than $20 if working at least 15 hours a week.
**250 times SAWW; includes permanent partial disability.
***Double compensation if injury due to employer's serious and willful misconduct. If no benefits are paid prior to final decision of claim, award is based on benefits in effect at time of decision instead of date of injury.

Mich. *Conclusive presumption of PT disability does not extend beyond 800 weeks from injury; thereafter determined in accordance with facts.
**Benefits reduced 5% a year after age 65 unless claimant is receiving Social Security or employer-funded pension or disability insurance.
***Maximum for 1983 determined to be $324 rather than $330 after date of publication.

Minn. *Actual wages if less, but no less than 20% of SAWW; $62.60 through 9/30/84. After 208 weeks' total disability, supplementary benefits bring compensation to 65% of SAWW; $204.00 through 9/30/84.
**Other government disability benefits from same injury also offset.

Mo. *Effective 9/28/83; increased to 75% of SAWW, effective 9/28/86.
**Compensation increased 15% if injury caused by failure to comply with statute or order, decreased 15% if caused by worker's failure to use safety device.

Mont. *Compensation terminates upon receipt of Social Security retirement benefits.

Nevada *Maximum monthly wages on which benefits are computed are $2,040.60, effective 7/1/83.

N.H. *Effective 8/22/83.

N.Y. *Effective 7/1/83. Increased to $275 as of 7/1/84 and $300 as of 7/1/85.

Ohio *After 200 weeks claimant examined to determine if disability is permanent.

Ore. *90% of actual wages, if less.
**Employer may be sued for damages for failure to comply with posted notice of violation of safety code.

Pa. *90% of wages if less, but no less than 33-1/3% of SAWW ($106.67, effective 1/1/83).

P.R. *May be paid in monthly installments of $100 to $125 for life.

R.I. *No compensation for PT disability if worker is earning pre-injury wages.

Tenn. *From date injury is determined to be permanent.

CHART VII INCOME BENEFITS FOR SCHEDULED INJURIES January 1, 1984

JURISDICTION	ARM AT SHOULDER	HAND	THUMB	FIRST FINGER	SECOND FINGER	THIRD FINGER	FOURTH FINGER	LEG AT HIP	FOOT	GREAT TOE	OTHER TOES	ONE EYE	HEARING ONE EAR	HEARING BOTH EARS
IN THIS GROUP OF STATES, COMPENSATION FOR TEMPORARY DISABILITY IS ALLOWED IN ADDITION TO ALLOWANCE FOR SCHEDULED INJURY														
ALABAMA	$40,848	$31,280	$11,408	$ 7,912	$ 5,704	$ 4,048	$ 2,944	$36,800	$25,576	$ 5,888	$ 2,024	$22,816	$ 9,752	$29,992
ALASKA*	59,000	45,400	14,000	8,700	5,700	4,700	2,800	54,400	39,700	7,200	3,000	30,200	9,800	37,800
AMERICAN SAMOA	PPD benefits paid at 66-2/3% of wages for specified number of weeks, no maximum.*													
ARIZONA	*43,725*	*36,437*	10,931	6,559	5,101	3,644	2,915	36,437	29,150	5,101	1,822	*21,862*	14,575	43,725
ARKANSAS*	30,800	23,100	9,240	5,390	4,620	3,080	2,310	26,950	19,250	4,620	1,540	15,400	6,160	23,100
CALIFORNIA*	*58,975***	43,540	7,595	3,360	3,360	2,520	2,520	64,575**	33,740	4,235	840	21,105**	6,335	43,540
COLORADO*	17,472	8,736	4,200	2,184	1,512	924	1,092	17,472	8,736	2,184	924	11,676	2,940	11,676
CONNECTICUT*	*107,640*	*86,940*	*32,775*	18,630	15,180	10,695	8,970	82,110	68,310	14,490	4,485	81,075	17,940	53,820
DELAWARE	55,945	49,232	16,784	11,189	8,951	6,713	4,476	55,945	35,805	8,951	3,357	44,756	16,784	39,162
DISTRICT OF COLUMBIA*	123,795	96,814	29,759	18,252	11,903	9,920	5,952	116,653	81,340	11,903	6,348	63,485	20,633	79,356
FLORIDA	No schedule. Benefits paid according to degree of impairment and loss of earnings.*													
GEORGIA	30,375	21,600	8,100	5,400	4,725	4,050	3,375	30,375	18,225	4,050	2,700	16,875	8,100	20,250
GUAM	39,200	29,680	7,140	3,920	2,520	2,380	980	34,720	24,220	3,640	1,120	19,600	7,280	28,000
HAWAII*	87,672	68,564	21,075	12,926	8,430	7,025	4,215	80,928	57,605	10,678	4,496	*44,960*	14,612	56,200
IDAHO*	45,705	41,135	16,759	10,665	8,379	3,809	2,285	30,470	21,329	6,399	1,066	*26,661*	—	26,661
ILLINOIS*	104,904	84,816	31,248	17,856	15,624	11,160	8,928	89,280	69,192	15,624	5,357	*71,424*	14,113	56,450
IOWA*	129,500	98,420	31,080	18,130	15,540	12,950	10,360	113,960	77,700	20,720	7,770	72,520	25,900	90,650
MAINE	85,286	70,361	21,322	13,646	11,940	8,529	7,249	85,286	70,361	10,661	4,264	42,643	21,322	85,286
MARYLAND*	83,200	69,264	10,400	4,160	3,640	3,120	2,600	83,200	69,264	4,160	1,040	69,264	13,000	69,264
MASSACHUSETTS*	*11,140*	*8,675*	—	—	—	—	—	9,900	7,425	—	—	9,900	7,425	19,800
MICHIGAN*,***	89,846	71,810	21,710	12,692	11,022	7,348	5,344	71,810	54,108	11,022	3,674	54,108	(**)	(**)
MINNESOTA	No schedule. Benefits paid according to degree of impairment and loss of earnings.*													
MISSISSIPPI	22,400	16,800	6,720	3,920	3,360	2,240	1,680	19,600	14,000	3,360	1,120	11,200	4,480	16,800
MISSOURI*	31,647	23,872	8,185	6,138	4,774	4,774	3,001	*28,237*	21,144	5,456	1,910	19,097	6,002**	22,917**
MONTANA*	38,780	27,700	10,388	5,540	5,125	3,463	2,078	*41,550*	24,930	5,125	2,216	*22,853*	5,540	27,700
NEBRASKA*	45,000	35,000	12,000	7,000	6,000	4,000	3,000	43,000	30,000	6,000	2,000	25,000	10,000	(*)
NEVADA	No schedule. Degree of disability determined in relation to whole man.*													
NEW HAMPSHIRE	87,780	79,002	31,768	19,646	15,884	7,942	3,762	58,520	40,964	7,524	1,254	35,112	12,540	51,414
NEW JERSEY*	61,710	37,485	5,100	3,400	2,720	2,040	1,360	58,905	31,280	2,720	1,020	30,600	4,080	23,800
NEW MEXICO	*57,840*	*36,150*	15,906	8,098	6,362	4,916	4,049	*57,840*	33,258	10,122	4,049	37,596	11,568	43,380
NORTH CAROLINA	62,880	52,400	19,650	11,790	10,480	6,550	5,240	52,400	37,728	9,170	2,620	31,440	18,340	39,300
NORTH DAKOTA*	*18,750*	*15,000*	*4,875*	*3,000*	*2,250*	*1,500*	*1,200*	14,040	9,000	1,800	720	9,000	3,000	12,000
OHIO*	37,688	29,312	10,050	5,862	5,025	3,350	2,513	33,500	25,125	5,025	1,675	20,938	4,188	20,938
OREGON*	19,200	15,000	4,800	2,400	2,200	1,000	600	15,000	13,500	1,800	400	10,000	6,000	19,200
PUERTO RICO*	10,000	9,000	3,375	1,800	1,350	1,125	675	10,000	7,875	1,350	675	(**)	2,250	9,000
RHODE ISLAND*	28,080	21,960	6,750	4,140	2,700	2,250	1,800	28,080	18,450	3,420	900	14,400	5,400	18,000
SOUTH CAROLINA	59,178	49,763	17,484	10,760	9,415	6,725	5,380	52,453	37,659	9,415	2,690	29,589	21,519	44,383
SOUTH DAKOTA	47,600	35,700	11,900	8,330	7,140	4,760	3,570	38,080	29,750	7,140	2,380	35,700	11,900	35,700
TENNESSEE	27,200	20,400	8,160	4,760	4,080	2,720	2,040	27,200	17,000	4,080	1,360	13,600	10,200	20,400
UTAH*	37,400	33,600	13,400	8,400	6,800	3,400	1,600	25,000	17,600	5,200	800	*24,000*	3,333**	20,000
VERMONT*	56,330	45,850	13,100	4,384	6,550	5,240	3,144	56,330	45,850	6,550	2,620	32,750	13,624*	56,330
VIRGINIA*	55,400	41,550	16,620	9,695	8,310	5,540	4,155	48,475	34,625	8,310	2,770	27,700	13,850	27,700
VIRGIN ISLANDS*	41,520	37,368	14,878	9,342	7,439	3,806	1,903	27,680	19,376	3,460	1,730**	17,300	—	26,988
WASHINGTON*	36,000	32,400	12,960	8,100	6,480	3,240	1,620	36,000	25,200	7,560	2,760	14,400	4,800	28,800
WEST VIRGINIA*	51,017	42,514	17,006	8,503	5,952	4,251	4,251	51,017	29,760	8,503	3,401	28,059	21,257	55,268
WISCONSIN*	50,000	40,000	16,000	6,000	4,500	2,600	2,800	50,000	25,000	8,333	2,500**	*27,500*	5,500***	33,000***
WYOMING	31,359	25,505	9,199	6,063	3,136	3,136	3,136	28,223	20,906	4,181	1,463	19,652	8,362	—
F.E.C.A.*	293,973	229,902	70,667	43,342	28,267	23,556	14,133	271,359	193,155	35,804	15,075	150,755	48,995	188,444
LONGSHORE ACT	171,082	133,795	41,126	25,224	16,450	13,709	8,225	157,922	112,410	16,450	8,773	87,734	28,514	109,668
IN THIS GROUP OF STATES, COMPENSATION FOR TEMPORARY DISABILITY IS ALLOWED IN ADDITION TO SCHEDULED INJURY WITH CERTAIN LIMITATIONS AS TO PERIOD														
INDIANA*	18,750	15,000	4,500	3,000	2,625	2,250	1,500	16,875	13,125	4,500	2,250**	13,125	5,625	15,000
KANSAS*	45,780	32,700	13,080	8,066	6,540	4,360	3,270	43,600	27,250	6,540	2,180	26,160	6,540	23,980
NEW YORK*	39,000	30,500	9,375	5,750	3,750	3,125	1,875	36,000	25,625	4,750	2,000	20,000	7,500	18,750
PENNSYLVANIA*	131,200	107,200	32,000	16,000	12,800	9,600	8,960	131,200	80,000	12,800	5,120	88,000	19,200	83,200
IN THIS GROUP OF STATES, COMPENSATION FOR TEMPORARY DISABILITY IS DEDUCTED FROM THE ALLOWANCE FOR SCHEDULED INJURY														
KENTUCKY	No schedule. PP benefits paid at 66-2/3% of wages up to 425 weeks according to degree of disability.*													
LOUISIANA*	49,000	36,750	12,250	7,350	4,900	4,900	4,900	42,875	30,625	4,900	2,450	24,500	—	—
OKLAHOMA*	39,750	31,800	9,540	5,565	4,770	3,180	2,385	39,750	31,800	4,770	1,590	31,800	15,900	47,700
TEXAS	37,800	28,350	11,340	8,505	5,670	3,969	2,835	37,800	23,625	5,670	1,890	18,900	—	28,350

NOTE—In Canada permanent physical impairments generally are compensated by degree of disability using medical rating schedules as guidelines.
Numbers in italics are computations for loss of major member, loss of leg precluding use of artificial limb, or loss of eye by enucleation.

CHART VII ☐ INCOME BENEFITS FOR SCHEDULED INJURIES ☐ January 1, 1984 (continued)

Alaska *Maximum dollar amount fixed by statute.

Am. Samoa *Arm—312, hand—244, thumb—75, first finger—46, second finger—30, third finger—25, fourth finger—15, leg—288, foot—205, great toe—30, other toes—16, one eye—160, one ear—52, both ears—200.

Ariz. *PP benefit is 55% of monthly compensation up to $1,325 (= $168.01 weekly).

Ark. *Maximum amount for PP is $63,000.

Calif. *Maximum PP benefit is $140.00, effective 1/1/84. Duration varies according to percentage of permanent disability, adjusted for age and occupation. Chart reflects standard rating for individual age 39 and loss of major arm.
**Chart reflects benefits for loss of eye if unable to wear artificial eye. Life pension up to $64.21 weekly also payable for loss of arm or leg.

Colo. *Maximum weekly benefit is $84.

Conn. *Commission may award additional benefits based on loss of earnings.

D.C. *Effective 7/26/82.

Fla. *Permanent impairment caused by amputation, loss of 80% of vision in either eye after correction, or serious facial disfigurement—$250 per 1% of disability up to 10%, and $500 per 1% of disability over 10%. Wage-loss benefits also payable in all permanent impairment cases—95% of difference between 85% of pre-injury wages and earnings after maximum medical improvement, up to 100% of SAWW weekly; Social Security retirement benefits are deducted from wage loss benefits.

Hawaii *In cases in which the disability is determined as a percentage of total loss or impairment of physical or mental function of the whole man, the maximum compensation is the corresponding percentage of 312 times SAWW (= $82,992 effective 1/1/83).

Idaho *Maximum weekly PP benefit is 55% of SAWW (= $152.35 for 1984).

Ill. *Effective January 15. Figures reflect benefits for amputation of member—maximum 133-1/3% of SAWW. Maximum for other PP benefits is 100% of SAWW (increase effective 1/15/84 not available at date of publication).

Ind. *Payable for 52 weeks; maximum weekly PP benefit is $75.
**Second toe—$2,250, third toe—$1,500, fourth toe—$1,125, fifth toe—$750.

Iowa *Maximum weekly PP benefit is 184% of SAWW (= $518.00).

Kans. *Additional healing period up to 15 weeks may be allowed. Maximum weekly PP benefit is 75% of SAWW.

Ky. *Maximum weekly PP benefit is 75% of SAWW (= $221.15). Degree of disability is determined by American Medical Association Guide or decrease in earning capacity, whichever is greater.

La. *Schedule applies to amputation or at least 50% loss of use. Supplemental earnings benefits are 74% of the difference between 90% of pre-injury wages and post-injury earnings, minimum 104 and maximum 520 weeks; cease 2 years after termination of temporary total disability (unless paid for 13 consecutive weeks during that time) or upon retirement or receipt of Social Security retirement benefits.

Md. *Maximum weekly PP benefit is 33-1/3% of SAWW (= $104.00); where benefits are payable for 250 weeks or more, the number of weeks are increased by 1/3, and maximum is 66-2/3% of SAWW (= $208.00).

Mass. *Benefits fixed at amount reflected in chart. Proportional benefits for functional loss of use of arm, hand, leg, or foot.

Mich. *Wage-loss benefits payable for life.
**Hearing loss compensable based on lost earnings.
***Maximum for 1983 held to be $324 rather than $330 after date of publication.

Minn. *For permanent partial disability, impairment compensation (IC) is paid ($75,000 to $400,000 according to percentage of disability), in lump sum if take job or at temporary total (TT) rate if refuse job. If lose job for economic reasons, monitoring period compensation is paid (600 to 1200 weeks according to percentage of disability), less weeks worked or IC, whichever is greater. If no job offer, economic recovery benefits (ERB) are paid (600 to 1200 weeks), less IC. If work stops for medical reasons, rehabilitation is provided and TT is paid for 90 days after maximum medical improvement, then ERB. IC and ERB are paid concurrently with permanent total disability benefits if claimant lives more than 30 days after injury. Minimum ERB is 120% of IC if claimant was entitled to IC.

Mo. *Maximum weekly PP benefit is 45% of SAWW ($136.41 effective 9/28/83); minimum is $40. If amputation or 100% loss of use, additional 10% compensation.
**Occupational hearing loss law provides benefits up to 40 weeks (1 ear) or 145 weeks (both ears).

Mont. *Maximum weekly PP benefit is 50% of SAWW (= $138.50, effective 7/1/83). Claimant may elect schedule or wage-loss indemnity.

Nebr. *Terms run consecutively for loss of, or loss of use of, more than 1 member but less than total disability.
**Permanent total loss of hearing is compensated as permanent total disability.

Nev. *Each 1% of impairment is compensated by .6% of worker's monthly wage up to maximum, payable for 5 years or until age 66 (rising 1 year annually until age 70 beginning 7/1/86), whichever is later. Maximum monthly wages are $2,040.60 as of 7/1/83.

N.J. *Computations include allowance for amputation of member (30% additional compensation). Compensation is payable weekly at 70% of pre-injury weekly wages, up to a maximum of 55% of SAWW for arm or leg, 45% of SAWW for hand, 40% of SAWW for foot or one eye, 35% of SAWW for hearing—both ears, 20% of SAWW for other scheduled injuries in chart.

N.Y. *Additional weeks for TT in excess of statutory healing period; maximum $125 weekly. Maximum increased to $135 as of 7/1/84 and $150 as of 7/1/85. Compensation for wage-loss in addition to schedule if impairment due to loss of 50% or more of member.

N.D. *PP benefit is $60 weekly for scheduled number of weeks.

Ohio *Maximum weekly PP benefit is 50% of SAWW (= $167.50 for 1983). Compensation payable for 200 weeks if percentage of disability is 90% or greater.

Okla. *Maximum PP benefit is 50% of SAWW (= $159.00 effective 11/1/82).

Oregon *Calculated at $100 per degree of injury.

Pa. *Healing period is 25 weeks for leg or foot; 20 weeks for an arm or hand; 12 weeks for great toe; 10 weeks for thumb, eye, or hearing; 6 weeks for finger or toe.

P.R. *Maximum PP benefit is $45 weekly.
**Permanent visual disability is compensated according to percentage of total disability; in addition, loss of eye by enucleation is compensated at 10% of permanent total disability.

R.I. *Maximum scheduled PP benefit is $90.00 weekly. Maximum is 100% of SAWW for unscheduled injury.

Utah *Maximum per week, including allowance for dependents, is 66-2/3% of SAWW (= $200 effective 7/1/83).
**Entry presumes total loss of hearing in one ear and no loss of hearing in the other (16-2/3 weeks). Benefits are based on the percentage of binaural hearing loss, adjusted for claimant's age.

Vt. *In addition to TT except for loss of hearing in 1 ear.

Va. *Benefits for scheduled injuries are payable in addition to compensation for temporary disability. *County of Spotsylvania v. Hart*, 218 Va. 565, 238 S.E.2d 813 (1977). After expiration of scheduled award, claimant may file for further benefits within 1 year if still incapacitated.

V.I. *PP benefit is 66-2/3% of SAWW weekly (= $173.00 effective 1/1/84).
**Third through fifth toes—$865.

Wash. *Benefits fixed at amount reflected in chart. 25% less for disability not involving amputation.

W.Va. *PP benefit is 70% of wages, payable in 4-week periods per 1% of disability up to 85% per week. Maximum is 66-2/3% of SAWW (= $212.57 effective 7/1/83).

Wis. *Maximum weekly PP benefit is $100 effective 1/1/84 and $108 effective 1/1/85.
**Second toe—$2,500, other toe—$2,000.
***Under occupational hearing loss law, maximum is $3,600/36 weeks for one ear and $21,600/216 weeks for both ears, as of 1/1/83.

Wyo. *PP benefit is 66-2/3% of SAWW.

F.E.C.A. *Includes allowance for dependents.

CHART X REHABILITATION OF DISABLED WORKERS January 1, 1984

JURISDICTION	SOURCE OF FUND	MAINTENANCE ALLOWANCE	SPECIAL PROVISIONS
ALABAMA	No fund established	Board, lodging, and travel, if away from home.	Physical and vocational rehabilitation to restore employee to gainful employment furnished at employer's expense. Employee's refusal results in loss of compensation.
ALASKA	No fund established	Board, lodging, travel, and temporary disability benefits. Additional $200 monthly if extreme financial hardship.	Employer pays full cost. Services available 37 weeks, extendable to 74 weeks. Compensation suspended for unreasonable refusal of evaluation or failure to participate in approved or agreed plan.
AMERICAN SAMOA	Second Injury Fund	$10 weekly paid by employer plus maintenance from Special Fund.	Commission arranges for vocational rehabilitation of permanently disabled workers.
ARIZONA	$1,150 in no-dependency death cases. Appropriations annually from general fund up to 2% of annual premium.	Commission may authorize additional necessary awards to persons undergoing vocational rehabilitation.	Vocational rehabilitation trainees considered an employee at $200 monthly wage rate for compensation benefits.
ARKANSAS	No fund established	Reasonable expenses for maintenance, travel, and other necessary costs for 60 weeks maximum.	Must apply to Commission within 60 days. Commission may authorize vocational rehabilitation if reasonable in relation to disability, but worker may refuse.
CALIFORNIA	No fund established	All additional necessary living expenses during rehabilitation.	Rehabilitation unit in Division of Industrial Accidents. Rehabilitation program is compulsory on part of employer or carrier. Rehabilitation trainee is considered employee of training employer for insurance purposes.
COLORADO	No fund established for vocational rehabilitation.	Maintenance, tuition, and transportation during 26 weeks.	Period of time may be extended another 26 weeks if necessary. Employee cannot receive disability benefits and maintenance simultaneously.
CONNECTICUT	2% tax upon compensation paid by insurers and self-insurers.	Weekly subsistence allowance during vocational rehabilitation.	Employer pays full cost of medical rehabilitation, which continues until employee reaches maximum improvement. Vocational rehabilitation is furnished by Division of Workers' Rehabilitation.
DELAWARE	No fund established	Reasonable board, lodging, and travel	Physical and vocational rehabilitation furnished at employer's expense. Employee's refusal results in loss of compensation.
DISTRICT OF COLUMBIA	No fund established	Not exceeding $50 per week	Employer must provide vocational rehabilitation. Benefits forfeited if worker fails to cooperate.
FLORIDA	Payments from Special Fund and assessments upon insurers and self-insurers.	Reasonable board, lodging, and travel.	Injured worker is entitled to prompt rehabilitation including retraining, provided by or at the expense of the employer. Rehabilitation may be up to 26 weeks extendable for an additional 26 weeks. Refusal to accept rehabilitation deemed necessary by deputy commissioner results in automatic 50% reduction in compensation for each week of refusal.
GEORGIA	No fund established	Board, lodging, and travel, if away from home	Vocational rehabilitation furnished for 52 weeks but may be extended if necessary. Employee's unreasonable refusal may result in suspension of compensation.
GUAM	State fund (appropriation)	$10 per week during retraining	Commission directs the vocational rehabilitation of permanently disabled employees and arranges with the appropriate public or private agencies for such education.
HAWAII	Payments from Second Injury Fund	Director of Labor to issue rules.	Rehabilitation unit within Department of Labor makes recommendation for physical or vocational rehabilitation.
IDAHO	.7% tax on insurers and self-insurers	Reasonable expenses for maintenance and travel	Rehabilitation Division administers. Temporary disability benefits payable up to 104 weeks where retraining required.
ILLINOIS	No fund established	Maintenance costs and incidental expenses	Physical, mental, and vocational rehabilitation as may be necessary. Institutional care, if required.
INDIANA	No fund established	No specific statutory provision*	
IOWA	No fund established	$20 weekly in addition to other compensation for 13 weeks.	May be extended additional 13 weeks. Medical care includes physical rehabilitation.
KANSAS	No fund established	If employer provides vocational rehabilitation, must pay reasonable board, lodging, and travel up to $2,000 for a 26-week period (may be increased to $3,000).	If vocational rehabilitation unavailable through public facility, employer must provide up to 26 weeks, extendable additional 26 weeks. Compensation suspended for worker's unreasonable refusal of physical or vocational rehabilitation; compensation canceled after 90 days' refusal. Rehabilitation Section of Division administers. Compensation paid during vocational rehabilitation is deducted from benefits for scheduled injury.
KENTUCKY	No fund established	Board, lodging, and travel, if away from home.	Unlimited medical rehabilitation; vocational rehabilitation up to 52 weeks (may be extended). Employee's refusal results in loss of 50% of compensation.
LOUISIANA	No fund established	Board, lodging, and travel paid by employer or carrier	Employer or carrier provides up to 26 weeks of vocational rehabilitation, extendable another 26 weeks. Benefits reduced 50% for refusal of necessary rehabilitation.
MAINE	No fund established	$35 per week for 52 weeks	Commission member may extend vocational or educational rehabilitation benefits for additional 52 weeks or for a 3rd period of 52 weeks.*
MARYLAND	No fund established	Up to $40 weekly paid by employer	Workmen's Compensation Commission investigates all claims and reports of injury or disability for referral to Division of Vocational Rehabilitation. Employee entitled to 24 months of vocational rehabilitation. Employee's unreasonable refusal results in loss of compensation. Employer pays compensation for temporary total disability plus expenses of vocational rehabilitation.
MASSACHUSETTS	No fund established. Paid the same as compensation.	Rehabilitation Commission may approve room, board, and travel expenses.	Necessary cost of rehabilitation subject to approval of Rehabilitation Commission.
MICHIGAN	No fund established	Transportation and other necessary expenses during 52 weeks training.	Medical and vocational rehabilitation services under Workers' Compensation Bureau. Bureau may extend training period additional 52 weeks, maximum total 104 weeks.
MINNESOTA	No fund established	Necessary expenses, including tuition, books, travel, board, lodging, and custodial daycare.	Employer must provide rehabilitation for up to 156 weeks, through approved plan.* Participant may request 25% benefit increase and is eligible for one-time relocation allowance. Employer may seek termination or suspension of benefits if worker fails to cooperate. Appeals of rehabilitation decisions are heard by Rehabilitation Review Panel.
MISSISSIPPI	No fund established	Up to $10 per week up to 52 weeks.	Commission cooperates with federal and state agencies.
MISSOURI	Second Injury Fund	$40 weekly for physical rehabilitation (by order of Division after 20 weeks).	Administered by Director of Worker's Compensation Division. Division may order employer to provide transportation.
MONTANA	Rehabilitation Fund by 1% tax upon compensation paid by insurers, self-insured, and state fund.	Additional $50 weekly for living expenses while in training plus transportation, tuition, books, and equipment.	Administered by Workers' Compensation Division in conjunction with Department of Social and Rehabilitation Services. Employee's refusal may result in loss of compensation.
NEBRASKA	Vocational Rehabilitation Fund by 1% premium tax on insurers and self-insurers (minimum $25) payable to Court.	Board, lodging, and travel in addition to compensation.	Insurer must furnish medical, physical, and vocational rehabilitation services voluntarily (if not, may be ordered to do so). Costs may be apportioned between the employer and the Vocational Rehabilitation Fund. Payments into fund suspended when fund reaches $400,000 (see Chart XII).
NEVADA	State Insurance Fund and self-insurance	Insurer may allow maintenance as needed.	Insurer is authorized to provide all necessary rehabilitation services. Employee's refusal results in loss of all benefits.
NEW HAMPSHIRE	No fund established	Board, lodging, travel, books, and basic materials in addition to compensation.	Insurer must furnish rehabilitation services voluntarily, or may be ordered to do so, for one year and further treatment if needed. Vocational and physical rehabilitation staff assist in program.
NEW JERSEY	No fund established		Permanent total disability benefits may be stopped after 450 weeks unless the worker has submitted to physical or educational retraining.

Ind. *State Rehabilitation Services Board administers vocational rehabilitation programs. Compensation suspended for refusal of suitable on employment by partially disabled claimant.

Maine *Parties may agree to 3-month trial work period during which compensation is suspended. Compensation resumed if unsuccessful.

Minn. *Surviving spouse may request rehabilitation.

CHART X ☐ REHABILITATION OF DISABLED WORKERS ☐ January 1, 1984 (continued)

JURISDICTION	SOURCE OF FUND	MAINTENANCE ALLOWANCE	SPECIAL PROVISIONS
NEW MEXICO	No fund established	Board, lodging, travel, and maintenance for family, $3,000 maximum in addition to other compensation.	Employer must furnish vocational rehabilitation services to render worker fit to engage in remunerative employment.
NEW YORK	$2,000 in no-dependency death cases	Up to $30 per week for rehabilitation maintenance.	Department of Labor cooperates with Department of Education.
NORTH CAROLINA	No fund established		Insurer must furnish rehabilitation services required to lessen disability. Employee's unreasonable refusal of services ordered by Commission results in loss of compensation.
NORTH DAKOTA	Benefit Fund	Rehabilitation allowance in lieu of and equal to compensation, plus 25%.	Bureau through its Director of Rehabilitation provides retraining. Employee's unreasonable refusal to cooperate shall forfeit compensation. Additional allowance of $5,000 maximum during lifetime, for remodeling living or business facilities, if required.
OHIO	State Insurance Fund	Same as for temporary total disability, minimum 50% of SAWW, for 6 months (renewable).	Rehabilitation Division within Commission administers. Division may make all necessary expenditures, medically including treatment of non-occupational conditions inhibiting return to work.
OKLAHOMA	No fund established	Board, lodging, travel, tuition, and books.	Court may order necessary rehabilitation up to 52 weeks.
OREGON	Rehabilitation reserve out of Administrative Fund	Worker receives temporary total disability compensation during rehabilitation.	Rehabilitation Reserve pays cost of physical rehabilitation. Need determined within 120 days after temporary total disability; benefits may be suspended for failure to participate. Vocational assistance may be provided by department, employer, or insurer. Department reimburses employer for temporary disability benefits paid after injury is medically stationary.*
PENNSYLVANIA	No fund established	Rehabilitation Board may provide cash payments for living expenses.	State Board of Rehabilitation may provide vocational rehabilitation, training, and services.
PUERTO RICO	No fund established	Administrator may grant $45 weekly for up to 26 weeks.	Rehabilitation center provides physical, medical, and rehabilitation services.
RHODE ISLAND	$750 in no-dependency death cases; 1% of insurance premium.	Board, lodging, and travel.	Rehabilitation clinic financed by the Curative Centre Fund. Compensation suspended for willful refusal of rehabilitation.
SOUTH CAROLINA	No fund established	No specific statutory provision	
SOUTH DAKOTA	State Fund to $15,000	Provided by Rehabilitation Division.	State Board of Education authorized to cooperate with federal board of rehabilitation. Employee paid compensation while undergoing rehabilitation.
TENNESSEE	No fund established		Division of Workers' Compensation refers feasible cases to Department of Education pursuant to plan providing full or partial recovery of expenses from employer or insurer.
TEXAS	No fund established		Insurer furnishes necessary medical care and services for physical rehabilitation. Board may refer employee to Texas Rehabilitation Commission for vocational services.
UTAH	$18,720 in no-dependency death cases	$1,000 maximum during rehabilitation of permanently and totally disabled person.	If cannot be rehabilitated, worker receives benefits for life from Second Injury Fund, minimum $85 per week.
VERMONT	No fund established	Board, lodging, travel, books, and tools	Commissioner may order vocational rehabilitation services. If employee refuses, compensation may be suspended.
VIRGIN ISLANDS	Government Insurance Fund	Board, lodging, and travel	Income benefits during rehabilitation suspended for employee's refusal to accept vocational rehabilitation. See Chart V—Total Disability Benefits.
VIRGINIA	Second Injury Fund		Commission may award compensation, medical care, and vocational rehabilitation. Employee's unreasonable refusal may suspend compensation.
WASHINGTON	No fund established	Compensation; board, lodging, travel, books, equipment, and child care allowance, up to 52 weeks (maximum $3,000).	Supervisor may extend period for another 52 weeks. Department operates a Rehabilitation Center and pays for maintenance and employer's cost of job modification. Compensation may be halved for refusing rehabilitation without good cause.
WEST VIRGINIA	State Fund used; no special account.	Up to $10,000 (includes tuition, books, supplies, travel, lodging, and tools), plus temporary total disability payments if totally disabled.	Fund-employed Rehabilitation Counselors provide referrals and direct services. Direct job placement preferred, but short-term training is provided when necessary. Medical services and devices are authorized for physical rehabilitation.
WISCONSIN	No fund established	Board, lodging, and travel up to 40 weeks. Temporary total disability paid during training.	Course of instructions must be undertaken with 60 days from date sufficiently recovered or as soon thereafter as State Board provides opportunity. 40-week period may be extended if necessary. Department employs rehabilitation specialists (physical, medical, and vocational) to evaluate and refer injured employee for treatment.
WYOMING	No fund established	Up to $10 per week (may be increased to $15 per week if insufficient) up to 72 weeks.	District judge grants maintenance allowance on recommendations of Board of Education.
F.E.C.A.	Employees' Compensation Fund	Up to $200 per month	If person fails to undergo rehabilitation, administrator may reduce benefit if rehabilitation would have increased earnings.
LONGSHORE ACT	50% of Special Fund*	Up to $25 per week	Surplus in Fund in any one year may be carried over. Appropriations authorized.
ALBERTA	Accident Fund	Discretion of Board	Board operates physical rehabilitation center. Board may make necessary expenditures to aid rehabilitation and may provide vocational rehabilitation to a dependent spouse.
BRITISH COLUMBIA	Accident Fund	Discretion of Board	Rehabilitation Clinic established. Board may make necessary expenditures to aid rehabilitation and may provide vocational rehabilitation to a dependent spouse.
MANITOBA	Accident Fund	Discretion of Board	Board may make necessary expenditures to aid rehabilitation.
NEW BRUNSWICK	Accident Fund	Discretion of Board	Board operates physical rehabilitation center. Board may make necessary expenditures to aid rehabilitation.
NEWFOUNDLAND	Accident Fund	Discretion of Commission	Commission may make necessary expenditures to aid rehabilitation.
NORTHWEST TERRITORIES	Accident Fund	$60 daily for first 7 days, $50 daily thereafter. Employer pays transportation cost.	Board may order rehabilitation and retraining.
NOVA SCOTIA	Accident Fund	Discretion of Board	Board may make necessary expenditures to aid rehabilitation.
ONTARIO	Schedule 1 cases—Accident Fund Schedule 2 cases—employers individually	Discretion of Board Discretion of Board	No limit on amount in any one case or in any year for rehabilitation.
PRINCE EDWARD ISLAND	Accident Fund	Discretion of Board	Board may make necessary expenditures to aid rehabilitation.
QUEBEC	Accident Fund Annex B—employers individually	Discretion of Board	Board may make necessary expenditures to aid rehabilitation
SASKATCHEWAN	Injury Fund	Discretion of Board	Board provides on-the-job training, employer assistance, and physical and occupational therapy. Vocational training is also available for spouse.
YUKON TERRITORY	Compensation Fund	Subsistence in Commissioner's discretion	Commissioner may make necessary expenditures to aid rehabilitation.
CANADIAN MERCHANT SEAMEN'S ACT	No fund established	No specific statutory provision	

Oregon *Field services division assists injured workers return to work as soon as condition permits.

Longshore *See Chart XII—Second-Injury Funds—Special Provisions

CHART XIII SECOND-INJURY FUNDS January 1, 1984

JURISDICTION	INJURIES COVERED	PAYABLE BY EMPLOYER	PAYABLE BY FUND	SOURCE OF FUND	SPECIAL PROVISIONS
ALABAMA	Second injury which combined with prior permanent partial disability results in permanent total disability.	Disability caused by second injury.	Difference between compensation payable for second injury and permanent total disability.	$100 in death cases	Employer must have knowledge of prior disabling injury affecting employability.
ALASKA	Second injury which added to pre-existing permanent physical impairment results in substantially greater disability than from second injury alone.*	Disability caused by second injury up to 104 weeks.	Compensation in excess of 104 weeks.	Up to 6% of compensation payable to fund; $10,000 in no-dependency death cases; civil penalties.	Vocational rehabilitation expense payable from fund. "Physical impairment" as listed or would support an award of 200 weeks or more.
AMERICAN SAMOA	Second injury which combined with prior permanent impairment results in death or compensable disability greater than from second injury alone.	Benefits for first 104 weeks.	Benefits beyond first 104 weeks.	$1,000 in no-dependency death cases, plus fines and penalties.	Employer must have prior knowledge of disability.
ARIZONA	Second injury involving loss of use of member or eye which added to pre-existing loss of use of member or eye results in permanent total disability. Also, aggravation of a pre-existing disease or condition whether or not work-related.	Disability caused by second injury.	Difference between compensation payable for second injury and compensation for combined disability. If earning capacity is reduced by more than 50%, fund pays half of award for reduced capacity in excess of 50%.	$1,150 in no-dependency death cases. Commission may allocate up to 1-1/2% of yearly premiums to special fund to keep fund actuarially sound.	For aggravation of pre-existing condition, combined disability must be greater than 40%. Payments are also made from fund for vocational rehabilitation.
ARKANSAS	Second injury which added to previous permanent partial disability or impairment results in additional disability or impairment greater than from second injury alone.	Disability caused by second injury.	Difference between compensation payable for second injury and permanent disability.	$1,000 in no-dependency death cases. $500 to Second Injury Fund and $500 to Permanent Total Disability and Death Fund; added penalty of 15% of benefits if due to employer's violation of health or safety regulations. Portion of premium tax.	Employer liable for combined disability of both injuries in same employment.
CALIFORNIA	Second permanent partial injury which added to pre-existing permanent partial disability results in 70 percent or more permanent disability. Second injury must account for 35 percent.*	Disability caused by second injury.	Difference between compensation payable for second injury and permanent disability.	Legislative appropriations and $50,000 in each no-dependency death case or unpaid balance.	Payments are made by State Compensation Insurance Fund.
COLORADO	Second injury which added to pre-existing permanent partial disability results in permanent total disability.	Disability caused by second injury.	Difference between compensation payable for second injury and permanent total disability.	$15,000 in no-dependency or partial-dependency cases.	Amount payable by fund is limited to 1/2 of average wage loss, in case employee obtains employment while securing benefits.
CONNECTICUT	Second injury or disease which added to pre-existing injury, disease, or congenital causes results in permanent disability greater than from second injury alone.	Benefits for first 104 weeks, less compensation payable for prior disability.	Benefits beyond first 104 weeks, less compensation payable for prior disability.	Tax equal to 3-1/2% of compensation paid by carriers and self-insurers during preceding calendar year plus fines.	Tax imposed each time fund balance is reduced to $500,000.
DELAWARE	Second injury or disease which added to existing permanent injury from any cause results in permanent total disability.	Disability caused by second injury.	Difference between compensation payable for second injury and permanent disability.	Tax of 2% of premiums received by insurance carriers and equivalent charge on self-insurers.	Payments suspended when fund reaches $85,000 and resumed when below $35,000.
DISTRICT OF COLUMBIA	Second injury or disease which added to pre-existing injury, disease, or congenital causes results in permanent disability greater than from second injury alone.	Disability caused by second injury for first 104 weeks and first $1,000 medical expenses.	Difference between compensation payable for second injury and permanent disability.	$5,000 in no-dependency death cases or unpaid awards. Pro-rata assessments upon carriers and self-insurers based on paid losses. Fines and penalties.	
FLORIDA	Second injury or disease which merges with previous permanent physical impairment and results in substantially greater disability than from the second injury alone.		Fund reimburses employer for 60% of impairment benefits, 60% of wage-loss benefits during first 5 years after maximum medical improvements and 75% thereafter, PT benefits after 175 weeks, 75% of death benefits and funeral expenses, and 50% of first $10,000 in temporary disability and medical benefits and 100% beyond $10,000.	Prorata annual assessment upon net premiums of insurers and self-insurers.	Assessment must equal sum of immediate past 3 years' disbursements.
GEORGIA	Second injury or disease which merges with prior permanent physical impairment and results in greater disability than from second injury alone.	Disability caused by second injury for first 104 weeks.	Employer reimbursed for 50% of medical expenses in excess of $5,000 up to $10,000, and 100% of medical expenses in excess of $10,000, plus income benefits beyond 104 weeks.	Assessments on carriers and self-insurers proportionate to 175% of disbursements from fund to annual compensation benefits paid. In no-dependency death cases, 1/2 of benefits payable or $10,000, whichever is less.	Employer must have prior knowledge of impairment. Assessments may be reduced or suspended when no funds are needed.
GUAM	Second injury which combined with a previous disability causes permanent disability.	Disability caused by second injury.	Difference between compensation payable for second injury and permanent total disability.	State fund (appropriation).	
HAWAII	Second injury which added to pre-existing disabilities results in greater permanent disability, permanent total disability, or death.	Disability benefits for first 104 weeks.	Benefits beyond first 104 weeks.	$8,775 in no-dependency death cases; and unpaid balance of compensation due in permanent total and permanent partial disability cases, if no dependents; 1/4% premium tax on insurers and self-insurers.	Premium tax suspended when balance exceeds $200,000, resumed when below $100,000.
IDAHO	Second injury which combined with prior permanent physical impairment results in permanent total disability.	Disability caused by second injury.	Difference between compensation payable for second injury and permanent disability.	Amount equal to 4% of award for scheduled or unscheduled injuries and $5,000 in no-dependency death cases.	When fund exceeds $500,000 excise may be suspended or reduced.
ILLINOIS	Second injury involving loss or loss of use of major members or eye which added to pre-existing loss of member results in permanent total disability.	Disability caused by second injury.*	Difference between compensation payable for second injury and permanent disability.	Semi-yearly employer payment of .125% of compensation payments.	When fund reaches $500,000 amount payable into fund reduced by 1/2. When fund reaches $600,000, payments cease. When fund reduced to $400,000, payment resumed.
INDIANA	Second injury involving loss or loss of use of hand, arm, foot, leg, or eye which added to pre-existing loss or loss of use of member results in permanent total disability.	Disability caused by second injury.	Difference between compensation payable for second injury and permanent total disability.	1% of compensation paid by insurers and self-insurers during preceding calendar year.	Payment suspended when fund reaches $400,000.

Alaska *Pre-existing disability must support 25% earnings loss or 90 weeks of benefits.

Calif. *Second injury must account for 35% unless prior disability involved a major member and second injury was to opposite and corresponding member and accounts for at least 5%. No benefits payable for subsequent unrelated noncompensable injury.

Ill. *Employer is liable in full if second injury is permanent and total without relation to prior injury.

CHART XIII □ SECOND-INJURY FUNDS □ January 1, 1984 (continued)

JURISDICTION	INJURIES COVERED	PAYABLE BY EMPLOYER	PAYABLE BY FUND	SOURCE OF FUND	SPECIAL PROVISIONS
IOWA	Second injury involving loss or loss of use of member or eye which added to pre-existing loss of use of member results in permanent disability.	Disability caused by second injury.	Difference between compensation payable for second injury and permanent disability, less value of previous loss of member or organ.	$2,000 in dependent death cases; $5,000 in no-dependent death cases; any contributions by the United States; payments due but not paid to non-resident alien dependents; and sums recovered from third parties.	Payments suspended when fund reaches $500,000, resumed when below $300,000.
KANSAS	Second injury related to 17 types of handicap as listed in statute—any physical or mental impairment.	Difference between fund payment and maximum award.	Compensation to the extent pre-existing handicap contributed to second injury.	$18,500 from employer in no-dependency death cases, and pro-rata annual assessment upon carriers and self-insurers based on losses.	Legislature oversees adequacy of workers' compensation fund, administered by Insurance Commissioner. Employer must prove knowledge of prior disability.*
KENTUCKY	Second injury or disease which added to prior disability or condition results in permanent disability greater than from second injury alone.	Disability caused by second injury or dormant condition.	Difference between compensation payable for second injury and greater disability, less amount paid for prior injury.	3/4% premium tax on carriers and self-insurers for administration and variable assessment based on need.	
LOUISIANA	Second injury which combined with prior permanent partial disability results in disability greater than from second injury alone, or in death.*	Total disability benefits for first 104 weeks; in death cases, first 175 weeks; 40% of partial disability benefits; 50% of first $10,000 medical benefits.	Employer reimbursed for balance of benefits.	1% premium tax on carriers and self-insurers, minimum $10.	Tax reduced when fund reaches $1,000,000; suspended when fund exceeds 200% of disbursements, resumed when below 125% of disbursements.
MAINE	Second injury caused by accident, disease, or congenital condition, which added to pre-existing impairment results in permanent total disability.	Disability caused by second injury.	Fund reimburses employer for difference between compensation payable for second injury and permanent total disability.	In no-dependency death cases, 100 x SAWW.	
MARYLAND	Second injury which combined with a pre-existing permanent impairment due to accident, disease, or cogenital condition results in a greater combined disability constituting a hindrance to employment.	Disability caused by second injury.	If permanent disability exceeds 50% of the body as a whole, employee is entitled to additional compensation for the full disability from the "Subsequent Injury Fund." Prior injury and second injury must each be compensable for at least 125 weeks.	5% of compensation paid for disability, death, or settlements.	Payments suspended when fund reaches $1,000,000, resumed when below $500,000.
MASSACHUSETTS	Second injury which added to pre-existing physical impairment results in substantially greater disability or death. Pre-existing disability must support 25% earnings loss or 90 weeks of benefits.	Benefits for first 104 weeks.	Employer reimbursed for half of benefits after first 104 weeks.	$500 in no-dependency death cases, and additional $500 in every death case; unpaid balance of scheduled awards.	Pro-rata assessment based on losses paid during preceding year by carriers and self-insureds.
MICHIGAN	Second injury involving loss of member or eye, which added to pre-existing loss of member results in permanent total disability.	Disability caused by second injury.	Difference between compensation payable for second injury and permanent total disability.	Assessments on carriers and self-insurers proportionate to 175% of disbursements from fund to annual compensation benefits paid.	Fund is credited with any balance in excess of $200,000.*
MINNESOTA	Second injury that results in substantially greater disability than would have resulted from second injury alone.	Disability caused by second injury.	Employer reimbursed for disability after 52 weeks, medical after $2,000. If second injury results in permanent partial disability, fund pays difference between compensation payable for second injury and greater disability.*	$25,000 in no-dependency death cases; 20% of compensation for injuries 6/2/71 through 12/31/83; percentage of indemnity benefits for earlier injuries; assessment based on various factors for injuries occurring 1/1/84; certain penalties.	Commissioner determines assessment base and rate, maximum total assessment $25 million for 1984 and increasing up to 10% annually thereafter.
MISSISSIPPI	Second injury involving loss or loss of use of member or eye, which added to pre-existing loss or loss of use of member or eye results in permanent total disability.	Disability caused by second injury.	Difference between compensation payable for second injury and permanent disability.	$500 in no-dependency death cases; $150 in dependency cases.	$150 payments suspended when fund reaches $35,000 and until reduced to $20,000.
MISSOURI	Second injury resulting in permanent partial disability which compounds either a greater permanent partial or a permanent total disability.	Disability caused by second injury.	Difference between compensation payable for second injury and compounded disability.	20% of 3% premium tax. Payment by carriers or self-insurers of 1/2 percent of total compensation paid.	
MONTANA	Second injury which combined with prior permanent physical impairment results in death or disability.	Benefits for first 104 weeks.	Employer reimbursed after first 104 weeks.	$1000 paid by employers, insurers, or accident fund in every death case. Carriers and self-insurers assessed 5% of losses paid in preceding year.	Division must certify unemployed worker as vocationally handicapped.
NEBRASKA	Second injury which combined with pre-existing disability causes substantially greater disability. Pre-existing disability must support 25% earnings loss or 90 weeks of benefits.[1]	Disability caused by second injury.	Difference between compensation payable for second injury and previous disability.	1% premium tax on carriers or self-insurers ($25 minimum) payable to Workmen's Compensation Court.	Payments suspended when fund reaches $400,000, resumed when below $200,000.
NEVADA	Second injury which combined with any previous permanent physical disability causes substantially greater disability.*		Compensation allocated between insurer and fund.	Subsequent Injury Fund in state treasury.**	Compensable claim considered "excess loss" in calculation of employer's experience rating. Employer must prove knowledge of prior impairment.
NEW HAMPSHIRE	Second injury which combined with any pre-existing disability results in substantially greater disability.[1]	Benefits for first 104 weeks.	Employer reimbursed after first 104 weeks.	Assessment against carriers and self-insurers proportional to total benefits paid by all carriers.	
NEW JERSEY	Second injury resulting in permanent partial disability which added to pre-existing partial disability, compensable or not, results in permanent total disability.	Disability caused by compensable injury.	Difference between compensation payable for second injury and permanent total disability.	Carriers and self-insurers assessed pro-rata for 150% of payments made from fund as it bears to total compensation paid during preceding year. Annual assessments paid quarterly.	When fund balance exceeds $1,250,000, up to $50,000 per year may be applied toward administration costs of Division.
NEW MEXICO	Second injury which added to pre-existing disability results in permanent disability greater than from second injury alone; or, second injury resulting in death.	Liability apportioned by judicial determination.	Liability apportioned by judicial determination.	$1,000 in no-dependency death cases. Employer or insurer pays quarterly assessment up to 1% of compensation paid during quarter, exclusive of medical benefits and attorney's fees.	

[1] In death cases it must be established that either the injury or the death would not have occurred except for such pre-existing permanent physical impairment. "Permanent physical impairment" means any permanent condition due to previous accident, disease, or congenital condition which is likely to be a hindrance to employment.

Kans. *Employer may file description of prior impairment to create presumption of prior knowledge.

La. *"Permanent partial disability" means any permanent condition due to injury, disease, or congenital causes which is likely to be a hindrance to employment. Certain scheduled conditions are presumed to be permanent partial disability if employer had prior knowledge.

Mich. *Compensation to certified vocationally handicapped persons payable from fund after 104 weeks.

Minn. *If injury, disability or death would not have occurred but for the preexisting impairment, the fund pays all benefits (except for a cardiac condition, impairment of at least 10% of the whole man, or as prescribed by rule).

Nev. *Pre-existing disability must support a rating of 12% or more of the whole man based on A.M.A. guides, which is likely to be a hindrance to employment.
**Fund is composed of assessments, penalties, bonds, securities, and all other property collected by administrator, Division of Industrial Insurance Regulation.

CHART XIII □ SECOND-INJURY FUNDS □ January 1, 1984 (continued)

JURISDICTION	INJURIES COVERED	PAYABLE BY EMPLOYER	PAYABLE BY FUND	SOURCE OF FUND	SPECIAL PROVISIONS
NEW YORK	Second injury involving loss or loss of use of member or eye, which added to pre-existing injury results in permanent total disability; second injury which added to pre-existing loss or partial loss of member or eye or other "permanent physical impairment" not resulting from a dust disease results in disability greater than from second injury alone or second injury or disease resulting in death, which is caused by pre-existing disability.[1]	Benefits for first 104 weeks.	Employer reimbursed after first 104 weeks.	Assessment against carriers and self-insurers proportional to compensation payments made by all carriers.	Employer or insurer pays awards and medical expenses, but is reimbursed from special disability fund for benefits after first 104 weeks.
NORTH CAROLINA	Second injury involving loss of member or eye which added to pre-existing injury results in permanent total disability, provided the original and increased disability were each 20% of the entire member.*	Disability caused by second injury.	Difference between compensation payable for second injury and permanent total disability.	Assessments against employer or insurer for each permanent partial disability, up to $50 for a minor member and $200 for a major member (currently $25 and $100, respectively).	
NORTH DAKOTA	Second injury or aggravation of any previous injury or condition which results in further disability.	Disability caused by second injury.	Percent attributable to aggravation or second injury.	Benefit Fund.	Compensation in excess of amount chargeable to second injury is charged to general fund.
OHIO	Second injury which aggravates pre-existing disease or condition (25 types of handicaps as listed by statute), resulting in death, temporary or permanent total disability, and disability compensable under a special schedule.*	Disability attributable to injury or occupational disease sustained in employment.	Amount of disability or proportion of cost of death award determined by Industrial Commission to be attributable to employee's pre-existing disability.	Reserve set aside out of statutory surplus funds.	In the case of a self-insuring employer, excess payments are made from the surplus fund. By rule of Commission in the case of State Fund employer, compensation in excess of amount chargeable to second injury is charged to surplus fund.
OKLAHOMA	Second injury to "physically impaired person" which results in additional permanent disability greater than from second injury alone.	Disability caused by second injury.	Difference between compensation payable for second injury and compensation for combined injuries.	2% of permanent disability losses by carriers, state fund, and self-insurers, and 2% of awards for permanent disability by employers.*	Permanent total awards are payable by the fund for 5 years or until age 65, whichever is longer.
OREGON	Injury caused by preexisting condition (may be congenital) or which combined with preexisting condition results in greater permanent disability.	First $1,000 claims cost and portion of claim for which relief not granted are charged to employer loss experience.	Claims cost above $1,000 and percentage of balance for which Department grants relief.	Employer and worker each pay 3¢ per worker per day.	Reimbursement from fund subject to funds available. Amount of reimbursement not reviewable. Settlement of claim requires Department approval if involves reimbursement.
PENNSYLVANIA	Second injury involving loss or loss of use which added to pre-existing loss or loss of use of member results in permanent total disability.	Scheduled benefits as a result of second injury.	Remaining compensation due for total disability.	Assessment against carriers and self-insurers proportional to compensation payments.	Payments are made directly by the Department.
PUERTO RICO	Second injury which aggravates or augments any former disability.		Job injury not caused by work accident is compensated in addition to second injury. Compensation for prior job injury is deducted from compensation payable for total disability, except where combined injury results in permanent total disability, which is compensated as such.	Insurance premiums.	The difference between expenditures by the Industrial Commission and the Manager of the State Insurance Fund and their maximum budget allotment are placed in the Reserve Fund for catastrophes except for medical expense surpluses; maximum $1 million.
RHODE ISLAND	Second injury which merges with pre-existing work-related disability resulting in greater disability or death.	Benefits for first 104 weeks.	Employer reimbursed after first 104 weeks.	2-3/4% tax on gross premiums collected by insurers and comparable tax on self-insurers, plus $750 in no-dependency death cases; also certain penalties.	Employer must prove knowledge of prior injury unless employee failed to disclose. Tax may be reduced when fund reaches $2 million.
SOUTH CAROLINA	Second injury which added to any previous permanent physical impairment results in substantially greater disability or death.	Disability caused by second injury for first 78 weeks' compensation and medical care.	Employer reimbursed for all benefits after 78 weeks, plus 50% of medical payments over $3000 during first 78 weeks.	Pro-rata assessments on carriers and self-insurers based on losses paid. In no-dependency deaths, unpaid benefits to fund.	Employer must prove prior knowledge of impairment or that worker was unaware of impairment.*
SOUTH DAKOTA	Second injury which added to any pre-existing disability results in additional permanent partial or total disability or death.	Disability caused by second injury.	Difference between compensation payable for second injury and compensation for combined injuries.	Carriers and self-insurers assessed 1/2% of losses paid during preceding year and $500 in no-dependency death cases.	Payments suspended at $100,000, and resumed at $50,000.
TENNESSEE	Second injury involving loss or loss of use of member or eye, which added to pre-existing loss or loss of use of member results in permanent total disability.	Disability caused by second injury.	Difference between compensation payable for second injury and permanent total disability.	$150 in death cases and $15 in each case of permanent partial disability.	
TEXAS	Second injury which added to pre-existing injury results in permanent total disability.	Disability caused by second injury.	Difference between compensation payable for second injury and permanent total disability.	Maximum $65,520* payable into fund in each no-dependency death case.	
UTAH	Second injury which combined with a previous permanent incapacity due to accident, disease, or congenital condition results in a substantially greater disability.	Disability caused by second injury.	Difference between compensation payable for second injury and compensation for combined injuries.	$18,720 in no-dependency death cases, less compensation paid; plus 3% premium tax on insurers and self-insurers. Fines from uninsured employers.	Medical panel determines percentage of disability attributable to prior disability and second injury. Fund is also used to extend the period of compensation above regular award for certain claimants who are permanently and totally disabled and who cannot be rehabilitated.
VERMONT	Second injury involving loss of use of member or eye which added to previous disability results in permanent total disability.	Disability caused by second injury.	Difference between compensation payable for second injury and permanent total disability.	$500 in no-dependency death cases.	
VIRGIN ISLANDS	Second injury which combined with prior impairment results in death or compensable disability greater than from second injury alone.	None. Employer's experience rating affected by disability payments after 104 weeks.	All benefits	Premiums paid by employers by classification and experience, plus fines, penalties, and interest.	Employer must have prior knowledge of disability.

N.C. *Epilepsy is considered a prior permanent disability.

Ohio *Does not apply to compensation for temporary partial or percentage of permanent partial disability.

Okla. *Payable quarterly, not later than the 15th day of the month following; total tax is 4% (2% of awards for permanent disability, total or partial). Tax is based on award and is payable regardless of whether award is paid. State political subdivisions pay 2% of permanent disability compensation paid in preceding year.

S.C. *"Permanent physical impairment" means any permanent condition due to injury, disease, or congenital causes which is likely to be a hindrance to employment. Certain scheduled conditions are presumed to be permanent physical impairment if employer had prior knowledge.

Tex. *360 times maximum weekly benefit.

CHART XIII □ SECOND-INJURY FUNDS □ January 1, 1984 (continued)

JURISDICTION	INJURIES COVERED	PAYABLE BY EMPLOYER	PAYABLE BY FUND	SOURCE OF FUND	SPECIAL PROVISIONS
VIRGINIA	Second injury involving 20% loss or loss of use of member or eye which added to pre-existing disability of 20% or more results in total or partial disability.	Disability caused by second injury.	Employer reimbursed for compensation after all other compensation has expired plus up to $7,500 each for medical and vocational rehabilitation expenses.	1/4% premium tax on carriers and self-insurers.	Payments suspended at $250,000, and resumed at $125,000.
WASHINGTON	Second injury or disease which added to pre-existing injury or disease results in permanent total disability or death.	Disability caused by second injury.	Difference between charge assessed against employer at time of second injury and total pension reserve.	Transfer of not more than cost from accident fund to second injury account. Self-insurers pay proportional to claims against self-insurers.	
WEST VIRGINIA	Second injury which combined with pre-existing impairment results in permanent total disability.	Disability caused by second injury.			Compensation in excess of amount chargeable to second injury is paid out of second injury fund at the Commissioner's disposal.
WISCONSIN	Second injury with permanent disability for 200 weeks or more with a pre-existing disability of an equal degree or greater.	Disability caused by second injury.	Disability caused by lesser of 2 injuries. If the combined disabilities result in permanent total disability, fund pays the difference between compensation payable for second injury and permanent total disability.	$4,000 for loss of a hand, arm, foot, leg, or eye. In no wholly dependent or partially dependent cases, 80% of death benefit otherwise available.	
WYOMING	Second injury in extra-hazardous employment which added to pre-existing loss or loss of use of member or eye results in permanent total disability.	Disability caused by second injury.	Difference between compensation payable for second injury and permanent disability.	$500 in no-dependency death cases.	Any payments for previous partial disability or payments which would have been made if the previous injury had occurred in an extra-hazardous employment are deducted from the award.
LONGSHORE ACT	Second injury resulting in permanent partial disability which added to pre-existing injury results in permament total disability.	Disability caused by second injury for first 104 weeks.	Difference between compensation payable for second injury and permament total disability.	$5,000 in no-dependency death cases or unpaid awards. Pro-rata assessments based on losses paid. Fines and penalties.	50% of fund is for second injuries and 50% for rehabilitation. Supplementary benefits for total disability or death payable by fund.
ALBERTA	No specific statutory provision*				
BRITISH COLUMBIA	Injury or disease superimposed on existing disability.	No	Proportion of disability attributable to second injury.	Accident Fund	
MANITOBA	All enhanced disabilities because of similar or other disabilities	No	Yes	Accident Fund	Compensation must be at least half the benefit payable if the entire disability were caused by the pre-existing condition. Condition includes neurosis or psychoneurosis.
NEW BRUNSWICK	Second injury coupled with other prior injuries or disabilities.	No	Yes	Reserve Fund	
NEWFOUNDLAND	All enhanced disabilities because of similar or other disabilities.	No	Difference between compensation payable for second injury and final result of disablement.	Reserve Fund	
NOVA SCOTIA	Injury that aggravates, activates, or accelerates pre-existing disease or disability; or injury that results in injury or disease caused partly by employment and partly by other causes.	No	Disability attributable to second injury.	Accident Fund	Board has authority to establish second injury fund.
NORTHWEST TERRITORIES	All disabilities due to pre-existing disease, condition or disability.	No	Difference between second injury and total cost.	Contingency reserve	
ONTARIO	All enhanced disabilities due to pre-existing diseases, condition, or disability.	No	Difference between second injury and total cost.	Accident Fund	Not restricted to permanent disability cases.
PRINCE EDWARD ISLAND	No specific statutory provision				
QUEBEC	Enhanced disability because of previous infirmity.				Commission has authority to establish second injury fund.
SASKATCHEWAN	All enhanced disabilities due to preexisting disease, condition, or disability.	No	Difference between second injury and total cost.	Injury Fund	
YUKON TERRITORY	All enhanced disabilities because of similar or other disabilities.	No	Yes	Compensation Reserve Fund. Assessment on employers' annual payroll.	
CANADIAN MERCHANT SEAMEN'S ACT	No specific statutory provision				

Alta. *Board has established reserve funds to cover enhanced disability or aggravation of previous condition.

AUTHOR INDEX

S

T

U

V

W

Y

Z

SUBJECT INDEX

J

K

L

M

N

O

P